Masculinity in Medieval Europe

WOMEN AND MEN IN HISTORY

This series, published for students, scholars and interested general readers, will tackle themes in gender history from the early medieval period through to the present day. Gender issues are now an integral part of all history courses and yet many traditional texts do not reflect this change. Much exciting work is now being done to redress the gender imbalances of the past, and we hope that these books will make their own substantial contribution to that process. This is an open-ended series, which means that many new titles can be included. We hope that these will both synthesise and shape future developments in gender studies.

The General Editors of the series are *Patricia Skinner* (University of Southampton) for the medieval period; *Pamela Sharpe* (University of Bristol) for the early modern period; and *Penny Summerfield* (University of Lancaster) for the modern period. *Margaret Walsh* (University of Nottingham) was the Founding Editor of the series.

Published books:

Masculinity in Medieval Europe
D.M. Hadley (ed.)

Gender and Society in Renaissance Italy
Judith C. Brown and Robert C. Davis (eds)

Gender, Church and State in Early Modern Germany: Essays by Merry E. Wiesner
Merry E. Wiesner

Gender, Power and the Unitarians in England, 1760–1860
Ruth Watts

Women and Work in Russia, 1880–1930: A Study in Continuity through Change
Jane McDermid and Anna Hillyar

The Family Story: Blood, Contract and Intimacy, 1830–1960
Leonor Davidoff, Megan Doolittle, Janet Fink and Katherine Holden

Masculinity in Medieval Europe

Edited by
D.M. HADLEY

Routledge
Taylor & Francis Group

LONDON AND NEW YORK

First published 1999 by Addison Wesley Longman Limited

Published 2014 by Routledge
2 Park Square, Milton Park, Abingdon, Oxon OX14 4RN
711 Third Avenue, New York, NY 10017, USA

Routledge is an imprint of the Taylor & Francis Group, an informa business

ISBN 13: 978-0-582-31645-4 (pbk)

British Library Cataloguing in Publication Data
A catalogue entry for this title is available from the British Library
Library of Congress Cataloguing-in-Publication Data
Set by 35 in 10/12pt Baskerville

Contents

List of Abbreviations

AHR	*American Historical Review*
BAR	British Archaeological Association Research Report
BIHR	Borthwick Institute of Historical Research
CSHB	*Corpus Scriptorum Historiae Byzantinae*
EETS	Early English Texts Society
EHR	*English Historical Review*
EME	*Early Medieval Europe*
HE	*Historia Ecclesiastica Gentis Anglorum*, ed., C. Plummer (Oxford, 1896, repd, 1975)
HWJ	*History Workshop Journal*
JEccH	*Journal of Ecclesiastical History*
JMH	*Journal of Medieval History*
JÖB	*Jahrbuch der Österreichischen Byzantinistik*
MGH	*Monumenta Germaniae Historica*
ODB	*Oxford Dictionary of Byzantium*, ed., A.P. Kazhdan, 3 vols (Oxford, 1991)
PL	*Patrologiae Cursus Completus, Series Latina*, ed., J.-P. Migne, 221 vols (1844–80)
RRAN	*Regesta Regum Anglo-Normannorum, 1066–1154*, vol. I, ed. H.W.C. Davies (Oxford, 1913)
s.a.	*sub anno*
Settimane	*Settimane di Studio del Centro italiano di Studi sull'Alto Medioevo*
TRHS	*Transactions of the Royal Historical Society*
YML	York Minster Library

List of Contributors

WILLIAM M. AIRD is Lecturer in Medieval History in the School of History and Archaeology at Cardiff University. He has published articles relating to the Norman impact on the Anglo-Scottish border, medieval saints' cults and dream narratives, and is the author of *St Cuthbert and the Normans. The Church of Durham 1071–1153,* (Woodbridge, 1998). He is currently researching medieval perceptions of the life-course and the portrayal of the somatomorphic soul in medieval visions of the Otherworld.

MARIANNE AILES is Lecturer in Early French Literature at Wadham College, Oxford and Sessional Lecturer in the Department of French Studies at the University of Reading. She has published articles in the journals *Medium Aevum, Reading Medieval Studies* and *Olifant.* She is currently working on a translation of Ambrose's *Estoire de la Guerre Sainte.*

ROSS BALZARETTI is Lecturer in Medieval History at the University of Nottingham. He has published articles on the ninth century in *Early Medieval Europe, Past and Present, History Workshop Journal* and the collections *Storia dell'alto medioevo Italiano (vi–x secolo) alla luce dell'archeologia* eds, R. Francovich and G. Noyé (Florence, 1994) and *Towns in Transition. Urban Evolution in Late Antiquity and the Early Middle Ages,* eds, N. Christie and S. Loseby (Aldershot, 1996). He has co-edited (with A.L. Erickson) a special issue of *Gender and History* (1995). He is currently preparing a book on the monastery of Sant' Ambrogio in Milan.

MATTHEW BENNETT is Senior Lecturer at the Royal Military Academy Sandhurst. He is a medieval military historian, and his research is largely concerned with using vernacular literature to explore warfare and the knightly ethos. His publications include, with Nicholas Hooper, the *Cambridge Illustrated Atlas of Warfare in the Middle Ages, 781–1485* (Cambridge, 1996) and numerous articles on battle tactics and knightly warfare in general.

MARK CHINCA is Lecturer in German at the University of Cambridge and a Fellow of Trinity College. He is the author of two books, *History, Fiction, Verisimilitude: Studies in the Poetics of Gottfried's 'Tristan'* (London, 1993) and *Gottfried von Strassburg: 'Tristan'* (Cambridge, 1997). He has also published articles and essays on fabliau, lyric and the *Rolandslied* and has co-edited special numbers of *Paragraph* (July, 1992) and *Forum for Modern Language Studies* (1997).

PATRICIA CULLUM is Senior Lecturer in the Department of History at the University of Huddersfield. She is the author of *Cremetts and Corrodies: Care of the Poor and Sick at St Leonard's Hospital, York in the Middle Ages* (Borthwick Papers, York, 1991) and a number of other articles on hospitals and charity in late medieval England. Forthcoming is 'Vowesses and veiled widows in the province of York, c.1300–1536' in *Northern History* (1997). She is currently working on a book *Hospitals and Charitable Provision in Medieval England.*

JEREMY GOLDBERG is Senior Lecturer in History in the Department of History at the University of York. He has published a number of articles on the later medieval English economy and society, and on medieval women in particular. He is the author of *Women, Work and Life-cycle in a Medieval Economy* (Oxford, 1992). He has also edited and contributed to *Woman is a Worthy Wight: Women in English Society, c.1250–1550* (1992) and has edited and translated a collection of primary sources in *Women in England, c.1275–1525* (Manchester, 1995).

DAWN HADLEY is Lecturer in Historical Archaeology in the Department of Archaeology and Prehistory at the University of Sheffield. She has published on aspects of early medieval society and economy, and on early medieval burial practices. She is the author of *Early Medieval Social Structures, c.800–1100* (Leicester University Press, 1998). She is currently researching aspects of the construction of gender in medieval society, and the social construction of the medieval landscape.

JULIAN HASELDINE is a Leverhulme Trust Special Research Fellow in the Department of History at the University of Sheffield. His publications include 'Friendship and rivalry: the role of *amicitia* in twelfth-century monastic relations', *Journal of Ecclesiastical History* (1993) and 'Understanding the language of *amicitia*', *Journal of Medieval History* (1994). He is currently preparing a critical edition and translation of the *Letters of Peter of Celle* for Oxford Medieval Texts, and is researching a book on *The Language of Friendship in the Middle Ages* with the support of the Leverhulme Trust.

CONRAD LEYSER is Lecturer in Medieval History at the University of Manchester. He has published articles on the early medieval ascetic tradition and on eleventh-century reform. His monograph *Gregory the Great and the Ascetic Imagination in the Early Medieval West* is forthcoming.

JENNY MOORE has just completed a PhD in the Department of Archaeology and Prehistory at the University of Sheffield, and is part-time editor for the Institute of Field Archaeologists. She has recently contributed to and edited a collection of papers on gender issues in archaeology entitled *Invisible People and Processes: Writing Gender and Childhood into European Archaeology* (London, 1996).

JANET L. NELSON is Professor of Medieval History and Director of the Centre for Late Antique and Medieval Studies at King's College, University of London, where she has taught since 1970. Her research interests have centred on the politics and ideology of the earlier Middle Ages. She is the author of *Politics and Ritual in Early Medieval Europe* (1986), *Charles the Bald* (1992) and *The Frankish World* (1996). She is currently working on a study of earlier medieval political ideas.

ROBERT SWANSON is Reader in Medieval Church History in the Department of Medieval History at the University of Birmingham. His most recent book is *Religion and Devotion in Europe, c.1215–c.1515* (Cambridge, 1995). His other publications include *Church and Society in Late Medieval England* (1989; rev. edn, 1993), *Catholic England: Faith, Religion and Observance before the Reformation* (1993), and contributions on many aspects of ecclesiastical history to numerous journals and essay collections.

SHAUN TOUGHER is Lecturer in Ancient History in the School of History and Archaeology at Cardiff University. His research interests range from eunuchs to Julian the Apostate to Byzantium's Macedonian dynasty. He is the author of *The Reign of Leo VI (886–912)* (Leiden/New York/Köln, 1997), and is currently working on eunuch monasteries.

CHAPTER ONE

Introduction: Medieval Masculinities

D.M. HADLEY

For a generation of scholars gender has been an important analytical category for the study of the Middle Ages.[1] It has come to be
accepted that gender is socially constructed; that is, that masculinity and femininity do not exist as fixed organic categories, but are
produced socially and vary. It has also been recognized in recent
work that we must be prepared to think in terms of a whole series
of masculinit*ies* and femininit*ies*. Much attention has been focused
on medieval women in recent years, but although this work is extremely valuable it has not really been about gender; it has served
to 'add' women to the historical picture, but has lacked insight into
the relational aspect of gender identity (the ways, that is, in which
men and women were defined in relation to one another), and the
various ways in which gender identity was formed and reproduced.
To develop the study of gender in the Middle Ages we need to
move beyond the separate study of women, and in order to do so
we have to address the gendered identity of men. There is a growing awareness that medieval men, and medieval masculinities, equally
require theorizing and detailed analysis. This volume is the first
multi-disciplinary contribution to that endeavour written for students of medieval history.[2] It proceeds through a series of case

1. Essential reading is J. Scott, 'Gender: a useful category of historical analysis',
AHR 91 (1986), pp.1053–75. For the medieval period, a comprehensive bibliography
of works which have been influenced by feminist scholarship and gender stud-
ies would be impractical here; see the bibliographical essay below, pp.256–72; and
J.L. Nelson, 'Family, gender and sexuality in the Middle Ages', in M. Bentley, ed.,
Companion to Historiography (London, 1997), pp.153–76. I am grateful to Trish Skinner,
Guy Halsall and Jinty Nelson for their comments on an earlier draft of this chapter.
2. Another notable volume, with a greater emphasis on medieval literature, is
C. Lees, ed., *Medieval Masculinities. Regarding Men in the Middle Ages* (Minneapolis,
1994).

studies ranging in time from the fourth to the sixteenth century, which draw on documentary and literary sources, and on the evidence of archaeology and material culture, from England, France, Italy, Germany, Byzantium and Scandinavia. Insights into medieval masculinities are offered from legal, political, ecclesiastical, social, literary and archaeological perspectives. The diversity of evidence and viewpoints presented enables the contributors to the collection to expose a myriad of masculinities. No one methodological or theoretical approach predominates in the collection, and this allows the contributors, and the reader, to explore the multi-faceted nature of male experience and identity in the Middle Ages.

Any study which takes masculinities as its central theme is, however, liable to be received with scepticism and suspicion: it is prone to accusations that it is 'an unwelcome take-over bid . . . unacceptably subversive . . . a modish irrelevance';[3] it is likely to be regarded as anti-feminist; it may even be regarded as being unnecessary on the grounds that 'the subjects of traditional historical discourse were for the most part men'.[4] The present collection is none of these things; the contributors have all been aware of the potential riskiness of the undertaking, and consequently three main concerns have predominated in the production of this volume. First, we have taken as our task the need to examine the divergent and constantly changing ways in which masculine identities were constructed throughout the Middle Ages, and in so doing to disaggregate the generality of the term 'men' in so much literature on the Middle Ages. Accordingly, in order to avoid a reductive approach, each of the contributors has examined the experiences of groups of men, and of individual men, in given historical contexts. It is apparent that when we begin to think of men as gendered beings we find divergent notions of masculinity, constructed in historically specific contexts, and this offers a necessary corrective to the premise, inherent in much scholarly writing on the Middle Ages, that masculinity is universal, unchanging and unquestioned. The chapters in this volume demonstrate that, on the contrary, masculinities were constructed, reconstructed and challenged; they were also situational constructs, created through social interaction. It has recently been observed that we must strive to elucidate the lives of 'the millions of men who were only men', rather than continuing with the apotheosis of the perceivedly important men.[5] In response to this, we offer

---

3. J. Tosh, 'What should historians do with masculinity? Reflections on nineteenth-century Britain', *HWJ* 38 (1994), p.179.
4. T. Fenster, 'Preface: why men?', in C. Lees, ed., *Medieval Masculinities*, p.x.
5. *Ibid.*

studies of a variety of medieval masculinities, as we recognize that the experiences of medieval men cannot be made visible through the continued concentration on the histories and experiences of kings, law-makers and bishops. Where such figures appear in this volume there is concern to assess the representativeness of the experiences and attitudes of such people, the extent to which their actions and ideas impinged on wider society, and the responses their stances elicited.

Second, we see this as a contribution to the valuable feminist scholarship on the Middle Ages which, although exploring the diversity of female experience during the period, has tended to ignore the gendered status of men; ironically privileging 'men' as universal, ahistorical, atemporal and genderless.[6] Men have commonly been projected as a single oppositional category. It is to be noted that the so-called 'men's studies' have made little impact on this collection. This results from a general unease with the 'men's studies' programme, which has recently been criticized as a reassertion of male prerogatives, as a re-presentation and repackaging of a fundamentally unchanged 'male power', and as the perpetuation of reductionist and essentialist notions of masculinity; its proponents have also failed to respond to issues raised by feminist scholarship.[7]

Third, we believe that by focusing on the construction of masculinities we will add important new insights into the study of the Middle Ages, and will, we hope, encourage the rewriting of traditional historical discourses. Recent studies elucidating the experiences of women in given historical periods have, for example, urged the need to reassess traditional approaches to historical periodization;[8] the disaggregation of male experience and identity may also contribute to such an endeavour.

A number of themes emerge and are explored in this volume: the plurality of masculinities, and the existence of dominant and subordinated masculinities; the fluidity of gender categories; the contested nature of gender identities; the relationship between age and gender; the ways in which masculine identities were constructed within all-male environments; the relationship between masculinity and power; the inadequacy of the blunt bi-polarities of male/female

6. For discussion of the relationship between feminist scholarship and the study of masculinities, see Fenster, 'Why men?, pp.ix–xiix; C. Lees, 'Introduction', in Lees, ed., *Medieval Masculinities*, pp.xv–xxv.

7. For an extended critique in another field, see A. Cornwall and N. Lindisfarne, 'Dislocating masculinity: gender, power and anthropology', in *idem*, eds, *Dislocating Masculinity. Comparative Ethnographies* (London, 1994), pp.27–34.

8. See, for example, J. Kelly-Gadol, 'Did women have a renaissance?', in *Women, History and Theory: The Essays of Joan Kelly* (Chicago, 1984), pp.19–50.

and masculine/feminine; the performative nature of gender and the importance of the repeated rehearsal of gendered identities; the role of material culture in the construction of masculinities and the importance of physical and sartorial appearance; the relationship between text and social 'reality', and the role of text as a medium for gender construction; and the complex nature of the relationship between sexuality and masculinity. These themes are worth examining in a little more detail.

The plurality of masculinities: dominant and subordinated variants

It is clear that 'masculinity' is problematic as an analytical category, and that such a universal category has to be questioned if not rejected. Masculinity was created and recreated in historically specific contexts; consequently we would be better advised to think in terms of a series of masculinities, and to explore the competing and contradictory forms present within any given society, or even within an individual member of that society. Although masculinity and femininity are often seen as 'relational constructs' defined by reference to each other, this is clearly an insufficiently subtle approach; equally important in the dynamics of gendering is the competition between different notions of acceptable masculine behaviour.

Within any given society there might be contrasting and competing forms of dominant masculinity; with men differentiating themselves from other men by a variety of means. For example, several of the chapters in this book discuss the relationship between ecclesiastical views of masculine behaviour, on the one hand, and secular notions, on the other. If ecclesiastical and secular men occupied 'the same moral universe', to use Conrad Leyser's words, then it was one constructed and disseminated largely by ecclesiastical authors through the medium of text, and it is apparent that there was resistance to the views of appropriate masculine behaviour presented in those texts, both within the Church and among the laity. Several chapters highlight the tensions exhibited between secular and ecclesiastical notions of appropriate masculine behaviour. Matthew Bennett contrasts the expectations expressed in literary texts concerning the appropriate appearance and behaviour of aristocratic warriors, with the consternation this caused in ecclesiastical circles. Janet Nelson discusses the cases of ninth-century aristocratic men who were offered divergent careers and who experienced actual physical symptoms as a result of the anxieties caused by the choices presented to them. In Nelson's chapter, and in some of the examples discussed by Robert Swanson and Patricia Cullum, we are introduced to a series of individuals who experienced variant notions of masculinity, and who had to respond to the competing, contradictory and undermining images with which they were presented. The transgressive clergy of the legal court and the literary *topos* show clearly the difficulties that certain groups of men might encounter in attempting to adhere to the restrictions placed on their actions, and, in particular, on their capacity to behave like other men. In the face of these competing models for behaviour some men found it very difficult to conform, whereas others, to use Nelson's phrase, 'learned somehow to live with dissonance'.

A number of the chapters draw out the ways in which dominant masculinities within given societies were both underpinned, and also challenged, by subordinated masculinities. William Aird demonstrates that part of the authority of William the Conqueror depended on his ability to control the behaviour of his eldest son, Robert Curthose: [his] inability to receive 'the public recognition and affirmation of his fully gendered adult self' was a cause of Robert's disaffection from his father. It is notable that Robert attempted to improve his status through an imitation of his father's behaviour, but that this was criticized by an early twelfth-century chronicler who drew on biblical images to present a model of what Robert's behaviour, as a son, should have been. It seems clear that in Anglo-Norman aristocratic society in the eleventh and twelfth centuries there were normative codes of masculine behaviour and that the aristocratic *iuvenis* was not permitted to adopt the attributes of adult masculinity until the adult had deemed it appropriate for him to do so. Both Aird and Matthew Bennett show that military prowess was only valorized when it was displayed in appropriate contexts and with the required level of caution: in itself, military prowess 'did not make the man'.

Intergenerational tensions between men were an important constituent factor in the construction of masculine identities. Patricia Cullum suggests that one of the tensions which the late medieval clergy experienced was their lack of social adulthood, and it was from this that their problems concerning their masculine status stemmed. Jeremy Goldberg details the relationship between late medieval English masters and apprentices in the urban environment: although the master and the apprentice were usually from the same social background, and of the same sex, they were distinguished by the fact that the former was usually married and a householder, while the latter was unmarried and a household dependant. Goldberg reveals that it was a relationship fraught with tension and the potential for conflict, in which the apprentice was expected to adhere to a strict code of behaviour within the household, and would be punished if he did not. Yet it was also one in which there was a community of interest when challenged by those beyond this relationship, as is demonstrated by the support the apprentice John Semer gave to his master Thomas Nesfeld against the latter's wife. What we witness here is the establishment of a dominant masculinity by the masters through the control of their apprentices, but which ultimately serves to ensure the 'defence of patriarchy' from any subversive influences, such as the transgression of acceptable behaviour by other men in the hierarchy and the challenges of women.

Jenny Moore and I discuss the ways in which the relationships between infant, adult and older males in early medieval society were both reflected in, and determined through, the burial rite and the grave goods with which their societies deemed it appropriate for them to be interred. The funerary ritual was a moment at which familial and communal relationships and identities were negotiated and reasserted; as such, it had more relevance for the living community than for the deceased. Ross Balzaretti points up the expectation in the writing of Liutprand that adult men should set an example to the young, and at the same time indicates that there was an expectation that the young might be prone to bad behaviour (here, sexual transgression), although their youth did not excuse that. Pope John XII is castigated for failing to set a good example ('how many chaste youths by his example have become unchaste?'), but is, to some extent, excused by the remarks of Otto I concerning his youth ('he is only a boy, and will soon alter if good men set him an example'). Liutprand makes Otto fill the gap created by the death of John's father, and casts John's behaviour as filial disobedience. In the didactic and polemical literature of the Middle Ages there emerges a concern not only to condemn the behaviour of young and subordinated versions of masculinity, but also to place a burden of responsibility on the more mature to set a good example.

This volume throws up an important point concerning the very notion of a plurality of gender identities. Although gender studies has urged on us the need to think in terms of pluralities of masculinities and femininities, we must be aware of the fact that many authors in the Middle Ages sought to impose very rigid modes of behaviour: Ross Balzaretti, for example, describes Ratherius of Verona as depicting a world characterized by a 'typically (deliberately?) simplistic gender divide'. Perhaps there was even a contemporary perception that there really only should be two fairly rigidly defined genders: masculinity and femininity. This is the conclusion that Robert Swanson reaches in his chapter. If the imposition of clerical celibacy and restriction of clerical marriage entailed the construction of a new gender identity, then it was an experiment that was doomed to failure; by the end of the period considered by Swanson, the reformer Justus Jonas commented that, 'If you are a man, it is no more in your power to live without a woman than it is to change your sex . . . it is the way that God has created and made us.' Attempts to polarize gender identity were, according to a study by Joan Cadden, made by some medical and scientific theorists in the later Middle Ages.[9] Similarly, recent work by Miri Rubin suggests that although hermaphrodites were not especially stigmatized, it was expected that they should choose between two polarized sexual identities, adopt the characteristic gendered behaviour related to the chosen sexual identity, and maintain this choice.[10]

Although from our perspective we may recognize a whole range of gender identities in the Middle Ages, we must, then, be sensitive to the possibility that contemporaries thought rather less theoretically about such matters, and that they broadly recognized only two essential gender categories. Indeed, a number of the chapters demonstrate that in discussing appropriate forms of behaviour many medieval authors tended to point up polarized identities: thus, for example, there is a single notion of societal masculinity held up by clerical reformers in the eleventh and twelfth centuries – of which marriage and procreation were essential elements – in opposition to which the clergy were attempting to construct a different gender identity. In this context Robert Swanson speaks appropriately of a third gender, even if some modern gender studies have disputed the use of the term if we are prepared to accept a range of masculinities

9. J. Cadden, *Meanings of Sex Difference in the Middle Ages* (Cambridge, 1993). It should be noted that some writers did allow for a range of possibilities in the male and the female (related to complexion, shape and disposition), but that individuals were also described by reference to what were believed to be masculine or feminine qualities: this is evident in terms such as the 'manly woman' and the 'womanly man', which serve to 'reassert a commitment to the ideal of a two-termed system' (p.225).

10. M. Rubin, 'The person in the form: medieval challenges to bodily "order"', in S. Kay and M. Rubin, eds, *Framing Medieval Bodies* (Manchester, 1994), pp.101–6.

and femininities.[11] On the other hand, Patricia Cullum's preference for the description 'a different form of masculinity' presents
an issue for future discussion. The difficulties which some of the
clergy encountered in fulfilling the expectations placed on them
highlights this dilemma: they may have sought to be 'like angels'
(Swanson's third gender) but were readily brought down to earth by
their desire to be men.

The reinforcement of masculine roles

Appropriate masculine behaviour, by both dominant and subordinated masculinities, was inculcated by a variety of means. The tales of
the aristocratic lovers which Mark Chinca discusses (which include
the ridiculing of men who play subordinate roles to women, and
those who run away), the deeds depicted in the epic and romance
literature which Marianne Ailes examines, as much as the more
overt condemnations of the behaviour of Robert Curthose and his
associates by Orderic Vitalis in Aird's study, all serve both to glorify
the actions of the dominant males *and* as a lesson, if not a warning,
to other males about what was expected of them in the hierarch-
icized masculine world. A number of the chapters reinforce the notion
that gendered identity was something which was learned through
processes of socialization, and shaped through social interaction
and social expectation. Janet Nelson comments 'on the theme of
training in masculine self-control', and Matthew Bennett examines
the ways in which appropriate notions of knightly masculinity were
inculcated through communal living, eating, hunting and sleeping.

The transmission of text is highlighted by a number of the
contributors as central to the underpinning of dominant forms of
masculinity. Some medieval authors drew on biblical and classical
authority to sustain their arguments: see for example, William Aird's
discussion of Orderic Vitalis' use of the stories of Absalom and
Rehoboam, and of Mosaic Law, and the biblical precedents utilized
by the monastic and episcopal authors discussed by Conrad Leyser
and Ross Balzaretti. The repetition of stereotyped imagery was central to the subordination of eunuchs in Byzantine society; Shaun
Tougher exposes the reality behind the stereotypes, and demonstrates that the perpetuation of myth was important to maintaining

---

11. For a variety of views, see G. Herdt, ed., *Third Sex, Third Gender: Beyond Sexual
Dimorphism in Culture and History* (New York, 1994); A. Cornwall, 'Gendered iden-
tities and gender ambiguity among *travestis* in Salvador, Brazil', in Cornwall and
Lindisfarne, eds, *Dislocating Masculinity*, pp.111–32.

the hierarchical relationship between eunuchs and the dominant secular male elite. Indeed, in this instance the subordinated masculinity became the repository for all that was not acceptable to the dominant male elite – lack of beards, sexual immaturity, inability to marry and have children, high-pitched voices – and, furthermore, this was a gender identity which was deliberately created both by a physical act and by legal prescription. Marianne Ailes and Matthew Bennett discuss the depiction in French epic and romance literature of a repertoire of male couples, some of which were comprised of men of equal status and others of which were not. This motif, repeated so often, served as an affirmation of what was expected of aristocratic males of varying status. The difficulties attendant on the imposition of clerical celibacy discussed by Robert Swanson and the resultant failures of some clerics to meet this new masculine – or emasculine – status culminated in an anti-clerical response which was articulated through a series of stereotyped images. The randy cleric who could not be trusted with the wives of his parishioners is a familiar character in late medieval literature: this literary motif impinged on social perceptions, and it is notable that rape was an accusation regularly levelled at the clergy, sometimes irrespective of the real crime, because it was an accusation which could be made to stick. Finally, the similarity between clerical characteristics and the alleged failings of women – primarily as gossips – was also commonly observed.

One further way in which dominant masculine behaviour was reinforced through the medium of text was through the absence of introspection in the writing of many medieval authors. In the epic literature it could be said that the association between aristocratic and royal masculinity and violence is both gendered and institutionalized through the lack of introspection in those texts, and also, implicitly, through the sparse roles for women in the tales depicted.[12] The twelfth-century letter-collections discussed by Julian Haseldine similarly underpin monastic masculinities through their lack of internal analysis of the friendships which they serve to maintain, and through their failure to distinguish between recent acquaintances, long-standing friendships and people completely unknown to the author. On the other hand, as Mark Chinca suggests, the context for the performance of late medieval literature introduces a different perspective on those texts, one in which a certain amount of debate might be allowed for, even if the words of the text do not

12. Fenster, 'Why men?', p.x.

suggest any level of debate. The presence of women in the audience
or the performance of some strophes in the guise of a female character would have greatly altered the range of meanings of those texts.

If we look to aspects of monasticism other than that considered
by Haseldine, we perhaps find evidence of some introspection and
debate. Caroline Walker Bynum's recent work on the imagery of
Jesus as a loving mother in monastic writing provides evidence for
anxiety in the monastic world. It was part of the rhetoric of the new
more affective piety, and of a growing concern, especially in the
Cistercian order, with the monastic role in pastoral care. It was also
part of a broader feminization of ecclesiastical language, in which
monks and bishops described their weakness and humility in feminine terms. The maternal imagery also arguably reflects the changing nature of monasticism in which child oblation ceased and those
who came to the monastic profession now had some experience of
family life.[13] Indeed, Patricia Cullum argues in the present volume
that late medieval monks may have had more of a problem in
dealing with their entry into the cloister than did their predecessors who would have done so, as child oblates, at much the same
age as they were acquiring their gender identity. Late medieval
monks, and also secular clergy, would have potentially faced great
anguish as they entered their chosen profession, since it contrasted
greatly as a way of life with the expectations of the gender identity
which they would already have adopted; hence, a complete renunciation of their extant gender identity was required. In contrast
to the confident images reproduced in the letters discussed by
Haseldine, other perspectives serve to remind us that reality was
not always as straightforward as some of the images with which we
are presented. Furthermore, it demonstrates the vulnerability of
the rarefied monastic notions of masculinity once they came into
contact with wider societal norms.

Strategies for undermining subordinated masculinities

Another means by which dominant masculinities maintained their
hegemony was through the feminization of forms of masculinity
considered to be inferior. A number of examples are cited in this

13. C. Walker Bynum, *Jesus as Mother. Studies in the Spirituality of the High Middle Ages* (Berkeley 1982).

collection: the feminizing of Robert Curthose in a dream narrative; the close associations made between eunuchs and royal and aristo- cratic women; the association made by Bishop Ratherius between women and lack of sexual control; the suspicion of late medieval clerics articulated through the perception of similarity to women, in their behaviour (as gossips, or riding side-saddle), their dress and through their use of speech (in the performance of their office) which was perceived as a feminine attribute. This feminization of subordinated masculinities also became a source of suspicion for other men. For example, the very characteristics for which the clergy were vilified were, conversely, deemed to make them attractive to women.

The link between different forms of masculinity and homosexual activity was also frequently made by those in dominant positions. In so doing, the latter effectively relegated homosexual masculinities to the bottom of a gender hierarchy among men. Byzantine eunuchs were characterized both as homosexual – an accusation which Tougher demonstrates was not always borne out in reality – and as being like women; at the same time they were accused of lacking courage and bravery and of being ineffective exponents of martial skills. In this characterization not only were eunuchs relegated to a subordinate gender status, but martial skills and their associated characteristics were explicitly gendered as heterosexual, elite, secular, masculine traits. Ironically, the whole of the Byzantine empire was liable to be depicted from an external perspective as being effeminate because of the very presence of the eunuchs whose subordination was funda- mental to notions of elite masculinity within the empire.

The association of dominant forms of masculinity with power was another means by which the gender hierarchy might be rein- forced. Because military prowess was gendered as an attribute of secular, masculine, elite identity, inability or inexperience in the military sphere was a sign of subordination, and associated expli- citly with those who did not belong to the dominant masculine group. Matthew Bennett discusses the fact that military prowess was a trait which a man might be expected to have inherited from his kins- men; William of Orange derides a young warrior until he realizes that he is his nephew but then encourages him to demonstrate his martial abilities, observing that he 'certainly ought to be a knight, for so were your father and your other kinsmen'. Conrad Leyser and Ross Balzaretti demonstrate that discussions by early medi- eval authors about the nature of authority were explicitly linked to masculine sexuality: self-control was expected of those who exercised authority, but women were not expected to be able to exercise the necessary self-restraint, and so were excluded from positions of authority. Jenny Moore and I discuss the relationship between 'power' (whether defined in political or military spheres, through wealth, or social status and position within the local community) and masculinity or symbols of masculine identity.

Other recent studies have discussed the ways in which women who exercised power or behaved in an heroic manner are not uncommonly described in masculine terms. The work of Carol Clover on the Scandinavian sagas – to which Moore and I draw attention – demonstrates this point very clearly.[14] A study of female cross-dressing by Valerie Hotchkiss reveals that women who wanted to exercise power (for example, as head of the household follow-ing widowhood or desertion, by rescuing captured husbands, and performing great acts of piety) had only male role-models on which to draw, and often responded to this by donning male clothing and passing themselves off as male; this was only condemned in his-torical or literary sources if the woman attempted to exercise control over men.[15] Powerful women may be forced, in some circum-stances, to adopt the trappings of masculinity.

It is important to analyse the ways in which relations of power and powerlessness are gendered in given societies, and the ways in which power was associated with particular forms of masculinity. In the societies with which this volume is concerned, as John Tosh has observed of nineteenth-century Britain, underlying all ideologies of masculinity was 'the incontrovertible fact of men's social power'.[16] The chapters in this volume demonstrate the range of ways in which that social power was reinforced and how challenges to it were met.

Resistance

Of course, there was also a certain amount of resistance to the dominant masculinities in medieval societies. Sometimes this took the form of actual confrontation. In other instances an act of rejec-tion of the trappings of a dominant masculinity was undertaken. Janet Nelson comments on the rejection of the sword-belt as a

14. C. Clover, 'Regardless of sex: men, women and power in early northern Europe', *Speculum* 68 (1993), pp.363–87.

15. V.R. Hotchkiss, *Clothes Make the Man. Female Cross Dressing in Medieval Europe* (New York, 1996).

16. Tosh, 'What should historians do with masculinity?', pp.183–4.

symbol of aristocratic masculine values and of the rejection of sexual activity by those aristocratic men who were experiencing difficulty in living out their assigned role. Patricia Cullum suggests that one strategy for dealing with the stigma of belonging to a minority group was to 'valorize the negative characteristics projected onto them', and that the ban on certain kinds of behaviour (notably fighting and fornication) 'may, paradoxically, have acted as a licence to behave in precisely those ways'.

Men in subordinated positions might also enhance their status, and to some extent resist the position in the masculine hierarchy to which they had been assigned, through the domination of women and men occupying the lowest-ranked masculinities. Perhaps more common, and arguably more effective, in resisting dominant masculine paradigms, however, was the solace found in the company of peer groups. We might think here of the 'coterie of similarly disaffected aristocratic youths' who surrounded Robert Curthose, of the drinking-partners of the urban apprentices, or of the male couples so prominent in late medieval epic and romance literature. However, although all-male associations were important in the construction of male identities it is important to note that desire between men was inadmissible.[17] So while associations of males were acceptable, homosexual activity was rather more problematic. As a result Marianne Ailes' chapter is an important corrective to recent studies which have interpreted many of the homosocial scenes of medieval literary and historical texts as homosexual. As Ailes reveals, such studies have started from a fundamental misunderstanding of literary *topoi* and symbolic gesture. Matthew Bennett observes that whether or not homosexuality was prevalent in court culture in the eleventh and twelfth centuries, it was not considered to be a positive attribute of military masculinity.

Masculinities and femininities

Crucial to the construction of gender roles is the relationship between varying notions of masculinity and of femininity. Few of the texts discussed by the contributors to this volume deal directly, or at length, with women or with the relationship between men and women, but that does not mean that we cannot explore the relationships between men and women in given societies. The very

17. *Ibid.*, p.187.

exclusion of women from texts, and from the events which the texts describe, has much to reveal about the roles which women were, or were not, expected to fulfil, which, in turn, determined the way in which masculinity was defined in given contexts; a man was commonly what a woman was not. Yet we have to remember that normative texts and literary works may have much to say about what was *expected* of men and women in given contexts, but that this may have been far removed from what they actually did.

The great emphasis placed on marriage in many of the texts discussed in this volume also had important implications for the relationships between men and women, even though many of the authors are mostly concerned with men and marriage. Marriage was controversial in the Middle Ages and was shaped by both the Church and the secular aristocracy.[18] Marital status was an important determining factor of gender identity, alongside age, social status and profession. In many respects marriage placed men in a socially dominant position over women, as they became responsible for their wives in the eyes of the law. Yet it also placed burdens and obligations on men: they were expected to provide for their wives and families; to look after their wife's dowry, which might bring them into conflict with the kinsmen of their wife; to perform sexually; and to beget children. Failure in any of these marital responsibilities might indicate that 'he had failed as a man'.[19]

The performative nature of gender and the role of material culture

Judith Butler has observed that 'gender is an identity tenuously constructed in time . . . through a stylised repetition of acts'.[20] The chapters in this volume demonstrate that performance and the public affirmation of identity were central to the construction of masculinities. Jenny Moore and I have located the burial rite in early medieval societies as a moment when gender roles were reinforced, and have highlighted the changing symbolic meanings of

---

18. For a discussion with extensive bibliography, see Nelson, 'Family, gender and sexuality'.

19. V.L. Bullough, 'On being a male in the Middle Ages', in Lees, ed., *Medieval Masculinities*, pp.31–45; S.M. Stuard, 'Burdens of matrimony: husbanding and gender in medieval Italy', *ibid.*, pp.61–71.

20. J. Butler, *Gender Trouble: Feminism and the Subversion of Identity* (New York, 1990), p.140.

grave goods. The funerary ritual was a public ceremony requiring a significant audience to be meaningful; it also required clear norms of behaviour, forming what has been termed a 'grammar of display'.[21] Mark Chinca looks not only at what twelfth-century German love lyrics *say* about masculine behaviour, but also considers the differing ways in which that message might be understood according to the performative context of these lyrics, determined by who was in the audience and whether the lover in the 'Falkenlied' was presented to the audience as a man or a woman. On the one hand these texts might be seen as a means by which 'sexist and patriarchal ideology' was reproduced and reinforced; on the other, they provide evidence that masculinity could be 'an object of discussion and debate'. Julian Haseldine describes twelfth-century monastic letters as the medium of the cultivation of friendship between monastic authors: 'letter writing was an art, and letter collections were refined and stylish compilations, carefully preserved for posterity', in which ideas were made available to a comparatively wide audience. Moreover, letters were part of an exchange, often including verbal messages and prayers, and the letter itself might be considered a gift; if we see letter-writing as a means by which the status and identity of monks and bishops was substantiated, we must see it as being largely public and performative. The sporting competitions of the urban apprentices described by Jeremy Goldberg provide another example of the importance of performance in the construction of gender identity.

Gesture and appearance are also instrumental in the performance of gender roles. The anxiety experienced by Gerald of Aurillac about the competing gender identities with which he had been presented caused him to have difficulties with what Janet Nelson describes as 'the very signs of his rank and of his masculinity': Gerald is said by his biographer, Odo of Cluny, to have neglected to acquire for himself a new leather strap by which he hung his sword, and he declined to have fine belt-fittings. Matthew Bennett shows that aristocratic military status was defined and determined in epic and romance literature by dress, hairstyle, physique, a 'handsome face', and even by the ability to consume large quantities of food; appearance and status are inextricably linked in these texts. The Byzantine eunuchs discussed by Tougher were characterized by their appearance – in particular their lack of beards – and in

21. G. Halsall, 'Female status and power in early Merovingian central Austrasia: the burial evidence', *Early Medieval Europe* 5 (1) (1996), p.13.

response to this the wearing of beards by the non-eunuch masculine elite became commonplace; indeed, the term 'bearded' was used to describe the latter by the ninth-century author Philotheos. I have already mentioned the ways in which the gestures and appearance of the late medieval clergy became the focus for much criticism and suspicion in anti-clerical literature. Significantly, Matthew Bennett highlights the discrepancy between aspects of aristocratic appearance valorized in epic and romance literature, and the more critical attitudes of clerical commentators. This reminds us that the 'meaning' of personal appearance was not static and might vary according to social context or the expectations and beliefs of the viewer.

Sexuality and the body

A number of the chapters in the volume reveal the extent to which sexuality and sexual activity were central to notions of appropriate and condemned gendered behaviour. Ross Balzaretti discusses the ways in which sexuality was considered to be part of a person's public persona in the writings of the three bishops his chapter examines. He argues that these authors (Ratherius of Verona, Atto of Vercelli and Liutprand of Cremona) deliberately linked men, sex, property and power, and associated political instability and corruption with 'an improperly sexual masculinity' and with lack of control by men. Also notable is the imposition of 'compulsory heterosexuality' through the stance taken by these authors, while marriage was considered to be the most appropriate means by which heterosexuality and proper sexual control might be ensured; however, this caused problems for the clergy who were simultaneously expected to observe a celibate lifestyle, and one reason advanced for clerical marriage was that it would avoid the clergy being accused of having sex with men. Indeed marriage proved a crucial testing-ground for gender identities, especially for those excluded from it by law, their profession, their status or their youth.

A common theme in the chapters by Leyser and Balzaretti is an emphasis on the constructed nature of 'the body' and sexuality: neither is natural or innate; each is socially conditioned, and aspects of both are considered to be more or less important according to circumstances. Both Leyser and Balzaretti reveal the monastic concern with control over bodily fluids; a capacity that was explicitly linked with suitability to hold public office. As Leyser also points out, concern about bodily functions is not simply 'infant trauma [or] cultural neurosis' but it stems from the fact that the body 'served as a crucial medium in which to discuss the social order'. Janet Nelson also discusses the ways in which bodily experience was central to the crises endured by ninth-century aristocratic men about their gender identity. Matthew Bennett comments on aspects of the appearance of warriors which were explicitly linked with expectations of military prowess and virility, but which caused consternation among clerical writers. In other words, the body was both socially constructed and contested.

It is important to note that although homosexual activity might be condemned there had not yet developed a concept of the homosexual figure. The 'stigmatization of homosexuals as an aberrant category of men set apart from the "normal"' is a modern phenomenon;[22] to medieval authors the euphemistic 'sins *contra naturam*' were possibilities open to all men, in contrast to 'modern notions of "innate homosexuality"', as Balzaretti puts it. Proper sexual restraint was what was expected and those who failed to exercise it were liable to criticism; ultimately it did not matter whether the failing was adultery, sex *contra naturum* or clerical marriage.

Conclusions

The various societies of medieval Europe had explicitly formulated theories of sexual inequality; they inherited the notion of male superiority from the classical world, a concept bolstered by biblical images of male and female behaviour and status. Yet we should not assume that medieval societies simply borrowed their notions of gendered behaviour; they actively constructed and reconstructed attitudes to gender identities. In addition to classical and biblical images, we also encounter a series of stereotyped literary *topoi* concerning expected male and female behaviour. These stereotyped images were commonly then enshrined in legal, religious, educational, scientific and political doctrines. There has been a tendency among scholars of the Middle Ages to present these notions as if they were the product of social consensus rather than of conflict. This volume challenges that view and shows that medieval gender roles and identities were themselves contested.

22. Tosh, 'What should historians do with masculinity?', p.191.

In conclusion, it can be stated that it is apparent that there is a wealth of evidence which may be used to contribute to a discussion of this subject. Recent theoretical work on gender identity, and masculinities in particular, can be explored and developed in the context of the Middle Ages from a variety of perspectives. This volume demonstrates that it is possible to explore normative codes of behaviour, societal expectation and subjective experience, and to assess the relative relationships between them. By drawing on these aspects of medieval society and culture we can further develop our understanding of medieval notions of masculinity. Furthermore, this volume also provides new perspectives on medieval society more generally, by asking questions of that which has for so long been considered to be unproblematic. Men were socially dominant in so many contexts in medieval society, yet the lack of analysis of the basis of this dominance has effectively rendered men 'everywhere but nowhere'.[23] This volume locates men as gendered beings in their historical contexts and reveals the multiple social meanings of masculinity. We hope that this volume will encourage further work on the historical construction of masculine identities.

23. *Ibid.*, p.180.

PART ONE

Attaining Masculinity

CHAPTER TWO

'Death Makes the Man'? Burial Rite and the Construction of Masculinities in the Early Middle Ages

D.M. HADLEY AND J.M. MOORE

Given the relative paucity of documentary sources in the early medieval period, much attention has been paid to the excavation of cemeteries and the nature of burial rite as a means of understanding and explaining social organization, ethnic identity, religious belief, political affiliations and so on. Many studies have, however, maintained a marked reluctance to deal with gender relations and find similarities, as much as differences, in the burial rites associated with males and females difficult to incorporate in their analyses of early medieval society. If the issue *is* addressed, stereotype is likely to dictate the approach taken. A more considered approach is clearly required: there are good reasons to suggest that burial was a major medium for the display of social status, of which gender was an important aspect. This chapter examines and challenges existing assumptions and biases in the interpretation of the construction of gender in early medieval cemeteries, and in particular rejects the fixed binary oppositions normally employed in discussions of male and female identity. There are undoubtedly common characteristics in the elaboration of male graves and in the signification of masculinity in early medieval cemeteries, but these patterns are not universal and do change over time. This suggests that masculinity was not constructed in a fixed and unchanging manner.

A massive body of data has been excavated from inhumation cemeteries in Anglo-Saxon England, Merovingian Gaul and Viking Age Scandinavia. Evidence for the construction of gender roles and relations – and, indeed, other forms of social identity – can potentially be deduced from the number, type and range of grave goods; the position of grave goods in graves; the position of the body

21

in the grave; differences in burial rites both within and between cemeteries; the relationship between age and grave goods; and changes over time in the nature and distribution of grave goods. This body of data offers new insights into the construction of masculinities in early medieval society and provides a perspective beyond the scope of textual analysis.[1]

Gender attribution and the search for material correlates

The relationship between archaeology and gender studies has been explicitly theorized in a number of recent publications and it is now recognized by many archaeologists that gender is a relational social process; a major structuring principle and dynamic of social and cultural life, providing guiding principles for the enactment of daily activities.[2] Furthermore, it is recognized that gender is constructed according to differing and changing social rules, and that we therefore have to look for the localized strategies by which gender identities were constructed – to 'disrupt the notion of fixity'[3] – and challenge monocausal and generalizing explanations. There has been much discussion of the means by which archaeologists may explore gender in their evidence, and a great deal remains to be done. The overriding emphasis on restoring women to the archaeological narrative in recent studies has proved a much-needed corrective to earlier work, but it needs to be balanced with a re-cognition that gender identities are formed in relational contexts in which femininities and masculinities are constructed both in relation to other femininities and masculinities and to each other. As such, the uncritical treatment of men and masculinity must also be addressed.

Medieval archaeology is widely regarded as the least theoretically well-informed branch of European archaeology; consequently it is tempting to draw on other branches for a theoretical framework. However, we must be clear about how successful archaeology has

1. We are grateful to Trish Skinner and Guy Halsall for their comments on an earlier version of this chapter.
2. A recent collection of papers which is based on this premise – and contains a number of studies about historical periods – is J.M. Moore and E. Scott, eds, *Invisible People and Processes. Writing Gender and Childhood into European Archaeology* (London, 1997).
3. J.W. Scott, 'Gender: a useful category of historical analysis', *AHR* 91(5) (1986), p.1075.

been in general at discussing gender before we take this route. Early attempts by archaeologists to discuss gender focused on the search for material correlates; that is to say, items which could be securely associated with either men or women. The underlying premise was that gender would become accessible to archaeologists as an analytic category if they could render women 'visible' in the archaeological record and this, in turn, would enable a challenge to be mounted against androcentrism in archaeology.[4] Ethnographic parallels were instrumental to the development of gender studies in archaeology, and these have been drawn upon to help understand the roles of men and women in given pre-industrial societies, because they show the potential variety of gender roles and relations.

These early efforts have, however, been the subject of critical reappraisal, and a variety of weaknesses have been identified. First, a number of studies offer little more than a sharp critique of existing androcentric approaches, and provide little with which to replace those interpretations. Second, archaeologists have tended to await the development of gender theory in other disciplines (notably history, anthropology, and other branches of the social sciences). This is problematic for two main reasons: gender theory does not offer a static or definitive body of theory from which archaeologists may borrow; and it perpetuates the myth that archaeology is only able to test theories developed elsewhere, rather than forming and questioning aspects of social theory. Third, we now recognize that gender structures were not static and that while attempting to undermine the 'biology is destiny' mantra archaeologists may unwittingly have underpinned it by imposing a fixed set of gender roles, relations and inequalities. Instead, emphasis has to be placed on the ways in which gender was actively constructed and reconstructed, and the extent to which it was historically and culturally specific; as a result, cross-cultural analogies might not be especially relevant, and should be treated with caution. Fourth, there is a tendency – especially in those studies which take as their aim the need to isolate the experiences of women – to reinforce existing stereotypes through the articulation of female experience in comparison with the criteria already established, though not questioned

4. For summaries see, M.W. Conkey and J.M. Gero, 'Tensions, pluralities, and engendering archaeology: an introduction to women and prehistory', in *idem*, eds, *Engendering Archaeology: Women and Prehistory*, (Oxford, 1991), pp.3–30; A. Wylie, 'Gender theory and the archaeological record: why is there no archaeology of gender?', in *ibid.*, pp.31–54. This, and the following, paragraph draw extensively on these two papers, as they provide a wide-ranging overview and substantive bibliographies; we have suggested additional reading where appropriate.

critically, for male-associated activities. There is also an inclination in some feminist scholarship to look for common patterns of female oppression and victimization without due attention being paid to the variability of female experience, and there is often a tendency to maintain the dichotomous opposition between males and females and thus to reproduce the biases inherent in androcentric approaches. Finally, the search for material correlates tended to reproduce the very assumptions it set out to challenge, since stereotyped models determined which items were thought to be associated with women and men.

There have, however, been some notable successes in early attempts to incorporate gender studies into archaeology, not least the undermining of the scholarly opinion which maintained that gender studies are not objective or scientific enough to be an acceptable part of the archaeological discipline. Some scholars attempted to develop a more rigorous 'scientific' approach to gender studies: in particular through the correction of previous 'biases'; but also through the development of an objective or ambivalent 'standpoint'.[5] Other scholars have opted rather to abandon the theoretical premises of the archaeology of the 1970s (so-called New Archaeology) and have instead derived theoretical underpinning from 'post-modern' critiques, which insist that 'no knowledge claims, nor any methods or criteria for establishing them, can be formulated independent of any particular (socio-political) standpoints'.[6] This is a rejection of the notion that there is any such thing as transcontextual 'knowledge', and an affirmation that all interpretations are contingent on the attitudes and opinions of the researcher. Furthermore, it has been argued that feminist experiences and perspectives are just one of many standpoints that exist, and that, therefore, totalizing explanatory frameworks must be abandoned as unattainable goals. Although the pluralism inherent in post-modern theory is appealing to gender studies, a fundamental problem remains for feminist scholarship because it cannot accept that the proclamations of 'sexist' science are not false.[7]

It has been necessary to explain these developments in archaeological theory, in part to locate this chapter in its broader archaeological context, but more pointedly as a prelude to a discussion of the general failure of medieval archaeologists to adopt – or

5. S. Harding, *The Science Question in Feminism* (Ithaca, 1986), p.195.
6. Wylie, 'Gender theory', p.43.
7. See, for example, A. Fausto-Sterling, *Myths of Gender: Biological Theories About Women and Men* (New York, 1985).

even to recognize – these theoretical debates, and to a series of proposals for how that might be achieved. A recent critique by Roberta Gilchrist has identified the tendency in studies of early medieval society to treat social categories of persons as 'single, uni-fied groups, discussed as objects'; and she suggests that a more theoretically well-informed approach to gender and early medieval cemeteries needs to regard the individuals buried in early medieval cemeteries not merely as objects but as social agents with 'the poten-tial to . . . engage in social practice'.[8] Many studies of early medieval cemeteries have – if they have considered gender issues at all – tended to concentrate on material correlates, and on assigning particular sets of grave goods to males and females respectively. They have tended to make simplistic statements about the role and status of the interred on the basis of these grave good assemblages: grave goods have often been viewed as being purely functional – therefore those buried with swords must have been warriors, for example – with little consideration given to the symbolic value of artefacts.[9] In traditional accounts far more attention has been placed on male burials, and these have been taken as the normative burial rite from which social structures and values may be determined, and against which female burials have been compared. Yet in react-ing against this a number of studies have done little more than to 'add' women to the archaeological record, commonly develop-ing a discussion of female status by citing exceptional, or 'deviant' female burials, and discussing 'unusual' female status-groups such as queens and 'cunning-women'.[10] These approaches are insufficient for three main reasons: burial rite and grave goods have been inter-preted in a somewhat functional manner; both have been interpreted from the perspective of a dichotomous opposition between males and females; and male burials have rarely been problematized. To some extent the first two of our observations have been addressed in recent studies,[11] but, as yet, the problematization of male burials, and of masculinity, has been barely attempted in a manner which is

---

8. Gilchrist, 'Ambivalent bodies: gender and medieval archaeology', in Moore and Scott, eds, *Invisible People and Processes*, pp.46–50, at p.46 for the quotation.

9. For a critique see H. Härke, 'Changing symbols in a changing society: the Anglo-Saxon weapon burial rite in the seventh century', in M. Carver, ed., *The Age of Sutton Hoo* (Woodbridge, 1992), pp.149–65.

10. C. Arnold, *An Archaeology of the Early Anglo-Saxon Kingdoms* (London, 1988), pp.154, 175–8; H. Leyser, *Medieval Women. A Social History of Women in England, 450–1500* (London, 1995), pp.3–18.

11. See, for example, the work of Guy Halsall, cited elsewhere in this article, and S.J. Lucy, 'Housewives, warriors and slaves? Sex and gender in Anglo-Saxon burials', in Moore and Scott, eds, *Invisible People and Processes*, pp.150–68.

informed by gender theory.[12] To transform a phrase used by Simone de Beauvoir: 'one is not born a man, but, rather, becomes one'. This 'becoming' is culturally compelled, and does not derive from biological sex alone.

Grave goods and the construction of social identity

It is necessary to begin our discussion by examining the role that burial rite played in societies, and how the evidence recoverable from this activity may be interpreted and what it may reveal about both the dead and the living community. Again this is an issue that has received more extensive consideration in other branches of archaeology, although we recognize that some early medievalists have also given sophisticated thought to this matter.

In prehistoric archaeology, the construction of identity can be explored through limited avenues, the main one being the nature of burial and associated grave goods, and therefore much attention has been placed on this aspect of social display in studies concerned which social structure and identity.[13] Burial is a deliberate act of deposition, and, although it should hardly need to be stated, it is important to remember that the dead do not bury themselves, and consequently 'the social identity of an individual as represented in their burial is to a large extent dependent upon the way that other people chose to represent the nature of the person in death'.[14] The call for material culture evidenced in burial remains to be read as 'text' has long been understood by many archaeologists. In an early medieval context, where documentary sources are scarce, the evidence from cemeteries is similarly of great importance in evaluating social relations, status, individual identity and gender relationships. Unfortunately, however, there is still a tendency among commentators of medieval burial rite to relate grave goods directly to the status of the individual through a crude method of adding up the number of items or assigning 'ranking scores' to particular artefacts.[15] Yet it has long been recognized that the status ascribed

12. See, however, Gilchrist, 'Ambivalent bodies', p.49.

13. See, for example, P. Garwood *et al.*, eds, *Sacred and Profane: Proceedings of a Conference on Archaeology, Ritual and Religion*, Oxford Committee for Archaeology Monograph no. 32 (1991).

14. J. Huggett, 'Social analysis of early Anglo-Saxon inhumation burials: archaeological methodologies', *Journal of European Archaeology* 4 (1996), p.338.

15. See, for example, C.J. Arnold, 'Wealth and social structure', in P. Rahtz, T. Dickinson and L. Watts, eds, *Anglo-Saxon Cemeteries*, BAR 82 (1980), pp.81–142.

to a person in life by the community within which they live is not necessarily or predictably reflected in death. Furthermore, traditional assessments of the significance of grave goods have tended to interpret grave goods in a functional manner, and to emphasize factors such as wealth, economic status, military capacity and political power, at the expense of familial status, role in the wider community, and gender identity.

The public nature of burial has to be taken into account when assessing funerary evidence. The great size of some cemeteries suggests that they were used over a period of time by several communities, who presumably had to travel to bury their dead. The lavishness of burials is suggestive of great social competition. There is also evidence from excavations to indicate the nature of the funeral ritual in the early Middle Ages. That it was a public ritual involving such activities as feasting is suggested by the evidence of ashes, potsherds and animal bones in pits and in grave-fills in cemeteries, and by food offerings in graves.[16] The meaning and significance of artefacts in this public burial context may have been very different from their meaning in other social contexts.

New interpretations of early medieval burial evidence are hampered by the traditional emphasis on grave goods; indeed, many nineteenth- and early twentieth-century excavation reports commonly failed to record anything about the burial beyond the grave goods. Furthermore, in the absence of modern techniques of biological sexing, grave goods have commonly been used to determine the sex of an individual. Vera Evison observed of the burials at Buckland (Dover) that 'when . . . a skeleton is provided with grave goods exclusively attributable to one sex, e.g. brooches and beads for a woman and a sword or spear for a man, it is regarded reasonable here to assume that the grave goods are a true indication of sex'.[17] There are various reasons why this emphasis on grave goods alone is inadequate. First, the 'meaning' of a particular burial may be determined from a whole series of factors, and not merely from the grave goods: the ceremony of the burial itself; the position of the body and the relationship of any associated artefacts to it; and the relationship of the burial and its grave goods to other burials in the vicinity.[18]

16. G. Halsall, 'Female status and power in early Merovingian central Austrasia: the burial evidence', *EME* 5(1) (1996), p.13.

17. V. Evison, *Dover: The Buckland Anglo-Saxon Cemetery* (London, 1987), p.123.

18. See, for example, E.J. Pader, *Symbolism, Social Relations and the Interpretation of Mortuary Remains*, BAR International Series 130 (1982); Härke, 'Changing symbols'.

Second, where biological sexing has been possible it has been demonstrated that the traditional association between, on the one hand, males and weapon burials and, on the other, females and jewellery assemblages cannot always be sustained.[19] Many graves do not have grave assemblages which fit the traditionally adduced weapon–jewellery dichotomy. While there clearly *is* a tendency for some adult male graves to be furnished with weapons, it is also apparent that female burials are sometimes accompanied by weapons (as is the case at Heslerton, Yorkshire), and that some male graves contain jewellery (as at Sewerby, Yorkshire). In addition, weapons and jewellery are sometimes found together (as occurs at Kempston (Bedfordshire), Harwell (Berkshire) and Salfleet (Isle of Wight)).[20] Work on Scandinavian burials of the Later Iron Age (c.AD550–1050) similarly reveals that jewellery and weapons were not uncommonly found together.[21] It is notable, however, that in some instances where this seeming discrepancy has been recognized the author has performed what Jenny Moore has termed 'interpretative gymnastics' in order to deny the possibility that stereotypes might be inaccurate and has looked instead to errors in the scientific method.[22] We would, however, add a number of caveats to these points. Although it is significant that weapons and jewellery are sometimes found together, in the absence of biological sexing of skeletons from many graves, it is difficult to state with any real conviction which burials contain males and which females. Furthermore, other studies *have* revealed that weapons and jewellery are not normally found together.[23] Finally, it should be noted that any assessment of the deposition of grave goods is dependent on how terms such as 'weapon' or 'jewellery' are interpreted.

Third, the emphasis on grave goods has tended to maintain the binary opposition between males and females, and masculinity and femininity, based on an assumption that sex and gender were articulated in an unvarying manner through the use of grave goods.

19. Lucy, 'Sex and gender'.

20. A. Meaney, *A Gazetteer of Early Anglo-Saxon Burial Sites* (London, 1968). Of course, the validity of this statement rests heavily on how the jewellery category is defined.

21. L.H. Dommasnes, 'Late Iron Age in western Norway. Female roles and ranks as deduced from an analysis of burial customs', *Norwegian Archaeological Review* 15 (1982), pp.77–8.

22. J. Moore, 'Conclusion: the visibility of the invisible', in Moore and Scott, eds, *Invisible People and Processes*, p.254; Lucy, 'Sex and gender', pp.155, 161.

23. G. Halsall, *Settlement and Social Organization. The Merovingian Region of Metz* (Cambridge, 1995), pp.75–109; K. Brush, 'Gender and mortuary analysis in pagan Anglo-Saxon archaeology,' *Archaeological Review from Cambridge* 7, 1 (1988), pp.80–1.

Less attention has been paid to assemblages of grave goods which do not contain artefacts so easily attributable to males or females – sometimes termed 'neutral' assemblages.[24] Still less has been said about the sex and/or gender implications of graves which have no grave goods. The extent to which grave goods may be correlated with males or females varies. Many burials are accompanied by grave goods which are not exclusively associated with either male or female burials (at Spong Hill (Norfolk), a late fifth- and early sixth-century cemetery, the inhumations contain items such as knives, buckles and strap-ends, pottery vessels, iron rings, iron pins and copper fragments which were seemingly not sex-linked).[25] As a result of such findings, the use of grave goods to determine biological sex has recently been dismissed as 'ridiculous'.[26]

Fourth, there has been an assumption that particular artefacts always carried the same significance; both functional analyses of artefacts and studies of 'symbolism' have been prone to ascribe static meanings to artefacts.[27] Instead, as Kevin Greene has put it, we must recognize that 'the same artefact could possess different meanings in different social settings, which could by implication change through time or even co-exist within a society which was itself changing'.[28] Recent work has recognized such changes and the differential ways in which grave goods were employed; for example we might expect to find that similar grave goods had different meaning according to whether they were placed in adult or infant graves.[29] Changes across regions and over time have also begun to be identified in the study of early medieval cemeteries.[30] Although weapon burials are commonly regarded as a typical trait of male burials, a recent discussion of a cemetery containing largely male burials at Oudenburg (Belgium) reveals the importance of context to the meaning of the weapon burial, and the social and cultural values attached to weapons. This cemetery contains 216 burials, of which about half are accompanied, but only two contain weapons. This cemetery is probably that of the fort's garrison, given

24. Lucy, 'Sex and gender', pp.157–64; Brush, 'Gender and mortuary analysis', p.81; Halsall, *Settlement and Social Organization*, p.80.

25. Brush, 'Gender and mortuary analysis', p.81.

26. Lucy, 'Sex and gender', pp.155 (for the quotation), 157–61.

27. Härke, 'Changing symbols'.

28. K. Greene, 'Gothic material culture', in I. Hodder, ed., *Archaeology as Long-Term History* (Cambridge, 1987), p.117.

29. See, for example, H. Härke, 'Knives in early Saxon burials: blade length and age at death', *Medieval Archaeology* 33 (1989), pp.144–8.

30. See Halsall, *Settlement and Social Organisation*.

its overwhelmingly male population. Yet the lack of weapon burials is not as surprising as might be thought, since, as Guy Halsall has observed, in this military community status would not have been very effectively displayed through weapons. Status appears to have been marked, instead, by brooches and belt sets.[31] This example also reminds us of the problem of determining what constitutes jewellery.

Clearly we have to seek, therefore, to explore 'the relationship between grave goods, gender and sex', rather than rely on assumptions.[32] We must think more broadly about the social significance of the burial rite. For example, who determined the nature of the burial? By whom were the messages contained in the burial rite meant to be 'read'? What was the relationship between status in death and status in life in a given society? In what ways was material culture used in the production and reproduction of social relationships?

The construction of masculinities in medieval cemeteries

We need to be clear what we understand by gender identities, and, more specifically, by the term 'masculinity'. Gender is taken to be the social construction of identities, which are fluid and, above all, changing. A whole range of gender identities is possible, which are related to social status, cultural and political affiliation and age, as well as to biological sex. Thus a variety of masculin*ities* can be posited. It is also implicit in our approach that masculinity was not formed solely as a result of a series of binary oppositions (such as, male/female or masculine/feminine) but rather that masculinities were also forged in the context of relationships between forms of masculinity. We want, finally, to highlight the relationship between masculinities and forms of social power.

As noted above, male burials have rarely been problematized. The work of Heinrich Härke comes close to doing this: in his discussion of weapon burials he has concluded from his skeletal analysis that those males who were buried with weapons were (to judge from the incidences of disabilities and congenital disease) not

31. G. Halsall, 'Archaeology and the late Roman frontier in northern Gaul', in W. Pohl, ed., *Frontiers in Late Antiquity* (forthcoming). We are grateful to Dr Halsall for allowing us to see his paper in advance of publication.
32. Lucy, 'Sex and gender', p.155.

necessarily fit for warfare, and the lack of any obvious correlation between incidence of wounds and weapon burial suggests that experience of battle was not a prerequisite for, nor did it guarantee, weapon burial. This would appear to indicate that weapon burials do not signify actual warriors so much as 'warrior status', which may have been bound up with notions of affiliation to descent groups and ethnic groups.[33] Härke did not explicitly discuss gender, but Roberta Gilchrist has commented that his work suggests that 'the rite of weapon burial was connected with the construction of masculinity'.[34] According to this interpretation material culture was utilized to make statements about gender and other social identities, that is to say, weapons had a symbolic meaning beyond that of their functional role.

Another important facet of Härke's work has been his revelation that weapon burials declined in frequency during the seventh and eighth centuries, and that knife burials became increasingly more common.[35] This suggests that the significance of these types of burial rite changed, and that the ways in which they were used to signify social status must have been transformed accordingly. Härke has observed that weapon burials are correlated with more elaborate grave structures, but large knives, as a group, are not; the only correlation being with age and sex, as knives with large blades are found mostly with adult males. To quote Härke: 'as the weapon burial rite became limited to an ever smaller number of comparatively rich burials, large knives became an alternative means of expressing adult status in poorer graves'.[36] One might add that with the decline of the weapon burial the blade length of knives became a symbol of masculinity, as males were consistently buried with knives having much longer blades than those buried with females. This is also a reminder that to divide grave goods into categories – knives, swords, tools, jewellery, and so on – may result in an oversimplification; aspects of design or ornamentation may be relevant to understanding the significance of artefacts in differing burial contexts, and they may show a greater correlation with sex or age than a simple analysis of the distribution of artefact types alone would suggest.

33. H. Härke, 'Warrior graves? The background of the Anglo-Saxon weapon burial rite', *Past and Present* 126 (1990), pp.22–43; *idem*, 'Changing symbols'. This is an area that would repay more attention. The identification of wound-trauma is not, however, straightforward, and may be missed or confused with other evidence for skeletal damage.

34. Gilchrist, 'Ambivalent bodies', p.49.   35. Härke, 'Knives', pp.144–8.
36. *Ibid.*, p.147.

Although there were certain norms attached to the burial of males with particular grave goods, there was also clearly competition; as may be witnessed by the fact that some graves were better furnished than others, and the fact that, in the cemeteries examined by Härke, the occurrence of weapon burials and knife burials overlapped, with the latter replacing the former gradually over time. There may be many reasons for the transition in the nature and frequency of grave goods in the early medieval period: the impact of Christianity on burial rites has commonly been cited as a major explanation for the disappearance of grave goods, although it should be noted that the early medieval Church is not recorded as taking any particular interest in this matter; the increasing availability of exchange networks for metal implements may be another explanation for the decline of weapon burials; changing burial strategies must also be considered; as must changes in the nature of the social competition in which burial rite was central.

In this study of Merovingian cemeteries Guy Halsall has detected a transition in burial rite between the sixth and seventh centuries, which he associates with the lessening of differences based on gender and age in favour of those based on class, wealth and rank. In the sixth century there was a clear correlation between grave goods and the age and the sex of the individual: infants rarely had artefacts buried with them which were gender-specific; adolescent males tended to remain artefactually 'neutral', whereas adolescent females received their full complement of gender-specific artefacts; from the age of about twenty males received their gender-specific items; between the ages of twenty and forty the number of artefacts buried with females declined; old age saw a decline in the numbers of artefacts for both males and females, although males were occasionally buried with gender-specific artefacts, whereas females almost never were. However, in the seventh century there was a clear change: earlier correlations between age, sex and artefacts disappear. This transition is best witnessed in the adoption by females of hitherto masculine artefact types (such as plaque buckles and knives).[37] The later cemeteries seem to be organized into familial plots, and this may suggest that social identities founded on status within the community based on gender and age diminished in favour of family identity. By the seventh century grave goods place greater emphasis on adult males and membership of a particular family, perhaps reflecting an emphasis on male hierarchy and

37. Halsall, 'Female status', pp.10–12.

inheritance. In sum, gender interrelationships were dynamic and ever-changing, almost within a life span.

The work of both Härke and Halsall demonstrates that burial rite and the ways in which status and identity were signified were neither uniform nor static. It has also been observed by Halsall that the range of grave goods found in male graves is commonly greater than those found in female graves. This might suggest that the symbolism of individual masculine objects was more fragile than that of feminine objects, requiring more underpinning through repetition.[38]

In discussing the construction of gender through the burial rite of a particular society we have to be aware that not all burials contained items which could be said to be gender-specific. For example, at Sewerby 57.6% of the burials contain either no grave goods, or assemblages described as 'neutral'; and at Heslerton the respective figure is 44.6% of the burials.[39] This feature of early medieval inhumation cemeteries has not been accorded much attention, yet it seems to be a common pattern. Karen Brush interpreted this phenomenon as a sign that gender may not have been 'a major structuring principle in the living society'.[40] However, aside from the fact that the connection between the living and the dead was perhaps more complex than such a statement implies, it presupposes that biological sex was the only determining factor in the construction of gender. This conclusion is belied by, if by nothing else, the diversity of ways in which those male and female burials *with* grave goods were signified, including the fact that grave goods were not always exclusively associated with either males or females. It seems clear that factors other than biological sex – such as social position, life style, religious or professional status, stage in the life cycle – determined gendered status. The contrast between accompanied burials and unaccompanied burials within the same cemetery is worthy, then, of further consideration. It may suggest that in such societies there was a social system in which social power and gender were closely interwoven; indeed, one could say that gender is itself a construction of power in society.

A recent study of early medieval Scandinavian society by Carol Clover, based on the saga literature, has described a gender system in which maleness and femaleness did not *necessarily* set parameters on individual behaviour or status.[41] Rather, actions and the relative

38. *Ibid.*, p.8.   39. Lucy, 'Sex and gender', p.157.

40. Brush, 'Gender and mortuary analysis', p.81.

41. C. Clover, 'Regardless of sex: men, women and power in early Northern Europe', *Speculum* 68 (1993), pp.363–87.

levels of power or powerlessness attained helped to determine gender status: as Clover puts it 'the "conditions" that mattered in the north – the "conditions" that pushed a person into another status – worked not so much at the level of the body, but at the level of social relations'.[42] Although there are clearly issues to be addressed concerning the historical reality portrayed by the sagas, which were written down much later than the events they purportedly describe, and about the universal applicability of the social organization they depict, the sagas do, at least, present an internally consistent society, which was believable to the intended audience.[43]

In the sagas what matters socially is power – as head of family, as landholder, in legal and governmental spheres, as victor in battle, as the honoured – and these attributes are commonly, although not exclusively, associated with males; powerlessness, in contrast, is subject to fear and loathing and is typically, but not inevitably, associated with females. In this society males were advantaged by their sex, but this did not protect them against failure. Through behaviour, wealth, prestige, marital status or force of personality a person could acquire and maintain power, which was apt to be described in masculine terms: 'there was just one "gender", one standard by which persons were judged adequate or inadequate, and it was something like masculine'.[44]

This has relevance and resonance for the study of early medieval Scandinavian cemeteries. Some difficulty has been encountered in explaining the occurrence of grave good assemblages typically associated with male burials (such as weighing scales or weapons) in the graves of females. Sometimes these have been explained away as aberrant, perhaps the result of status acquired from a husband now dead or temporarily away, or the product of the incorrect sexing of the body.[45] However, the power/gender model provides an alternative perspective: power and status in a particular social or economic context was marked in death by a particular burial rite, which was normally associated with males but which might be accorded to females who had achieved the requisite status. Perhaps the most famous example of this in the sagas concerns Unn the Deep-Minded (in *Laxdæla Saga*), who had through her efforts

42. *Ibid.*, pp.378–9.
43. There have been numerous studies of the 'historical' content of the sagas; for a summary see, G. Palsson, ed., *From Sagas to Society. Comparative Approaches to Early Iceland* (Enfield Lock, 1992).
44. Clover, 'Regardless of sex', p.379.
45. A. Stalsberg, 'Women as actors in north European Viking Age trade', in R. Samson, ed., *Social Approaches to Viking Studies* (Glasgow, 1991), pp.75–83.

acquired and exercised power, and had attained a status which might be described as masculine, according to the norms of the sagas, and was accordingly provided with a lavish ship burial when she died.[46] At the other end of the social spectrum powerlessness rendered men and women in the same category, and this may begin to explain why it is that in death such people were buried without grave goods or with similar assemblages irrespective of their biological sex. Of course, such a hypothesis needs further investigation; in particular the age and sex profile of those buried without artefacts and with gender-'neutral' artefacts requires much greater attention.

We also have to address the fact that there *are* commonly differences between the grave goods found in male burials and those in female burials. It may suggest that on the one hand there was an opposition between the powerful and the powerless (as determined from a variety of perspectives), but that at the same time within the ranks of the powerful there was a variety of means of articulating status, of which some, but not all, were related to biological sex. The construction of gender operated at more than one level even through the single medium of burial.

When discussing the relationship between power or status and gender we need to be clear that there may have been aspects of authority and status which were enjoyed in life but which were not expressed in death. Guy Halsall has identified aspects of status which might be expressed through lavish funerary displays, related to intra- and inter-community issues, particularly alliances formed through marriage and reproduction. This may explain why, for example, females acquire lavish burial displays in sixth-century cemeteries, because of their childbearing ability and marriageable status. To reiterate, the dead do not bury themselves, and burial rite involves the conferment of a status perceived by the remaining members of a community; as such, any death which affected wider relationships within and between communities might be expected to be afforded a more lavish treatment in burial than a death which did not. The death of marriageable females of childbearing age might well have created a greater rupture in society because of its ramifications for communal power strategies. The status expressed through burial display was not absolute, but was contingent on social context and the need to respond to the social rupture created by the death of

46. *Laxdœla Saga*, ed. and trans., M. Magnusson and H. Pálsson (Harmondsworth, 1969), pp.51–7.

an individual. In sixth-century Merovingian cemeteries burial displays were much more lavish, on the whole, than in the seventh century; an important reason for this might be because of the very great size of sixth-century cemeteries which must have been used by several communities, whereas in the seventh century individual communities seem to have had their own cemetery. Therefore, the level of public display in the sixth century was potentially much greater, involving a substantial audience, perhaps reflecting 'the instability of north Gallic society'.[47]

Gender and the life cycle

Another important aspect of gender roles and relationships is related to position in the life cycle. Neither children nor the elderly have been adequately dealt with in any branch of archaeology, and here even anthropological comparisons prove disappointing. Both archaeological and anthropological studies commonly eschew consideration of the life cycle in favour of an emphasis on prestige, power, economy or politics, often identified with the male. Yet, male status may fall with age in many societies and the role of males within the community changes because – even though the wisdom which has come with age may be of importance – they are less able to perform the roles for which they were previously valued, such as forging allegiances with other communities through marriage and reproduction, or participating in warfare. As their status changes they are not uncommonly feminized. This may provide an interesting contrast with older females, who, once freed from child-bearing, are able to undertake activities previously forbidden to them, enabling them to gain a new status, although not one necessarily marked in death.

If stages in the life cycle were central to gender roles then how may we explore this from early medieval cemetery evidence? The ageing, as much as the sexing, of skeletons is a prerequisite, although one subject to limitation. The skeletons of pre-pubertal children are difficult to age and sex securely, and the ages of adults over about forty years tend to be truncated. Only rarely do we have the ideal of a fully excavated cemetery coupled with the ageing and sexing of all skeletons, against which the distribution and the nature of grave goods can be analysed. Guy Halsall was able to make

---

47. Halsall, 'Female status', p.13.

use of such data in his study of Merovingian cemeteries in the Metz district of Gaul. As important as the careful correlation of sexed and aged skeletons was the change in interpretative ideology; from this study it is clear from the burial evidence that stage in the life cycle affected identity within society. Male and female elderly were buried with little in the way of grave goods, and gender divisions broke down with age. As Halsall puts it:

> In old age, people of both sexes received little attention in burials. Graves of the elderly are frequently 'neutral' or unfurnished, and often small too . . . men lost their most important social roles as family heads, seeing their sons now reach the 'active family head' or 'older warrior' age. Their deaths created less tension and required less lavish marking.[48]

It is important to remember that although social status might have changed with age, and it was not uncommon for burial provision to become less lavish, this does not necessarily mean that individuals became less important. It was, rather, the case that the aspects of status which were signified in lavish burial displays were no longer relevant to them, but this does not preclude them from having been important figures in other spheres. Their social roles within the family, in military or political contexts may have been replaced by communal or even religious roles.

Conclusion

Masculinity was not a fixed status, but a dynamic and heterogeneous aspect of social identity. Gender roles and relationships developed through time, varied across regions, and were determined by aspects of social status and position in the life cycle. We should think in terms not of a single universal gender system, but of multiple gender systems. It seems clear that gender was an important structuring principle in early medieval society, and that we can begin to uncover aspects of it from the funerary archaeology of the period. Clearly, the burial rite was only one medium for the negotiation of gender roles, but as a particularly visible medium it has much to offer the discussion of medieval gender, and medieval masculinities. In particular it emphasizes the importance of the public negotiation of gender identity, and the role of symbolism

---

48. Halsall, *Settlement and Social Organization*, p.257.

and display in the construction of this aspect of social identity. It will be necessary in future to discuss other means by which we may uncover the gender structures of early medieval societies; as we have suggested here, the relationship between historical and archaeological evidence would repay greater emphasis and analysis. In sum one might observe that although death did, in part, 'make the man', the kind of man and the nature of his relationship to men in the living community are open to a great deal of future enquiry.

CHAPTER THREE

Frustrated Masculinity: The Relationship between William the Conqueror and his Eldest Son[1]

W.M. AIRD

The *Worcester Chronicle* in its annal for the year 1079 reported that:

> King William, while fighting with his son before the castle of Gerberoi, which King Philip [I of France] had offered to him, was wounded by him in the arm and unhorsed; but soon, after he had recognized his father's voice, [Robert] hastily dismounted and ordered him to mount his own war-horse, and then allowed him to depart. And with many of the king's men slain and some taken prisoner and with his son William and many others wounded, he [William] began to retreat.[2]

As well as being an early indication of the chivalrous nature of Robert Curthose's behaviour, the encounter between William I and his eldest son outside the castle at Gerberoi on the eastern frontier of Normandy was the most dramatic of a number of incidents in the stormy relationship which punctuated the later years of the reign of the Conqueror.[3] Robert quarrelled with his father between

---

1. I would like to thank Dr Marjorie Chibnall, Prof. John Gillingham, Dr Matthew Bennett and Dr Helen Nicholson, who were kind enough to comment on this chapter, for their constructive criticism and suggestions. I am also very grateful to the members of Cardiff University, School of History and Archaeology Staff/Postgraduate seminar who helped me to clarify my ideas.
2. *Florentii Wigornensis monachi Chronicon ex Chronicis*, ed. B. Thorpe, 2 vols. (London, 1848–49), II, p.13 *s.a.* 1079; cf. *The Anglo-Saxon Chronicle*, eds, D. Whitelock, D.C. Douglas and S.I. Tucker (London, 1961), D, E, *s.a.* 1079, p.159.
3. D.C. Douglas, *William the Conqueror* (London, 1964), pp.238, 239, 279, 405–407; D. Bates, *William the Conqueror* (London, 1989), pp.161–2. For Robert Curthose as a model of chivalry, see his portrayal by Geffrei Gaimar, *L'Estoire des Engleis*, ed., A. Bell (Oxford, 1960), especially lines 5738 *Suz ciel n'aveit meillur barun* ('under heaven there was no better baron'); 5741 *Mainte bunté e maint barnage* ('[he performed] much good and many brave deeds') and 5744 *E mainte bele chevalerie* ('And [he performed] many worthy knightly exploits'). See John Gillingham, '1066 and

1077 and 1079, and although they were reconciled by May 1080, a further estrangement occurred in 1083, and following this it is doubtful whether Robert ever saw his father alive again.

This chapter looks at the relationship between these two men in terms of the specific gender roles which late eleventh-century Norman society assigned them. These masculine roles were constructed for both father and son according to a normative code of behaviour which, although given explicit expression by members of the clerical and monastic hierarchy of the period, was also accepted and made implicit in secular society.[4] Essentially, we are dealing with the social dynamics of patriarchy, which involved not only the subordination of women, but also that of other men, either younger, weaker or simply different. The ecclesiastical and secular aristocracies of this period were closely associated with one another and often members of the same family occupied positions of authority in both social spheres.[5] Given this normative code of aristocratic masculine behaviour, the purpose here is to examine the underlying causes of the tension between father and son and to relate them to ideas about dominant or hegemonic masculinity and challenges to this hegemony within the context of the aristocratic society of Northern France in the late eleventh century.

Robert Curthose's conflict with his father has been seen as almost inevitable by some historians, the result of the father's refusal 'to give his impatient heir as much power as he thought he deserved'.[6] But was the conflict between Robert and William a simple matter of the exclusion from power of one individual by another? What effect did the fact that Robert was William's eldest son have on their relationship? How did they perceive their respective gender roles, not only within society at large, but also within the microcosmic power arena of the family, and did this inform and affect their attitudes and behaviour towards each other? It is hoped that,

---

the introduction of chivalry into England', in G. Garnett and John Hudson, eds, *Law and Government in Medieval England and Normandy. Essays in Honour of Sir James Holt* (Cambridge, 1994), pp.31–55 at 34–5, n.12.

4. On the subject of masculine identities and gender history in general, see David Buchbinder, *Masculinities and Identities* (Melbourne, 1994); M. Roper and J. Tosh, 'Historians and the politics of masculinity' in M. Roper and J. Tosh, eds, *Manful Assertions: Masculinities in Britain since 1800* (London, 1991), pp.1–24; and John Tosh 'What should historians do with masculinity? Reflections on nineteenth-century Britain', *HWJ* 38 (1994), pp.179–202.

5. In this context the career of Odo, Bishop of Bayeux and Earl of Kent provides a useful example: D. Bates, 'The character and career of Odo, Bishop of Bayeux', *Speculum* 50 (1975), pp.1–20.

6. Bates, *William*, p.99.

in addressing these questions by focusing on issues of gender and social roles, this chapter will offer a commentary on the dynamics which characterized the relationships between these two men, joined in one respect by their biological connection as father and son, but separated in other respects by their being representative of different and often competing masculine generations. The study also throws some light on the strategies employed by the patriarch in his management of the tensions and rivalries within the family, which, at times, threatened his position as *paterfamilias*. In terms of the gender roles assigned to individuals by medieval society at large, therefore, William and his son represent two distinct masculine identities, two different images of medieval masculinity.

For historians of the Anglo-Norman *regnum* Robert Curthose's career has almost universally been seen as something of a failure.[7] The measure of this failure was his inability to succeed his father to the throne of England in 1087 and his subsequent ineffectual responses to the political machinations of his younger brothers, Rufus and Henry, which eventually led to his defeat and capture at the Battle of Tinchebrai in September 1106. Robert spent the last twenty-eight years of his life in captivity, ending his days in early February 1134, writing Welsh poetry in Cardiff castle.[8] According to twelfth-century writers, most especially Orderic Vitalis, whose *Ecclesiastical History* provides us with the most detailed account, Robert's personal rule of the duchy of Normandy was characterized by administrative incompetence and the triumph of anarchy. Although the most informative of the twelfth-century sources for the history of Normandy, Orderic is also the most contentious and his description

7. See, for example, E.A. Freeman, *The History of the Norman Conquest of England*, 6 vols. (Oxford, 1870–79), III, p.111, '. . . Robert, the eldest, twice failed of the Crown of England, and ruled Normandy to his shame and sorrow'; C.H. Haskins, *Norman Institutions* (Cambridge, Mass., 1918), p.62; and C. Warren Hollister, 'The Anglo-Norman civil war: 1101', reprinted in his *Monarchy, Magnates and Institutions* (London, 1986), especially pp.84–5. More recently, David Bates has hinted that perhaps Robert's government of Normandy was not as incompetent as has been thought; 'The Conqueror's charters', in Carola Hicks, ed., *England in the Eleventh Century* (Stamford, 1992), p.11 and *idem.*, 'Normandy and England after 1066', *EHR* 104 (1989), p.868.

8. Historians of the First Crusade have a very different view of Robert as an effective and charismatic war leader and the crusading hero commemorated in the stained glass of Suger's Saint-Denis: C.W. David, *Robert Curthose* (Cambridge, Mass., 1920), pp.89–119 and frontispiece. Despite his exploits on the successful First Crusade, modern historians are still heavily influenced by the traditionally negative views of Robert's character; see, e.g., John France, *Victory in the East. A Military History of the First Crusade* (Cambridge, 1994), pp.80–1. For Robert's bardic career, David, *Curthose*, pp.187–9.

of Robert's relationship with his father must be located within the moralizing discourse which Orderic employed in his portrayal of contemporary figures and events.[9]

For Orderic, and the majority of medieval writers, the model for the proper behaviour of sons towards their fathers was derived principally from the Bible, with some additional *exempla* abstracted from a knowledge of the Classics.[10] Orderic makes reference to Mosaic Law and to the stories of Absalom and Rehoboam in order to construct an explicit ideology of the appropriate conduct of a son towards his father.[11] This ecclesiastical model of the normative relationship between father and son stressed the biblical admonition that the son should respect and obey the father in all things and it is certain that such a model had obvious parallels for a monk writing within the strictly hierarchical institution of the monastery.

Orderic was not the only ecclesiastical figure to employ this discourse when dealing with the problem of the relationship between William I and Robert. In a letter written in 1080 to the rebellious son recently reconciled with his father, Pope Gregory VII reminded Robert of two fundamentals of Mosaic Law embodied in the injunctions, 'Honour thy father and thy mother: that thy days may be long upon the land which the Lord thy God giveth thee,' and 'He that curseth his father or his mother, shall surely be put to death.'[12] The crux of this biblical teaching was that rebellion against the father was contrary to God's law and consequently infringed the natural order and would be punished. The tendency of medieval

9. *The Ecclesiastical History of Orderic Vitalis*, ed. and trans. Marjorie Chibnall, 6 vols (Oxford, 1968–80) (hereafter *OV*). On Orderic's historical methodology, see Marjorie Chibnall, *The World of Orderic Vitalis* (Oxford, 1984) and Jean Blacker, *The Faces of Time* (Austin, TX, 1994). Orderic's account of the dispute may have been well informed as he had spoken to a fellow monk, Samson, Queen Mathilda's messenger, who had fled to St-Évroul when William I threatened to have him blinded: *OV*, III, p.105.

10. Given the contours of the discourse employed by Orderic, it seems difficult to accept that his account can 'credited with some degree of objectivity'; see S. Mooers, ' "Backers and stabbers": problems of loyalty in Robert Curthose's entourage', *Journal of British Studies* 21 (1981), p.2, n.6.

11. William I himself points out to his son the lessons to be learned from the fates of Absalom and Rehoboam, to which Robert replied (p.101), 'I did not come here to listen to a lecture for I have had more than enough of these from my schoolmasters and am surfeited with them', *OV*, III, pp.98–101. While reflecting on the rebellion of the young King Henry against his father Henry II, Ralph de Diceto produced a list detailing examples of sons rebelling against their fathers, including Robert Curthose's revolt: *Radulfi de Diceto decani Londoniensis Opera Historica*, ed., W. Stubbs, Rolls Series, 2 vols (London, 1876), I, p.365.

12. Exodus, 20:12; 21:17. Gregory's letter printed in P. Jaffé, ed., *Bibliotheca Rerum Germanicarum, Volume II, Monumenta Gregoriana* (Berlin, 1865), pp.420–21.

historians to see in historical events the working out of divine will suggests that Orderic's portrayal of Robert's career was adversely coloured by the latter's typological representation as the disobedient son. In this light Robert's unsuccessful government of Normandy and his defeat at Tinchebrai become the inevitable results of his filial disloyalty.[13] The appeal of this ecclesiastical discourse for secular society lay in the definitive nature of its statement about the relative power of father and son when, increasingly, the focus of dynastic ambition was the preservation and transmission from one generation to the next of the patrimony as a single unit. The attainment of this goal necessitated the son's co-operation in remaining a patient and dutiful member of his father's household until he could inherit the patrimony *in toto*.

Thus this ecclesiastical discourse on the proper relationship between men of different generations stressed the subordination of the younger to the older man; the son to the father. The dominant or hegemonic construction of masculinity therefore belonged to the father. In Orderic's account of Robert's relationship with his father much is made of his youth and the corollaries of his youthful behaviour. The implication is, therefore, that Robert's conduct betrayed an immaturity which impaired his attainment of full adult status. Robert remained a *iuvenis* or 'youth' in this society and he was prevented from attaining the status of manhood which had its own attendant and defining characteristics.[14] In the aristocratic society of late-eleventh-century Northern France, an individual did not attain manhood or full adult masculine status simply by growing older but, rather, this status was recognized and conferred as the result of the display of a learned or imposed pattern of behaviour appropriate to that society's construction of adult masculinity.[15] Robert's goal was to assume a particular social identity which would enable him to function as a fully gendered adult male in this society but, as we shall see, the main obstacle in his path was the figure of his father. Medieval social ideology had constructed a

13. *OV*, V, pp.300–2.

14. For medieval notions of the stages of life see Shulamith Shahar, *Childhood in the Middle Ages* (London, 1990), pp.21–2 and the references in note 3, and *idem*, *Growing Old in the Middle Ages* (London, 1997). On 'youth' as a specific stage of social development, G. Duby, 'Youth in Aristocratic Society. Northwestern France in the twelfth century' in *idem*, *The Chivalrous Society* (London, 1977), pp.112–22. Orderic describes Robert as *iuveni regis filio* and his companions as *seditiosi tirones*, *OV*, III, p.97.

15. Robert was born c.1053/54 and was, therefore, in his mid-twenties when the dispute with his father, who was fifty, broke out. Mooers '"Backers and stabbers"', p.1, n.1 suggests that Curthose's birth should be assigned to 1051.

different role for Robert's father and William I felt his own position threatened by his eldest son's aspirations.[16] It was, then, the
conflicting goals of these two men, operating according to their
assigned gender roles, which produced the often violent struggle
between them.

In what ways, therefore, did William I frustrate his eldest son's
attempts to attain his manhood? To answer this question it is necessary to suggest some defining characteristics of adult masculinity in
this period and in this particular society. Fundamentally, independence of action in a number of social contexts seems to have been a
prime indicator of manhood achieved in this society. Three key
areas will be examined: access to power; the establishment of an
independent household; and, finally, the public recognition and
affirmation of the fully gendered adult self.

'I am not prepared to be your hireling for ever':
Robert and his search for independence

First, Robert needed to have access to real political power, for it was
only in the exercise of independent power that he could demonstrate that he was worthy of enjoying the status of a fully adult male
in this society. Robert probably felt that he could reasonably expect
to exercise such power as he had been formally recognized as heir
to the County of Maine and the Duchy of Normandy by the time of
William's invasion of England in 1066 and later, as a result of the
Treaty of Blanchelande, Robert again did homage for Maine to
Fulk of Anjou in 1081.[17] In addition, it is probable that Robert had
been given some responsibility in the government of Normandy
during his father's absences in England and possibly also some

16. Matthew Bennett (personal communication) has suggested that perhaps
William I's fears – the result of his own illegitimacy, his insecure childhood, and the
struggles to secure the duchy – heightened his sense of vulnerability.

17. Robert had previously done homage for Maine to the Count of Anjou in
around 1063. F.M. Stenton, *William the Conqueror and the Rule of the Normans* (London, 1908), pp.314–15; Douglas, *William*, pp.73, 143, 174, 242; and Bates, *William*,
pp.38, 41, 46, 104–5, 138 and 165. C. Warren Hollister makes the point that the
Anglo-Norman kings adopted the strategy of having their sons perform homage for
Maine and Normandy in order to avoid placing themselves in the subordinate position of a vassal; see 'Normandy, France and the Anglo-Norman *Regnum*', reprinted
in his *Monarchy, Magnates and Institutions*, pp.17–57.

measure of personal rule in Maine.[18] It was common practice among the heads of the royal and noble dynasties of Northern France and elsewhere in this period to designate their heirs and associate them with their government during their own lifetime. William, too, had followed this dynastic expedient; initially, in the case of the County of Maine, to advance his own claims to an important border zone lying between his own lands and those of his principal political rival, the Count of Anjou, and later, in the case of Normandy, to ensure the smooth transition of power should his expedition to England fail disastrously.[19] These provisions and those of the Treaty of Blanchelande gave Robert the promise of power, but it is more than likely that he was denied any personal role in government and this political exclusion was reinforced by his father, who was given to using Robert's title to the lordship of Maine.[20]

As he grew older, and especially in the aftermath of his father's conquest of England, Robert seems to have felt that he had been denied his proper right as Count of Maine and designated heir to Normandy. Although William had employed his son as co-regent with Queen Mathilda in the king's absence, Robert, according to Orderic, felt like a *mercennarius* or hireling. In a telling exchange between father and son that immediately preceded his first break with William, Robert (then aged around twenty-four – in other words three years over his majority) demanded Normandy but was rebutted by his father, who refused to surrender the duchy as long as he lived. Orderic's text encapsulates Robert's dilemma, and he has the frustrated youth state:

> I am not prepared to be your hireling for ever. I want at last to have property of my own, so that I can give proper wages to my own dependants. I ask you therefore to grant me legal control of the duchy, so that, just as you rule over the kingdom of England, I, under you, may rule over the duchy of Normandy.[21]

18. Douglas, *William*, p.185; and Bates, *William*, pp.85, 99, and 105 on his government of Maine. A donation by a canon of Saint-Vincent of Le Mans was dated by reference to 'Robert, son of King William of the English governing the city of the men of Maine' (*Robertoque, Willelmi regis Anglorum filio, Cenomannicam urbem gubernante*), which might imply that Robert had some independent control; David, *Curthose*, p.10 and n.35.

19. On the significance of the designation of heirs by their fathers, see A.W. Lewis, 'Anticipatory association of the heir in early Capetian France', *AHR* 83 (1978), pp.906–27.

20. Stenton, *William the Conqueror*, p.315. See *RRAN*, I, Nos. 103, 105, 140, 147, 149, 150, 171.

21. *OV*, III, pp.98–99. It should be noted that William's reluctance to surrender any control may be associated with his defeat at Dol in 1076; see Douglas, *William*, p.234.

Although, ideally, Robert sought access to independent power, he was prepared to compromise and hold Normandy under the direction of his father. Nevertheless, the power which he would exercise in the duchy would enable him to fulfil another essential of the social role which he perceived for himself, that of creating and heading an independent household. As long as his father refused to grant him access to power and the attendant ability to distribute resources, Robert felt that he was being treated like a landless knight, which, in his own mind, was a status wholly unbecoming the eldest son of a duke, let alone the heir of a king.

The foundation of a household both as the focus for a military retinue and as the venue for the expression of adult, that is marital, sexuality was a *sine qua non* of eleventh-century aristocratic society and the ambition of every noble son who was not called to the spiritual life. Robert had been educated in a society in which the concerns of the dynasty were increasingly paramount and it was his duty to see that the line was continued into the next generation. In addition, the reforming Church gradually and ever more vociferously came to insist that only the sons and daughters of ecclesiastically sanctioned unions would be recognized as legitimate heirs.[22] Among the nobility of Northern France in this period marriage was far too potent a political and dynastic weapon to be left to the romantic inclinations of the offspring, so matrimonial alliances were arranged with the utmost care and invariably with an eye to the best interests of the dynasty. While still a young boy Robert had been betrothed to Margaret, the infant heiress of Maine, but the marriage never took place as Margaret died in childhood.[23] After his negotiations with Anjou over Maine, William seems to have been reluctant to commit his sons to other marriage alliances, preferring instead to use his daughters to cement political unions.[24] William's control over his sons' matrimonial status probably reflected his concern to maintain the integrity of the Anglo-Norman *regnum* which would have been threatened by the need to provide any future alliances with dowers drawn from the patrimony. The heads of

22. C. Brooke, *The Medieval Idea of Marriage* (Oxford, 1989) and G. Duby, *Medieval Marriage: Two Models from Twelfth-Century France*, trans. E. Forster (Baltimore, 1978), and *idem*, *The Knight, the Lady and the Priest*, trans. B. Bray (New York and Harmondsworth, 1983).

23. *Guillaume de Poitiers, Histoire de Guillaume le Conquérant*, ed., Raymonde Foreville (Paris, 1952), pp.93, 95; see also David, *Curthose*, pp.7–11 and R. Latouche, *Histoire du Comté du Maine pendant le Xe et le XIe siècle* (Paris, 1910), p.32.

24. R.V. Turner, 'The children of Anglo-Norman royalty and their upbringing', *Medieval Prosopography* 11, no. 2 (1990), p.37.

medieval noble families had to tread a fine line between ensuring the continuation of the dynasty by marrying early and siring sons or delaying marriage so that the sons would mature just as the father was in his declining years. Although William's marriage to Mathilda at the beginning of the 1050s, when he was in his early twenties, was a shrewd political move, in terms of engineering the smooth transmission of power from one generation to the next, it was perhaps a little early and far too fruitful. This may also explain why William was reluctant to arrange another marriage for his eldest son, as this would have strengthened Robert's demand for the resources to support his own household. Robert's liaisons while in exile may, therefore, have been seen as relatively safe outlets for his sexual appetite, although he later had to face a woman who claimed that her children were Robert's and was willing to undergo the ordeal of hot iron to prove it.[25]

Robert needed to establish an independent household in order to take up a position as a fully adult male member of Anglo-Norman aristocratic society. Until he moved away from his father's court he could never be anything but his father's son and thus a member of a subordinate masculinity and a social inferior. Temporary respite came when Robert absented himself and went into voluntary exile, but this could never be anything but an interim expedient as by accepting help from figures outside the Anglo-Norman realm Robert was once again placing himself in a dependent position. According to the normative criteria of Anglo-Norman society, Robert needed to build up his own military retinue and bind it to him with displays of largesse. The fully functioning retinue would then act as the expression of his own successful lordship and independence, or, in other words, of his successfully attained manhood. Without the wherewithal to support a retinue and living at his father's court, Robert was constantly made aware of his own subordinate position as a *iuvenis*. It is in the nature of patriarchy that, not only is there the subordination of women to men, but there is also the dominance of the *paterfamilias* over other men.[26] In his father's household, therefore, Robert shared a subservient position with other subordinated groups, namely, women and his social inferiors.

25. *OV*, V, pp.282–83. Robert also had an illegitimate daughter who was later married to Helias of Saint-Säens; *OV*, IV, p.182 and David, *Curthose*, pp.38–39.

26. There is a very useful discussion of gender and social roles in S.H. Rigby, *English Society in the Later Middle Ages. Class, Status and Gender* (London, 1995), pp.243–83.

Allied to the need to establish an independent household was Robert's desire to receive the public recognition and affirmation of his fully gendered adult self. Medieval society, secular as well as ecclesiastical, was characterized by a series of public rituals which invariably involved a change of status for the men and women participating in them. In aristocratic circles displays of military prowess were not, in themselves, sufficient evidence of the attainment of manhood, thus the public ceremony of dubbing admitted a young male into the fellowship of arms, but it was not a definitive *rite de passage* imparting manhood on the newly dubbed knight. Knights were expected to act in a certain fashion, but it was recognized that in the heat of battle they might not 'act like men'. In other words, *chevaliers* were still 'youths' until they had attained the other essentials of manhood. Neither did acts of reckless bravery make the man, for, far from being seen as the actions of adult male warriors, they were, paradoxically, the occasion for criticism. In recent years it has been emphasized that medieval warfare was rarely a matter of heroic encounters on the battlefield where the actions of individual knights could make the difference. The more usual form of warfare was the campaign based on the siege and a war of attrition conducted in enemy territory.[27] In this sense Robert's father's victory at Hastings was atypical. The wise and mature warrior or general held back his forces and waited for the most advantageous moment to strike or, indeed, wheeled away from an encounter the outcome of which, he felt to be uncertain. Criticism was often levelled at young knights who recklessly charged into battle without heeding the wiser counsel of their elders. Restraint was the virtue exercised by the mature man; impatience and derring-do were the faults of the *iuvenis*. Chivalric literature often stressed the heroism of the individual – perhaps in response to the less appealing realities of medieval warfare (see below, chapter 5). Thus military prowess did not make the man.

The tensions between father and son

If manhood is constructed on the understanding that to wield power is a necessary characteristic of the adult male's gender identity, then the son's exclusion from power by his father undermined his

27. J. Gillingham, 'William the Bastard at war', in C. Harper-Bill, C. Holdsworth and J. Nelson, eds, *Studies in Medieval History presented to R. Allen Brown* (Woodbridge, 1989), pp.141–58.

self-image and weakened the force of the *persona* which he presented to his peers and to social inferiors within this hierarchical
society. As well as the son having certain aspirations in his social
roles, the father was obliged to ensure that he himself met certain
essential criteria for the successful fulfilment of his own social role.
In an aristocratic society increasingly defined by dynastic rather
than kinship structures, the essential feature of the father's gender
role was his ability to produce a son who would ensure that the
dynasty would continue and so perpetuate the father's achievements.
The father, in his capacity as the head of a noble dynasty, was also
anxious to ensure that the unity of the patrimony which he himself
had received and embellished was maintained and handed on to
the next generation intact. Thus the father not only provided the
role model for his son, he also embodied the major obstacle to the
consummation of his son's ambitions. William's reluctance to yield
responsibility to his eldest son frustrated Robert's attempt to fulfil
his expected gender role and this disempowerment by his father
prompted his rebellion, which may be seen as his attempt to define
a separate adult and independent masculinity. Given Robert's early
designation as heir and his brief taste of rule in Maine, he may have
felt that his father was being wholly unreasonable in his parsimoni-
ous attitude.[28] Robert may also have been aware of the practice in
other neighbouring principalities where heirs were allowed some
support from a portion of the family's property until they came
into their full inheritance.[29] It was even possible for aged fathers to
hand over the government of their lands to their sons and allow
them to exercise full political power as can be seen in the case of
Fulk Nerra's abdication in favour of Geoffrey Martel.[30]

If William's power represented that of hegemonic masculinity
then Robert's actions may be seen as an attempt to subvert that
hegemony. Robert's challenge to his father's hegemony essentially
took the form of an imitation of William's modes of behaviour or,

28. It may be that Robert's rule in Maine proved so unsuccessful that his father
felt that he could not be trusted with any further exercise of authority. Robert's
obvious military prowess was not, therefore, necessarily all that was needed in order
to become a successful ruler.

29. Lewis, 'Anticipatory association', p.916.

30. This was not an entirely successful arrangement as Fulk was forced to
humble his son and resume control after Geoffrey's alleged misuse of power. See
B.S. Bachrach, 'Henry II and the Angevin tradition of family hostility', *Albion* 16
(1984), pp.111–30 and *idem, Fulk Nerra, the Neo-Roman Consul, 987–1040* (Berkeley,
1993), pointing out that Fulk was perhaps not wholly convinced of Geoffrey's suitability for government but handed over the reins of the County before his departure
on pilgrimage.

in other words, those associated with manhood. Robert tried to mirror the essential attributes of his father's power, but his imitation was necessarily a youthful distortion or exaggeration. It is in his descriptions of Robert's behaviour that Orderic employs his most ardent condemnations of the son's youthful and reckless actions.[31] Similarly, Robert's retinue was composed of rash, youthful, unwise and deceitful counsellors. Robert's sexuality was expressed through the casual liaison devoid of the political and dynastic significance of the fully adult marriage. In failing to achieve full recognition of his adult status within Anglo-Norman society, Robert was forced to absent himself from that society. He could not operate successfully within that social arena while his father obstructed his ambition and his rebellion was thus an expression both of his frustration and of his recognition of the hopelessness of his subordinate position.

Around Robert Curthose gathered a coterie of similarly disaffected aristocratic youths from some of the most powerful of the Norman noble houses.[32] Robert's *maisnie* was an imitation of his father's mature military retinue and Orderic, following his biblical *exemplum* of Rehoboam, is careful to make explicit the point that, whereas William's men gave him measured and mature counsel, Robert's youthful companions could only offer ill-considered advice and make rash demands.[33] The essence of the complaints made to Robert by his companions was that they were not being treated as the members of a retinue of a great lord should be. Robert needed to be able to reward them adequately for their service and if he could not then it was a matter of great disgrace. This was a society where perceptions of public shame were acute and Orderic's account of the youths' advice to Robert in 1077–79 makes it clear that Robert's lack of resources was the cause of considerable embarrassment:

> Royal prince, they said, how long can you live in such wretched poverty? Your father's minions guard the royal treasure so closely that you can scarcely have a penny from it to give to any of your

31. For example, *OV*, III, pp.97, 103; IV, p.125; V, p.302.
32. *OV*, III, pp.100–102 and David, *Curthose*, p.22, n.20. For a detailed discussion of the longevity of the loyalty to Robert of these individuals, see Mooers, '"Backers and stabbers" ', pp.1–17 at 3 and n.14.
33. Duby, 'Youth', pp.114–5, pointed out that these youthful associations also had a positive effect in that they helped to form the bonds of cohesion for the next generation of a lordship's vassals. For Rehoboam, see 1 Kings 12: 6–11 and *OV*, III, pp.99–101 where William advises Robert to accept the counsel of wiser heads, such as the archbishops of Rouen and Canterbury.

dependants. It is a great dishonour to you and injury to us and many others that you should be deprived of the royal wealth in this way. A man deserves to have wealth if he knows how to distribute it generously to all seekers. How sad that your bounteous liberality should be thwarted, and that you should be reduced to indigence through the parsimony of your father who sets his servants or rather your servants over you. How long brave lord, will you bear this? Come now, rise up boldly, claim a share of the realm of England from your father; or at least ask again for the duchy of Normandy which he has already granted to you publicly before a great body of magnates who are able to testify to it. It is not fitting that you should continue to allow those who are born your slaves to lord it over you, and to deny you the riches of your inheritance as if you were a nameless beggar.[34]

Here Robert's companions recognize their lord's desire to be generous and able to display that essential of medieval lordship, largesse. However, it is interesting to note that in Orderic's eyes Robert's generosity becomes the wasteful dissipation of wealth as displayed by the prodigal son of the Gospels.[35] It is also noticeable that Robert's companions stress how inferior Robert appears within society and how the natural order of servant and master has been overturned by William's unreasonable treatment of his son. As Orderic portrays it, there is no understanding of the father's concerns among members of the next generation.

Robert's challenge to his father's hegemonic masculinity was met by William in a number of ways. William's displays of anger towards his eldest son expressed his own frustration that Robert was incapable of obeying him according to the normative standard of behaviour dominant in this society. In admonishing his son William invoked this norm, pointing out the kind of conduct which he and the model derived from biblical *exempla* expected. The Conqueror may also have employed ridicule, which in itself denotes that the person being ridiculed is not worthy of receiving the respect due to obedient members of society.[36] Ridicule could sometimes become ritual humiliation, as demonstrated in the relationship between Fulk of Anjou and his son, when, in order to punish Geoffrey, Fulk made him carry a saddle on his back.[37] In behaving contrary to the expected norm, Robert also exposed himself to association with other individuals who were marginalized in this society. Thus

34. *OV*, III, pp.98–9.   35. *OV*, III, p.102; cf. Duby, 'Youth', p.115 and nn.18, 19.
36. *OV*, III, p.113.

37. William of Malmesbury, *De gestis Regum Anglorum*, ed., W. Stubbs, Rolls Series, 2 vols (London, 1887, 1889), II, p.292. On the meaning of this ritualized submission by Geoffrey, see Bachrach, *Fulk Nerra*, pp.234–36.

Robert's government of Normandy after 1087 was seen as being characterized by the ascendancy of whores, effeminates and other socially liminal groups.[38] These individuals, like Robert himself, threatened the stability of the dynasty and the family, the very foundations of eleventh-century aristocratic society.

William appears to have temporarily placated Robert after his first revolt, possibly by entrusting him with the task of stabilizing the relationship with King Malcolm III of Scotland in 1080.[39] Unlike many of his less virile contemporaries, William also had another strategy of control open to him, that is, the manipulation of sibling rivalry within the family. William can be seen actively promoting his younger sons, William Rufus and Henry, against their elder brother in an attempt to control Robert's ambition. Orderic notes that when Robert was in rebellion, Rufus and Henry were favoured by their father.[40] This strategy was, of course, only open to a father who had been successful in siring a number of potential heirs and in less productive dynasties it may have been the case that fathers were necessarily forced to seek more amiable accommodations with their heirs. This mention of Robert's brothers brings us to a consideration of the arena within which notions of masculinity were primarily constructed, that is, the family.

Family politics at the Anglo-Norman court

The relationship between father and son needs to be located within the wider context of the Anglo-Norman royal family in order to determine what roles Robert's mother and his younger brothers and sisters played in the construction of his gender identity. His mother, Mathilda, may have had an early part in the formation of Robert's social ambitions, although it must be admitted that it was usual for young male aristocrats in this period to be given over into the care of guardians and tutors from an early age.[41] Given this

38. *OV*, III, pp.107–109.
39. *Historia Regum s.a.* 1080 in *Symeonis Monachi Opera Omnia*, ed., T. Arnold, Rolls Series, 2 vols, (London, 1882–5), II, p.211; David, *Curthose*, p.31.
40. *OV*, III, p.115, 'Just as William, a father angered by the attacks I have related, had from time to time cursed his presumptuous son and wished him many and various misfortunes, so he blessed and favoured William and Henry, the sons who supported him.' William of Malmesbury maintained that William the Conqueror spoilt Rufus; *Gestis Regum*, II, p.359 and Turner, 'Childhood', pp.41–2.
41. Turner, 'Childhood', and N. Orme, *From Childhood to Chivalry: The Education of the English Kings and Aristocracy 1066–1530* (London, 1984).

tendency of the medieval nobility to hand over their offspring to others for rearing, some historians, notably Philippe Ariès and Lawrence Stone, have doubted whether deep affective bonds were characteristic of the medieval family. This view has understandably been challenged and, indeed, Orderic has Mathilda say that she would willingly lay down her life for her eldest son.[42] Mathilda supported Robert in his struggle with his father, sending him money and offering prayers for his safety.[43] William expressed great anger at her support for Robert and this may be significant for an alliance between these two representatives of subordinated groups within a patriarchal society, the wife and the younger male, posed a severe threat to the authority of the *paterfamilias*.[44] The theme of female complicity in the perpetuation of patriarchy is a commonplace of gender studies, but here it seems as though Mathilda acted on her son's behalf, if not in direct opposition to her husband, then at least in the role of mediator between Robert and William. Mathilda's aim seems to have been to establish that degree of co-operation between her husband and son which was essential in the successful noble dynasty.[45] It may be significant that Robert's second period of exile came around the time of his mother's death in 1083. It is tempting to view the loss of his mother and perhaps also the imprisonment of his uncle Odo, Bishop of Bayeux, as removing two figures who had managed to mediate successfully between father and son.[46]

According to Orderic, Mathilda was so concerned for her son that during his first exile she consulted a hermit living in Germany in order to discover what would become of Robert.[47] The hermit dreamt of a meadow covered in grass and flowers in which was feeding a spirited horse. All around stood cattle that desired to graze in the meadow but they were driven away by the horse. However, the horse died and a wanton cow took charge of the field and the whole herd rushed in, devouring the grass and flowers and

42. P. Ariès, *L'Enfant et la vie familiale sous l'ancien régime* (Paris, 1960); English trans., *Centuries of Childhood* (London, 1962); L. Stone, *The Family, Sex and Marriage in England, 1500–1800* (London, 1977); cf. Turner, 'Children', p.43; *OV*, III, pp.102–5.

43. Robert Curthose's sister, Adela, was instrumental in securing the County of Blois for her second son, Theobald, in preference to his elder brother, whom she considered incompetent; Turner, 'Childhood', p.20 and the references therein.

44. *OV*, III, pp.102–5.

45. William's counsellors also advised a reconciliation, although some of them may have been motivated by their own dynastic concerns as their own sons were in Robert's entourage: *OV*, III, pp.112–13.

46. A point made by Marjorie Chibnall, *OV*, III, p.112, n.4.

47. *OV*, III, pp.104–9.

covering the meadow in their dung. The dream narrative is interesting – not least for its portrayal of William as a horse, an animal pre-eminently associated with battle, and his son as a cow, closely linked with lasciviousness. This feminizing of Robert reinforces the theme of the inversion of the natural order of things and the inevitable outcome of such unnatural arrangements was the ruin of the land and the rule of social outcasts, the sexually ambiguous and the sexually deviant.[48] According to this social ideology of gender roles, mothers and sons should obey the *paterfamilias*.

It has already been mentioned that in response to Robert's actions, William promoted his other sons, Rufus and Henry. Robert's rebellion thus excluded him from occupying what he saw as his natural position as eldest son at the head of the familial hierarchy. Although primogeniture was by no means the norm at the end of the eleventh century, Robert had been designated William's heir and he seems to have expected his younger brothers to behave towards him with due deference. William's acquisition of the kingdom of England also raised the stakes considerably, for the Norman inheritance after 1066 was of a different order. The king's sons were now competing not only for a duchy but for one of the wealthiest kingdoms in the medieval west.[49] Therefore, although subordinate to his father, Robert expected to dominate others within the family, namely his younger brothers and sisters. The insubordination of his brothers undermined his power within the family group and thus his gender identity, thereby sharpening his sense of outrage. Orderic reports an incident which occurred at Laigle on the Norman frontier shortly before Robert's first period of exile, when Rufus and Henry insulted their elder brother by urinating on him and his companions. Once again Robert's youthful counsellors offered a commentary on the significance of the incident:

> Why do you put up with such insults? Just look at the way your brothers have climbed up above your head and defile you and us with filth to your shame. Don't you see what this means? Even a blind man could. Unless you punish this insult without delay it will be all over with you: you will never be able to hold up your head again.[50]

48. J. Chevalier and A. Gheerbrant, *A Dictionary of Symbols*, trans., J. Buchanan-Brown (London, 1994), pp.237–8 (*sv.* 'cow') and 516–26 ('horse').

49. Marjorie Chibnall, (personal communication). It is possible to see William's management of the rivalries between his sons as an attempt to leave the strongest possible candidate to inherit the Anglo-Norman realm.

50. *OV*, II, pp.357–9.

Robert's response was to set about his younger brothers until his father intervened. Far from supporting Robert's case, William seems to have defended the younger males, whereupon Robert rather ambitiously attacked Rouen castle. Thus not only had Robert's sense of honour been infringed, but his sense of self-worth had also been undermined and the only response open to him was to rebel in order to assert his own masculine identity.

Conclusion

The view of medieval masculinity which emerges from this study highlights the complexities of the father–son nexus, where the son both embodied the ambitions of the father and yet, through his physical presence, reminded the patriarch of his mortality and appeared as a rival for his position as *paterfamilias*. William's conception of his own power would not allow even a part of it to be relinquished, as the loss of Maine or Normandy would expose him to additional demands from his other sons. Within eleventh-century aristocratic society in Northern France, the father's concern was to pass on the patrimony to the next generation undiminished. It appears that the Conqueror's seemingly stubborn attitude towards his eldest son may have been the result of this imperative. His task was a difficult one in that he had three ambitious sons to control and he had to develop effective strategies to deal with their demands. It is significant that none of William's sons married early and perhaps his main strategy in seeking to maintain his own power was to prolong the youth of his sons and, in so doing, deny them the status of manhood. Whether we view the conflict between William and Robert as the inevitable corollary of the overriding concern with the integrity of the patrimony, or whether it is discussed in Oedipal terms as a result of the personal hatred between father and son, underlying all this are the specifically constructed gender roles and expectations which medieval society imposed on its men.[51] Where one man sought to prevent another from fully expressing his masculine identity and attaining manhood, it should not be surprising that conflict was the result.[52]

51. Bates, *William*, p.162 suggested that Robert came to hate his father.
52. Ralph de Diceto (I, 355–65) made a direct link between Robert Curthose's rebellions against his father and those of the Young King Henry against his father, Henry II, which began in 1173. The parallels are striking and the motives for Young Henry's rebellions might be examined in the manner which has been attempted here.

CHAPTER FOUR

Masters and Men in Later Medieval England

P.J.P. GOLDBERG

The purpose of this chapter is to explore the relationship between artisans and the workers they employed, but particularly that between apprentices and their employers in later medieval England. Taking as a starting point urban society in the later fourteenth century and early years of the fifteenth century, by using such sources as poll tax returns, wills, cause papers (i.e. records of litigation within the Church courts), we can distinguish between those households headed by members of the franchise, who were invariably guild masters, and hence that were associated with workshops, and those households associated with persons who did not run their own businesses, but were piece-rate workers, labourers, and journeymen.[1] At a rough estimate, about a third of urban households were probably associated with workshops and were hence liable to employ labour other than family labour. By implication, piece-rate workers, labourers, and journeymen constituted the remaining two-thirds of households.[2] In considering dependent labour employed within the workshop, we need to distinguish between workers employed by the day (journeymen) and those in service (i.e. persons resident within the employer's household and employed on long-term contracts). The former, who included both men and women, were invariably adult and might often be married. They worked in their employer's workshop during clearly defined hours and had few ties to their employers beyond those implicit in their employment. Servants, however, were invariably adolescents or young adults, were single, and, as members of the employer's household, were

1. The most useful recent discussion of the organization of workshops is Heather Swanson, *Medieval Artisans* (Oxford, 1989).

2. P.J.P. Goldberg, *Women, Work, and Life Cycle in a Medieval Economy: Women in York and Yorkshire c.1300–1520* (Oxford, 1992), pp.160–3.

subject to the moral authority and discipline of the employer. Indeed, the employer stood in effect *in loco parentis* to those in his service.[3] But we must distinguish further between ordinary servants, who usually stayed with one employer only a year or two at a time, and the apprentice, who was bound to the employer – usually for a term of seven years. Whereas the former might be male or female, the latter, with a few exceptions, were male. Servants, moreover, might come from a variety of backgrounds. This would be particularly true of female servants, who could equally be daughters of merchants, of artisans, or of poor labourers. Apprentices, in contrast, appear to have come exclusively from comparatively more well-to-do and affluent backgrounds. They were thus the sons of merchants, artisans, and solid peasant agriculturalists. The apprentice, unlike the servant, aspired, moreover, to become a craft master, a head of a workshop, and employer of labour in his own right at some future time after completing his apprenticeship.

The relationship between master and apprentice

In focusing on apprentices, and exploring the relationship between employer and apprentice, we are thus focusing on an essentially masculine population, and a relatively privileged level of urban society. Certainly, female apprentices can be found, but largely only in London, and only in respect of a relatively narrow range of crafts primarily associated with the silk trade and with embroidery. It may also be that women were sometimes apprenticed because they had been orphaned and apprenticeship offered young women thus deprived of paternal protection a degree of security up until such age as they might marry.[4] Equally, we should probably distinguish between the boy engaged as an apprentice to a mercer, draper, or grocer, and the boy so contracted to a cordwainer, tailor, or weaver.

3. *Ibid.*, pp.168–86. Borough law invariably held employers answerable for the misdeeds of their servants and apprentices. The clearest statement is from Waterford c.1300, namely that, '. . . each citizen is bound to answer for his apprentice for any wrong or injury that he has done by day or night . . . just as for his son, if he is of age, that is when he knows how to count 12d. as is the law in respect of the citizen and the burgess': Mary Bateson, ed., *Borough Customs*, I, Selden Society, 18 (1904), p.222.
4. Caroline M. Barron, 'The education and training of girls in fifteenth-century London', in D.E.S. Dunn, ed., *Courts, Counties and the Capital in the Later Middle Ages* (Stroud, 1996), pp.139–53, probably overstates the significance of female apprenticeship in London.

There was always some sort of hierarchy of crafts, and mercantile trades would always have enjoyed positions at the top of that hierarchy and would have drawn apprentices only from like backgrounds. The essential point remains, however, that the relationship between master and apprentice was invariably between persons of the same social status and the same sex. The only substantial differences between master and apprentice were those of age and household status. The master was a householder and, unless a widower, a married man. The apprentice was a servant, a household dependant, and unmarried.[5] The master had achieved social adulthood through marriage and the headship of a workshop. The apprentice only aspired to these. The relationship may thus not have been between equals, but involved a greater degree of equality than the master's relationship with his other servants or his journeymen. It was also in some ways an intense and highly competitive relationship, pregnant with potential for friction and for conflict.

Some of these tensions are illustrated by a cause from the consistory court of York in 1417. The case concerned the attempt by one John Waryngton to have annulled his contract of marriage to Margaret Barker, formerly his fellow servant in the employ of the cordwainer John Bown.[6] Waryngton's case rested on the allegation that he was forced by his master to marry against his will, an allegation that the court ultimately upheld, not least because his master gave testimony in his support in the consistory. Waryngton was discovered by his master in compromising circumstances with Margaret Barker. We are told that he had on a previous occasion seduced another of Bown's female servants and Bown was accordingly furious. Although Waryngton is not specifically identified as an apprentice, it is implicit that it is his breach of the apprentice's contractual obligation not to sleep with female members of the employer's household that explains his master's threat to have him committed to prison. Bown, however, first consulted one John Gamesby, who advised caution and suggested that Bown first discover if Waryngton were willing to marry Margaret. Bown followed

---

5. That masters were invariably married is illustrated by the exceptional case of a York founder, one Giles de Bonoyne, who was permitted an additional apprentice by his guild because he lacked a wife, presumably because widowed at the moment (c.1390) that the ordinances were being drawn up: Maud Sellers, ed., *York Memorandum Book*, I, Surtees Society, 120 (1912), p.106. Apprenticeship indentures invariably specify that the apprentice cannot marry without the master's consent. Apprentices were therefore by implication unmarried.

6. BIHR, York, CP.F.127. I have translated the pertinent depositions in P.J.P. Goldberg, *Women in England c.1275–1525* (Manchester, 1995), pp.110–14.

this advice, but Waryngton denied both having sex with Margaret and having promised her marriage, both of which denials were repudiated by Margaret. Margaret's version of events is unfortunately lost since only the depositions of John Waryngton's witnesses survive, but it would not be unusual for an older female servant to engage in courtship with a fellow servant, nor would it have been regarded as particularly reprehensible for a young woman to have sexual relations with a man after a promise of marriage.

Waryngton then went on to claim that what he had actually said to Margaret was that his master 'was able to make it so and be sufficiently good and generous to him that he would be willing to make Margaret a wife and do honour to her so far as he was able'. This appears to have been said as much as a threat, or at least as a bargaining strategy, than as an objective retelling of a past conversation. Bown returned the threat by reminding him of 'the transgressions committed by the said John Waryngton *within the dwellinghouse* . . . and how he was able for that reason to have John Waryngton substantially burdened and punished according to the common law', and then asked him again if he would marry Margaret.[7] Waryngton merely repeated his observation, 'You are able to be so good and so generous towards me and can show me favour such that you can make me more willing to betroth and have her to wife,' protested that he would not betroth Margaret if his father were present, but ultimately capitulated and contracted her before witnesses using words of present consent.

For Waryngton his master could assist him towards gaining a workshop, to mastership, and hence to social adulthood. Thus provided, he would be willing to marry. Indeed, marriage to a woman for whom he clearly felt no great love was a reasonable price. It may well be, moreover, that Waryngton could hardly conceive of marrying without having already obtained access to a workshop. From his perspective, marriage and the acquisition of a workshop were inseparable. For Bown, Waryngton's behaviour was an affront to his authority and indeed a challenge to his reputation within the wider community as a householder. Similar emotions no doubt explain the ritualized beating in the London drapers' guildhall of one John

---

7. It is a not uncommon feature of apprenticeship contracts to specify that the (male) apprentice was not to have sexual relations *within* the master's house or with women of the household, cf. YML, consistory court book, M2(1)e, fo.23 (contract dated 1428); Ruth Mazo Karras, *Common Women: Prostitution and Sexuality in Medieval England* (New York, 1996), n.41, p.166; Mary Bateson, ed., *Records of the Borough of Leicester*, III (Cambridge, 1905), p.50 (contract dated 1543).

Rolls found by his master 'upon Passyon Sonday . . . in naked bed, within hys seid hous' with his fellow servant Margaret Byllyngton.[8] Gamesby's deposition repeatedly stresses that John Waryngton's transgression was committed within the household. The concern is not so much with sexual morality or that Waryngton was committing sin by engaging in fornication, but that he was so misbehaving under his master's roof. The depositions are also used to demonstrate that Bown acted firmly to restore his authority. Gamesby deposed that when Bown had discovered Waryngton's seduction of a previous servant 'in his home' he had made Waryngton 'swear on a book' that he would not so transgress again. After the second alleged seduction, Bown threatened Waryngton with imprisonment, warned the parish constable, and sought advice of an older friend. According to his wife, Margaret Bown's deposition, Bown even told Waryngton, 'You said yesterday when I told you the transgressions you had committed in my house and within my dwelling that to make amends you wished to do as I pleased and to place yourself at my will, and thus you placed yourself to act according to my will.'

This show of authority was sufficient to persuade the York consistory that Waryngton had indeed been forced into marriage with Margaret and hence to grant an annulment, although ironically Bown showed himself the 'good and generous' master Waryngton had appealed to by supporting him in his cause before the consistory.[9] Bown thus demonstrated his concern was more for his own reputation as a householder than for Margaret Barker, the seduced servant, and indeed, that ultimately he identified more with the needs of his apprentice than with a woman servant who had allowed herself to be seduced within his own house. Even Margaret Bown's loyalty has ultimately to be with her husband rather than with the women servants of whom Waryngton took advantage, for her testimony substantiated that of Thomas Gamesby and of her husband. But her deposition provides a further clue to the dynamics of the household. It is she who observed that Waryngton did not seem well disposed towards Margaret after their marriage. She also recalled that Waryngton complained to her, as his mistress, that 'his master

8. William Herbert, *The History of the Twelve Great Livery Companies of London* 2 vols (London, 1834–7), I, p.424. Another London apprentice who had 'irreverently' attacked his mistress in 1456 was similarly stripped and publicly beaten by his master in the kitchen of the goldsmiths' guildhall: *ibid.*, II, pp.169–70.

9. It is apparent that Waryngton's concern was to free himself of any claim by Margaret Barker so as to be free to marry one Margaret Foghler: BIHR, CP.F.74. Waryngton's master was present at this contract, which took place in his master's house and was subsequently solemnized at the church door.

had done ill towards him'. If Waryngton constructs Bown as a Godlike figure who can dispense good things with one hand and terrible chastisement with the other, then Margaret Bown is constructed as a Virgin Mary whom he hopes can intercede with her master and ask mercy.

It is implicit in this case that both Bown and Waryngton had a clear sense of what constituted acceptable behaviour by the one towards the other. This Waryngton transgressed by seducing Bown's female servants within his own home. But Waryngton believed that Bown had done him wrong by making him then marry the young woman. Here, as so often, we see the dynamic only when it breaks down. Some London evidence suggests that apprentices had a clear notion as to the work that was proper to them. Thus John 'in the Lane', an apprentice goldsmith, secured an oath in 1365 binding his master not to send him out of the city to thresh corn or engage in other agricultural work. Similarly, in 1366 Nicholas Salmon had his indentures as a draper's apprentice cancelled when a jury upheld his claim that his master employed him as 'son hostiller' ('his ostler') at 'mean tasks both in and outside his house'.[10] Apprentices expected, according to their contracts, to be fed, clothed, and trained in the craft. There are numerous instances where apprentices complained that their employers had, through debt, imprisonment, or neglect, failed in this obligation. Occasionally, it appears, employers also contracted to school their apprentices. Thus John Holand complained in 1415 that his master Thomas Hert, barber, had failed through poverty to feed or clothe him properly or to send him to school until he could read and write.[11] Masters had the right to chastise their apprentices, but not to abuse them.[12] When physical examination of the brothers Thomas and William Sewale showed that they had both been 'cruelly beaten', they were consequently exonerated from their apprenticeship.[13]

More positive aspects of the relationship between master and apprentice can still be found. Just as masters stood *in loco parentis* to their apprentices, so they might act in support of their dependants. Thus Nicholas Myn was able to ask his master John Burnett to help him negotiate dowry terms when he visited his prospective

10. A.H. Thomas, ed., *Calendar of Plea and Memoranda Rolls of the City of London, 1364–1381* (Cambridge, 1929), pp.18, 58.

11. A.H. Thomas, ed., *Calendar of Plea and Memoranda Rolls of the City of London, 1413–1437* (Cambridge, 1943), p.41.

12. Employers could chastise their apprentices, but equally could be sued for assault if they stepped beyond the mark: Bateson, *Borough Customs* I, pp.62–3, 228–9.

13. Thomas, ed., *Plea and Memoranda Rolls, 1364–1381*, pp.128–9.

mother-in-law.[14] York probate evidence shows that employers could at times be quite generous to their apprentices. The merchant Alan de Hamerton left some silver, a dagger, and the sum of £20 to Richard Gumays in 1406 on condition that he serve his widow for a further two years, presumably the remainder of his contract, and the mercer Thomas Curtas made similarly generous provision in 1460 to one Thomas Wrangwys, whom he also named as one of his executors. Employers of lesser rank made more modest provision. John Rodes, a fishmonger, left his apprentice a small boat in his will of 1457, and in 1391 the cordwainer William de Kirkby left John Cotyngwyth all his tools, the sum of 3s. 4d., and in addition made him one of his executors.[15] Such generosity may be atypical. Certainly some employers, such as the tanner John de Thorlethorpe, who left his apprentice an obligatory 40d., seem neither to have formed the close and trusting relationship suggested by the appointment of their apprentices as executors, nor to have seen their obligations to extend beyond those contained within their contracts, but age may be a factor here. A young man in his early twenties, nearing the completion of his apprenticeship, may have been more of a companion and trusted business partner than a lad of fourteen, fresh from the country, perhaps equally ignorant of the craft and of city mores.

Masters were expected to exercise authority over wives as well as servants. This is illustrated by a second York cause.[16] Significantly, it is a former male servant, and from his length of service almost certainly in fact an apprentice, who is made to articulate this defence of patriarchy. In 1396 one Margery Nesfeld attempted to obtain judicial separation from her husband Thomas through the consistory court on the grounds of his alleged unreasonable violence. She produced two witnesses who described a brutal, and apparently unprovoked attack on her by her husband, armed with a club and a dagger, some four years earlier. Thomas contested his wife's suit and brought two witnesses to make depositions in his support. One was merely a character witness, but, as such, a commentator on Thomas' public reputation as a good husband. The other, John Semer, the former apprentice, described two occasions that allegedly took place four years before and with the obvious

14. BIHR, CP.G.115.

15. BIHR, Exchequer court probate register, Prob. Reg. 3 fo.244(Hamerton); 2 fo.357Av(Rodes); 2 fo.438v(Curtas); 1 fo.35(Kirkby).

16. BIHR, CP.E.221. Three of the four surviving depositions are translated in P.J.P. Goldberg, *Women in England*, pp.141–2.

implication that one of these corresponded to that alleged by Margery's deponents. On one occasion, Margery left the house without her husband's permission and stayed out until dark, an obvious hint of unchastity at least of character if not in fact. When challenged on her return, she asserted her desire to go wherever she wished, a 'rebellion' that Thomas reasonably chastised by striking her with his fist. On a subsequent occasion, so John related, Margery told her husband that she could kill him in bed at night if she wanted. When he made to strike with his hand as punishment for this second act of rebellion, she ran crying hysterically out into the street. John Semer's deposition thus constructs his former master as entirely reasonable and proper in his behaviour. He corrects his wife's actions, tellingly described as 'rebellion' because they are against the will of her husband who is her lord, for not to have done so would have been to condone a perversion of the divinely sanctioned order, but he shows himself both stoical and moderate in his responses. He constructs Margery, however, no doubt at the instruction of the canon legal counsel, as the harlot from the Book of Proverbs, wayward, loud, disobedient, and unchaste.[17]

The master's control over the sexuality of his household dependents, whether wife, children, servants, or apprentices can be seen as central to the authority of the master. Only he, as invariably a married man, was permitted a sexual relationship within the household. Waryngton's transgression was to subvert the authority and sexual monopoly of his master, hence the righteous anger implicit in John Bown's response. Similarly, Margery Nesfeld's 'transgression' and implied unchastity struck at the heart of patriarchal order within the household. Where the sexual hierarchy was undermined, the household became dysfunctional. An act book for the Capitular court of York recording presentations for fornication and adultery over the later fourteenth and fifteenth centuries allows an insight into certain such dysfunctional households. Thus the pewterer Thomas Peny was presented in 1442 for fornication with one Joan Smyth, formerly the servant of Henry Forster, a goldsmith in Petergate, an affair that was still going on in 1457. But Thomas was also presented for fornication with one Agnes Banyster in 1444, and was having an affair with Marion, the wife of John Bosse in 1454, 1455 and 1457. It is no surprise then to find in this household headed by a single man conducting a series of simultaneous affairs that we find his servant Joan Wilson presented for fornication

17. Cf. *Proverbs* 7: 10–12.

with the cordwainer John Vyntener, by whom she was pregnant.[18] Of perhaps greater interest to us, however, is the household of the goldsmith William Snawschill. In 1442 his servant John Smyth was presented for fornication with Isabella Atkynson and also with his fellow servant Isabella. The following year another of his female servants, Alice, was presented for fornication with a vicar choral. William Snawschill was evidently an unsatisfactory master, but the ultimate clue to the dysfunctional nature of this unhappy household lies in the presentation only two years later of his wife Joan for adultery with one John Kendale.[19]

Urban recreation

If we turn now from the dynamics of the workshop to recreation outside the workshop, we may find further clues as to the particular brand of masculinity manifested by apprentices and other male workshop dependants. Many recreational activities observed in contemporary records seem to have involved only males. This is true for example of football, tennis, wrestling, archery, or the now lost sport of shooting at cock. It is difficult to know what sorts of men were involved, but, with the exception of archery, which was as much a civic responsibility as a recreation, there is reason to believe that they were primarily – though perhaps not exclusively – young men's activities.[20] A London proclamation of 1479 forbidding such activities as football, tennis, dicing, and cards (following parliamentary legislation of two years earlier) was specifically addressed to labourers, servants, and apprentices, although it was probably this group in society the civic authorities were most concerned to regulate. There may also be social boundaries being constructed

18. Peny was also presented for fornication with Elizabeth Scott at Rufforth in 1447. Latterly he was said to be living with Marion Bosse. Agnes Hudson was presented in 1447 as a procuress for Peny: BIHR, capitular act book, D/C AB.1, fos 102v, 104, 105v, 108, 110v, 112v, 126, 136, 137.

19. BIHR, D/C AB.1, fos 103, 104, 107, 107v.

20. A large group of Pocklington (Yorks.) men are, for example, remembered as shooting at butts near the township one Sunday after vespers in July of 1422: BIHR, CP.F.152 (deposition of Robert Barbour). The civic authorities in Coventry in the early sixteenth century seem regularly to have required exercise at the longbow whilst proscribing other games, but these measures reflect parliamentary statutes: Mary Dormer Harris, ed., *The Coventry Leet Book*, EETS, 134–5, 138, 146 (1907–13), pp.196, 338, 572, 652, 661; *Rotuli Parliamentorum* VI (London, 1832), p.188. The statute of 1511 required heads of households to provide boys in their care between the ages of seven and seventeen with a bow and to train them in its use, whereas men over seventeen years were to provide their own bows: *Statutes of the Realm* III (London, 1817), 3 Hen. VIII c.3.

here as a Coventry (Warws.) ordinance of 1518 forbad 'pore Craftes-
men to vse bowlyng . . . levyng ther besynes at home that they shuld
lyve by'.[21] A London ordinance of 1411 against wrestling in public
places ran, 'that no manere man ne child of what estate or
condicioun he be', that might again suggest that a relatively youthful age group was involved.[22] A further clue is provided by one
Thomas Newby's 1423 alibi that he could not have married Beatrix
Pullane one Sunday evening because he was playing football all
afternoon until sunset and then went off drinking. In this instance
we know the ages of three of the men involved in the game: one
was said to be forty years old, but the two others were said to be
twenty and twenty-four respectively. Newby was probably himself in
the latter age group because implicitly unmarried.[23]

These sports were competitive. This is reflected for example in
the murder of a Lynn (Norf.) man as a consequence of a dispute
arising out of a game of football.[24] They were also, at least in the
case of football, a group activity of young males. Margaret Pyper of
Wistow (Yorks.), to cite a non-urban example, deposed in 1422 that
William Kyng and Alice Cok contracted marriage together on Ash
Wednesday at the time when the men of Wistow play football.[25]
Sports were an opportunity for young males to show off their
strength, their athletic skills, indeed their manliness. A game of
tennis played between two Beverley (Yorks.) men one late summer
evening in 1445 was watched by several male onlookers, two of
whom placed bets on the outcome.[26] Wrestling in particular seems
to have been very much a spectator sport. A proclamation made in
1385 temporarily forbidding all wrestling matches within seven miles
of London appears to have been made to prevent large gatherings of
people at a time of rumours of attack.[27] Manuscript illuminations of
wrestling matches, such as that in the early-fourteenth-century Queen
Mary Psalter, likewise suggest that wrestling contests could attract
large crowds. Wrestling was thus an opportunity to show off manly

21. Harris, ed., *Coventry Leet Book*, p.656. Hunting and hawking were at much the
same date restricted to 40s. freeholders: *ibid.*, pp.629–30, 690. It may be that status
boundaries were being more clearly demarcated by the early sixteenth century than
a century earlier.

22. R.R. Sharpe, ed., *Calendar of Letter-Books of the City of London: Letter-Book 'I'*
(London, 1909), p.93; Sharpe, ed., *Calendar of Letter-Books: Letter-Book 'L'* (London,
1912), pp.163–4.

23. This is rural evidence from Church Fenton (Yorks.): BIHR, CP.F.137.

24. D.M. Owen, ed., *The Making of King's Lynn*, Records of Social and Economic
History, new ser., 9 (1984), no. 13, p.428.

25. BIHR, CP.F.133.   26. BIHR, CP.F.241.

27. Sharpe, ed., *Calendar of Letter-Books: Letter-Book 'H'* (London, 1907), p.272.

vigour, reflected further in the award of cocks (as in the Queen Mary Psalter illumination) or rams as prizes; Chaucer wrote of his Miller, 'At wrastlynge he wold have alwey the ram'. It may also have been an opportunity to show off before young women.[28] A group of women is certainly shown at the back of the crowd of spectators in the Queen Mary Psalter illumination. A mid-fourteenth-century didactic text addressed to women, which continued to circulate through the fifteenth century, warned the adolescent not to watch wrestling matches or the sport of shooting at cock lest she be taken for a loose woman. Since this was a text designed to restrict the opportunities open to young women to meet members of the opposite sex and to engage in courtship, we could perhaps read against the text and conclude that young women went to wrestling matches specifically to see and be seen by young males.[29] This was indeed the perspective of one early modern observer who noted that the audiences at wrestlings 'consist of a small Party of young Women'.[30]

These male leisure activities were an opportunity to show off masculine athletic prowess and strength, to socialize with other males, but, as we have just seen, also to show off to young women. Much the same may be said of some other aspects of well-to-do young men's behaviour, notably a tendency to dress nattily and an interest in dancing. Chaucer's fragmentary 'Cook's Tale' describes the apprentice, Perkyn, who kept his black locks 'ykemd ful fetisly' and 'At every bridale would he synge and hoppe'.[31] The youngster addressed in the *Book of Curtesye* is advised to dress 'not appeishe'. Young men seem also have enjoyed drinking. The Wise Man taught his Son in the didactic verse of that name to 'Be waar of usinge of þe taverne', but social drinking was in fact a normal part of leisure activity.[32] A cause of 1394 reveals how a group of four young York

28. British Library, Royal MS 2B.VII, fo.160v, reproduced in G. Warner, *Queen Mary's Psalter* (London, 1912), plate 193; Chaucer, *Canterbury Tales*, General Prologue, l. 548. Much the same use of wrestling matches as an opportunity for young men to display before potential wives has been described among the Mehinaku Indians of Brazil: David D. Gilmore, *Manhood in the Making: Cultural Concepts of Masculinity* (New Haven, 1990), p.90.

29. Felicity Riddy, 'Mother knows best: reading social change in a Courtesy Text', *Speculum* 71 (1976), pp.68–86.

30. Sir Thomas Parkyns quoted in John R. Gillis, *For Better, For Worse: British Marriages, 1600 to the Present* (New York, 1985), p.28.

31. Chaucer, *Canterbury Tales*, 'The Cook's Tale', ll. 4369, 4375. Of Perkyn the tale further relates that '. . . in the toune nas ther no prentys / That fairer koude caste a paire of dys': *ibid.*, ll. 4385–6.

32. F.J. Furnivall, ed., *Caxton's Book of Curtesye*, EETS, extra ser., 3 (1868), ll. 484–90, p.49. 'How the wise man taught his son', in F.J. Furnivall, ed., *The Babees Book*, EETS, 32 (1868), l. 59, p.50 (the two subsequent lines warn against playing with dice and lechery).

journeymen saddlers, all probably in their early twenties and all unmarried, spent their weekend visiting the village of Crayke (Yorks.) together to view property that one of their number had just inherited. They returned to York late on Sunday, arriving some time after ten o'clock and then spent time drinking together at the house of one of the four. The three others then went off just before midnight and two of them, Thomas de Horneby and Thomas Gasgill, went to Gasgill's room by the cemetery of St Michael, Spurriergate, and passed the night together in the same bed.[33] There is, however, no reason to think that social drinking was exclusively a male activity. The Goodwife advised her daughter not to get drunk too often, but did not forbid her from visiting taverns.[34] A cause of 1472 reveals a mixed group of young people drinking and making jokes together in a York tavern in Christmas week.[35]

One final recreation we may usefully consider is fornication. Implicitly, male servants, but not female servants, might engage in sexual activity outside the household. Indeed, male servants and apprentices are often regarded as important clients of prostitutes, if only because the apprenticeship contract specifically forbad resort to brothels.[36] Unfortunately, very little work has yet been undertaken on the clients of prostitutes in later medieval England.[37] The Capitular act book already noted may, however, undermine this assumption. The court had jurisdiction over an area around York Minster, including the important commercial thoroughfares of Petergate and Goodramgate. Clergy appear very prominently among the clients of those women who, from frequency of presentation, appear to have been engaging in commercial sex. This is discussed in chapter 11, but is in part a reflection of the neighbourhood. Males identified as servants appear much less frequently and it would seem that they are rather more likely to be associated with other servants, or at least with women whose names do not reappear in the record. The implication is that these presentations arise out of sexual activity within courtship, very much the context we

33. The testimony was given in this form to establish an alibi for Thomas de Horneby who allegedly contracted marriage the same weekend, but this does not detract from the value of the narrative: BIHR, CP.E.159; translated in P.J.P. Goldberg, *Women in England*, pp.103–9. It was common for persons of the same sex to share a bed and it does not here carry any implication of sexual activity; see chapter 13.

34. 'How the Goodwife taught her daughter', in Furnivall, ed., *The Babees Book*, ll. 74–80, p.39. The female apprentice was directed by her indenture not to frequent taverns ('*tabernas ex consuetudine non frequentabit*'): Norfolk Record Office, Hare MSS no. 2091; Corporation of London Record Office, Misc. MSS. 1863 (I am grateful to Dr Caroline Barron for these references).

35. BIHR, CP.F.252.   36. Owen, ed., *Making of King's Lynn*, no. 14, p.428.

37. Only pp.76–81 of Karras, *Common Women* are focused on clients.

have already seen in the Waryngton case, rather than commercial transactions. Thus we find in 1446 one Joan, the servant of John Bene, pregnant by Robert Parkour, servant in the same household.[38] In fact, there is every reason to believe that older men, identified by occupation and hence journeymen or even masters, are at least as conspicuous among the clients of actual prostitutes.

Conclusion: the transition into the early modern era

Thus far I have portrayed an essentially static picture focused on the hundred years or so following the Black Death. It is, however, increasingly evident that the period from the later fifteenth century saw quite profound changes in the urban economy and in the gender dynamics of the urban workshop. Consequently, the position of the dependent male workforce, both apprentices and non-apprentices, changed and this has implications for our study of masculinity. We seem to see a shift from a world in which males and females enjoyed a lot of contact in the workshop, and socialized, even engaged in courtship, comparatively freely, and in which hierarchies of age and status were perhaps as important as those of gender, to a world in which the genders were much more segregated, and were perhaps much more conscious of separate gender identities. This is revealed in a number of ways.

First, the actual sexual composition of the workshop changes. Whereas female servants regularly worked alongside males in the labour-starved decades of the later fourteenth and earlier fifteenth centuries, by the later fifteenth century a marked shift can be observed.[39] In craft households only male servants tended to be employed, whereas numbers of female servants came to characterize mercantile households. At the same time wives may have become less involved in the day-to-day activities of workshops. Certainly, widows seem to have been less likely to continue to run workshops after their husbands' deaths. This was no doubt a consequence of social pressures, though it was sometimes reinforced by specific guild ordinances. It may follow from a historical perception that widows were not competent to head workshops. Indeed, a number of London cases concerning allegations by apprentices that they

---

38. BIHR D/C AB.1, fo.107v.
39. Goldberg, *Women, Work, and Life Cycle*, pp.194–202.

had not received proper instruction relate to workshops managed by widows. In the long run, widows were forced to marry their apprentices in order to retain some control over inherited businesses. The concern here was to ensure that as many workshops as possible were available to young men finishing their apprenticeships, but in the context of rapid demographic recovery outstripping any economic growth, such young men increasingly found themselves forced to remain journeymen.

It is within this hostile economic environment that we find men specifically articulating arguments against women's employment. At the same time the better off were probably more likely to keep their daughters, and perhaps even their sons, at home than to allow them into service. Work on early modern parish listings shows that households were more likely to retain daughters than sons throughout the seventeenth and until the later eighteenth century. The evidence is more ambiguous if analysed by social status, though at Eccleshall (Staffs.) in 1693/8, for example, craftsmen were much more likely than labourers to retain their adolescent daughters at home. Courtship became less free and men may more readily have turned to prostitutes to find sexual satisfaction. It also became harder for women to support themselves singly. Those that did were often forced into the twilight zone of the alehouse, prostitution, and petty crime. We can also discern indicators that certain domestic chores were considered unsuitable for more well-to-do urban women by the later fifteenth century. A London man observed in a matrimonial cause of 1487, for example, objected to his fiancée, who was then in service, carrying clothes to be washed in the Thames.[40] Women's place was thus increasingly seen as in the home. It was for men to go out and become breadwinners. But young men, before they achieved social adulthood through marriage and householding, with its associated responsibilities, may themselves have absorbed some of the misogynistic propaganda designed to put women in their place and to enforce a new gender order. They may have preferred to shun ordinary social intercourse with women and at the same time sought ways of asserting their masculine identity. We may for example notice an ordinance of the merchants' guild of Newcastle-upon-Tyne made in 1554 which declares rhetorically that 'never amonge apprentices, and chiefelye of this said Feoloshipe, hathe bene more abused and inconvenyent behavour than ys of

40. R. Wall, 'Leaving home and the process of household formation in pre-industrial England', *Continuity and Change* 2 (1987), pp.93–4, tab. 6, p.96; S. McSheffrey, *Love and Marriage in Late Medieval London* (Kalamazoo, 1995), pp.58–9.

theim at this daye frequented, for what dyseng, cardeng and mumming; what typlinge, daunseng, and brasenge [embracing] of harlots; what garded [edged] cotes, jagged hose, lyned with silke, and cutt shoes; what use of gitterns by nyght; what wearynge of berds [beards], what daggers ys by theim worn crosse overthwarte their backs, that theis theire dooings are more cumlye and decent for rageng ruffians than seemlye for honest apprentizes'.[41] The whoring, the heavy drinking, the fighting, and the outrageous dressing may thus be more an aspect of early modern culture than has perhaps been hitherto supposed.

41. J.R. Boyle, ed., *Extracts from the Records of the Merchant Adventurers of Newcastle-Upon-Tyne* I, Surtees Society, 93 (1895), pp.20–1.

CHAPTER FIVE

Military Masculinity in England and Northern France c.1050–c.1225

M. BENNETT

The figure of the mounted knight is still, to many people, the most potent image of the medieval period. He is often portrayed, in both medieval literature and in manuscript illuminations, in front of 'his' castle, at once both a representative of the military ideals of the Middle Ages and an oppressor of the peasants whose labour provided the upkeep of the knightly class. Although there is much that is wrong with this stereotype of the knight, it does contain elements that would have been recognized by his contemporaries. This chapter explores the image of the male military figure in texts of the period c.1050–c.1225. What physical and sartorial attributes were required by men of the aristocracy in order to fulfil social expectations of the warrior? How did they learn how to be knights? How were knights expected to behave? How far were the images presented in epic and romance literature challenged in other sources? Were the images of knightly behaviour socially acceptable? What happened to knights who failed to fulfil the expectations placed on them?

It is important to be aware that the image of the knight was not fashioned solely by the secular aristocracy; the medieval Church also had an investment in determining the behaviour of the military classes. The doctrine of the 'Three Orders' was prevalent in much ecclesiastical writing; it divided society into those who prayed (*oratores*), those who fought (*bellatores*) and those who worked the land (*laboratores*).[1] The clerics, whose literacy made them masters of the medium of communication both with contemporaries and with historians who use their texts to study the period, naturally placed

---

1. G. Duby, *The Three Orders: Feudal Society Imagined*, trans. A. Goldhammer (Chicago, 1980).

themselves on a higher plain. The period under consideration in this chapter saw much tension between secular and ecclesiastical lords, and a great deal of debate about the nature of the relationship between secular and ecclesiastical authority. Over the two centuries covered by this chapter, Church leaders made strenuous efforts to control the temporal warriors and to direct their violent energies towards spiritual ends: by taking part in the Crusades, for example. Male violence needed to be controlled if Christian society was to flourish peacefully.

Of course, women were also involved in warfare, and recent studies have examined instances where women played a role in warfare, not just at the strategic levels, exercising regal or princely power, but also as active participants on campaign or in battle. Examples of the latter are extremely rare for the period in question, however, and where they do occur they attracted attention from contemporaries for their exceptional roles.[2] This chapter concentrates on the majority, the male warriors of medieval Europe, and focuses in particular on the elite of that group. When considering the image of military masculinity between the mid-eleventh and the early twelfth century, there are a number of sources upon which the historian can draw, in both Latin and the vernacular languages. Latin chronicles in the form of narrative histories contain descriptions of military hero-figures, which help to illustrate what were considered important masculine characteristics. The extensive corpus of Old French literature, with its many genres, exemplifies the way a society uses poetry to examine, and criticize, some of its most important precepts. The visual arts also provide significant pointers as to the ways in which the male military image was constructed through, for example, the depiction of lords as mounted knights on their seals. The Bayeux Tapestry is also an extremely valuable source when examining this type of representation.

What defined masculinity in the context of the warrior – the knight – and how is it represented to us in the sources? This chapter will start by examining the chronological development of a boy into a man in the eleventh and twelfth centuries. It will then look at exterior signs of masculinity (including physical presence and dress), and, finally, will consider the interior qualities which made a knight (a sense of breeding and honour, courage and expressions of love towards other men and women).

2. M. McLaughlin, 'The woman warrior: gender, warfare and society in medieval Europe', *Women's Studies* 17 (1990), pp.193–203.

Growing up

The education of the prospective knight began in childhood, and it is possible to uncover much about the processes by which a boy learned the behaviour that would be expected of him as a man. According to the tradition inherited by medieval writers, a man's life before his majority at twenty-one was divided into three periods: infancy, adolescence and youth. From birth to seven years old was considered infancy. The second age, adolescence, involved training as a squire, the third age, youth, knighting and bachelordom (see below). Learning to walk and to ride were practically simultaneous experiences in medieval society. A three year-old was not considered competent at either, but he needed to be able to perform both tasks by the age of seven, at which time he was deemed ready to learn his trade as a knight, usually serving as a squire in the household of a relative. Shulamith Shahar sums up the experiences of young boys in this context:

> Training was conducted in groups, and children constituted a single group (of mixed ages) within the population of the castle . . . However, [unlike children in a monastery] no attempt was made to separate future knights from adult society. They were raised in the male world of sweat, weapons, stables, horses and hounds, with its ethos of courtly culture, as well as its lusts and unrestrained urges. A central role in the child's education was played by approval, and by the sanctions of group pride and shame.[3]

A term frequently found in vernacular texts for boys brought up together is '*nurri*' (literally 'nourished' in the same household). They formed close ties as they learnt their trade together. In addition to acquiring military techniques, they also had to face danger together when out hunting, which was both an introduction to, and a substitute for, war itself. The bonds formed during this apprenticeship were close, and often proved to be long-lasting. Certainly, the boy who became Edward the Confessor remembered his upbringing at the Norman court, together with the sons of Duke Richard, when he was exiled from England. Like all medieval aristocrats, Edward was a keen hunter:

> Hunting was one of the basic parts of military training, for it perfected horsemanship under conditions very similar to those met on campaign. It taught boys and youths how to move in company across the countryside, instilled in them the arts of scouting and selecting a

---

3. S. Shahar, *Childhood in the Middle Ages* (London, 1990), pp.210–11.

line of advance, and gave excellent training in arms, the bow against many running animals and the sword and spear against the wild boar.[4]

The quote comes from Frank Barlow's book on William II Rufus, whose behaviour is often seen in stark contrast to the 'saintly' Edward; yet they actually shared this masculine interest. Hunting together provides a fine example of the creation of small group loyalties deemed essential to a successful army. Shared risk and the need to co-operate as a team helped to produce in military males the required skills, attitudes and bonds of affection which would stand them in good stead in war. It also inculcated in them a sense of shared values.

Communal eating also provided informal moments for socializing and strengthening group loyalties. Sleeping in the same room did the same. In his work on household knights, John Medding has stressed that it was these kinds of association which produced the most dependable followers: trusted and devoted to a lord and to each other.[5]

Each knight had to learn how to handle a sword, lance and shield on horseback. These skills made the Franks feared warriors and made possible the mounted charge which was their trademark in battle. The prospective knight also had to learn how to serve, in all its senses, from serving at table, to demonstrating obedience to his sworn superior, his lord, and as the chivalric ethos grew from the 1130s onwards, to devote himself to a lady. By the age of fifteen he was old enough to be knighted, since by that age a young man should be competent in military skills. William of Poitiers has a description of William the Bastard at just this age:

> Our duke, already adult in sagacity and bodily strength if not in years, took up the arms of knighthood; whereat a tremor ran though all Gaul. It was a sight at once delightful and terrible to see him managing his horse, girt with sword, his shield gleaming, his helmet and lance alike menacing'.[6]

As a modern commentator puts it: 'For a boy to become an adult he must prove himself – his masculinity – among his peers'[7] (a theme discussed in other chapters in this volume).

---

4. F. Barlow, *Edward the Confessor* (London, 1979); *idem, William Rufus* (London, 1980), p.23.
5. Dr John Medding, personal communication.
6. *Guillaume de Poitiers, Histoire de Guillaume Le Conquérant*, ed., R. Foreville and trans. (into French) (Paris, 1952). This passage, trans. R. Allen Brown, *Documents of Norman Conquest* (Woodbridge, 1994), p.18.
7. M.Z. Rosaldo quoted by J. Tosh, 'What should historians do with masculinity? Reflections on nineteenth-century Britain', *HWJ* 38 (1994), p.184.

In fact, we might doubt the enthusiasm of William's panegyrist, for a fifteen year-old was not quite the finished article in military terms, and his first taste of battle did not come until he was nine-teen, and then under the tutelage of his overlord, Henry I of France. Extracts from *La Chanson de Guillaume,* a vernacular *chanson de geste* of a century later, provide an ironic counterpoint to such fulsome-ness.[8] The nephew of the epic hero William of Orange, named Guy, is described as 'very young, not yet fifteen, and [he] had no beard, not a single hair except on his head that he was born with' (ll. 1,441–42). Guy promises to defend his childless uncle's lands, should William die. William replies 'Scoundrel, you are better suited to sit among the cinders than you are to rule my domain!' (ll. 1,455–56). Guy responds 'Why should you criticize me for being young. There is no great man who was not born small' (ll. 1,463–64), which brings the following response from William: 'You have a child's body but the speech of a fighter. After my death, my fief will be yours' (ll. 1,479–80). Then Guy is armed, but he is left behind when the men ride out the next day. The debate about Guy's age and size carries on throughout the poem, and William's wife Guiborg chides him that 'You are only a child of tender years. You could not undergo the hardships, watching by night and fasting by day nor endure and suffer the fierce fighting' (ll. 1,525–27). Guy pleads his case to join the battle, and so he is armed again, with 'little' arms and armour, and instead of a grown man's charger he is given Guiborg's palfrey to ride, but even this is too large for him. 'Guy was small and the horse was large. He sat only a foot-and-a-half above the pommel and his spurs but three inches below the saddle-cloth, yet he bore arms better than a man of thirty' (ll. 1,553–56).

Guy arrives at William's council of war to hear his uncle say, 'Now listen, noble and well-tried knights. No great battle can be well fought unless by the endurance of the warriors and the staying power of the young fighters, the strong and vigorous, the bold and famous' (ll. 1,610–15). William derides the tiny knight until he realises that he is his nephew. He then demands that Guy demon-strate his ability with horse and arms (again like Duke William) and when he does so to good effect praises him: 'You certainly ought to be a knight, for so were your father and your other kinsmen' (ll. 1,670–71). This vignette neatly encapsulates attitudes to the integ-ration of the young warrior into the adult setting. It is a fantasized account, of course, but this point is worth developing. Military

8. *La Chanson de Guillaume,* ed., D. MacMillan, Société des Anciens Textes Français, 2 vols (Paris, 1949–50); this text is translated by L. Muir, in *William, Count of Orange: Four Old French Epics,* ed., G. Price (London, 1975), pp.131–203.

virtues are believed to be inherited from other men, from the
father and the wider kin. Those who display such virtues are worthy
of the group they represent: whether the family, the kin or the
wider Christian community. Those who fail to live up to expectations
of appropriate military values and behaviour are no better, and often
worse, than the enemy, the Saracens. The *chansons de geste* deal with
the idea of good and bad 'lignage'. A warrior from a good lineage
is expected to embody the qualities of his forefathers. A nobleman
was expected to live up to his inheritance and display proper military characteristics. Someone from a bad line – most notoriously
Ganelon, the villain of the *Chanson de Roland*, who intrigues with the
Saracens to plot the downfall of the hero – will naturally embody
evil traits. Such characters always give themselves away at crucial
moments. They may be brave, but, through greed, anger, pride or
resentment, they will not sustain it in the face of a true hero.

Breeding was clearly important in producing a brave man. *Le
Couronnement de Louis*, another *chanson de geste* of the William of
Orange cycle, provides good examples of how courage was understood. William is slighted by the faction in the court of Charlemagne which believes in peace rather than war. This faction gains
favour over William from Charlemagne's son, Louis the Pious, who
has monastic tendencies. Charlemagne is outraged by this turn of
events, and as a result suspects that Louis might not be his son.
Failure to possess the necessary military attributes of courage and
enthusiasm for military action might result in questions being asked
of a man's parentage.[9]

Youth and 'bachelers'

Young men had a particular role to play in warfare. After training
as squires, those wealthy enough to own – or lucky enough to be
given – horse and armour were dubbed knights. The word is French
– derived from *adouber*, 'to equip' – and is expressive of the need
to have the right equipment. This means not just weapons and
armour, but several horses and, hence, a squire and a groom to
manage them. 'Dubbing' also refers to the formal ceremony which
marked the passage into military manhood. John Gillingham has
pointed out that the word first appears, surprisingly perhaps, in the

9. *Le Couronnement de Louis*, ed., E. Langlois, Classiques français du moyen âge
(Paris, 1925) ll. 79–98; a translation by D. Hoggan is in *Four Old French Epics*, ed.
Price, pp.1–59 (pp.2–3, for this passage).

Anglo-Saxon Chronicle entry for 1086, when William the Conqueror '*dubbade to . . . ridere*' (dubbed a knight) his youngest son, Henry. Its first use in a French text comes in the work of the first 'chivalric' author, Gaimar, written in the 1130s.[10] Latin texts of the 1170s describe elaborate ceremonies for the dubbing of princes, such as Geoffrey of Anjou and Frederick Barbarossa. Later ceremonies include vigils, special baths and clothing; but the original ceremony seems to have been a straightforward arms-giving to the new warrior. This reveals the influence of the Church on these ceremonies, which become more 'religious' in nature, in imitation of royal coronation rituals.[11]

When first knighted, the young man was known as a *bacheler*, and was expected to pursue a career in the *mesnie* (household) of a great man, or to make his way in the world in some other manner, such as tourneying or finding a rich heiress. The latter course of events gave rise to the ideal and the reality of the knight errant; later enshrined in the romances of the late twelfth century onwards as the pursuit of a noble object, such as a woman worthy of love, or an even greater goal, the Holy Grail. These are idealizations of the very real need for young warriors to earn money in military service. Georges Duby identified a group he called 'Youth' (*iuvenes*), who pursued lives of military adventure. They were often led by the sons of rulers. Robert Curthose, eldest son of William the Conqueror, ran a bachelor court and caused his father endless problems over the last decade of the king's life (see above, chapter 3). This inter-generational conflict is a classic example of masculine competition. Both the older man and the youth define themselves in the context of disputes with men of another generation. In many ways the youth was practising the exercise of 'real' power, a right that would come to him in due course.

War was also something that could be practised. In many ways war was seen by the military classes as a combination of a kind of sport and profitable recreation. Sometimes this spilled over into illegitimate warfare. Contemporary rulers were unhappy with out-breaks of this kind of fighting, unless they themselves instigated it, because it could interrupt the revenues which they expected to receive from a prosperous peasantry or from merchants plying their

---

10. J. Gillingham, 'Kingship, Chivalry and Love: political and cultural values in the earliest history written in French: Geoffrey Gaimar's Estoire des Engleis', in C. Warren Hollister, ed., *Anglo-Norman Political Culture and the Twelfth Century Renais-sance* (Woodbridge, 1997), pp.33–58, at p.39 & n.35.

11. See J. Flori, *L'Essor de la Chevalerie* (Paris, 1986) for a detailed study of dubbing.

trade peacefully, and it also caused scandals, such as the robbing of churches. However, to interpret all low-level military activity as destructive feud is to misunderstand its purpose.[12] The knightly classes enjoyed fighting and it enabled them to inculcate the necessary skills in their fighting men, which could then be employed in the service of the ruler when he needed them. *Bachelers* needed to be exercised in the use of arms and blooded in border raids on neighbouring lands.

Another well-known demonstration of masculine prowess and military skill was jousting. It also served as an important way for young *bachelers* to make a living. Mounted warriors had always practised some form of martial skills on horseback, but the form known as tournament apparently originated in the mid-eleventh century. Contrary to popular perception, jousting across a tilt was not the most common form of tourney in the twelfth century. Tournament was properly a mêlée 'fought over several miles of open countryside' between opposing teams often grouped on a regional or national basis.[13] The aim of the competition was for the knights to unseat their opponents, who were promptly picked up by supporting squires or foot-soldiers and ransomed for the defeated man's horse and arms. There were no clear rules to differentiate the tournament from real warfare, except that it was not intended to kill an opponent. The events were clearly demonstrations of masculine prowess. They might even take place outside besieged fortresses between the two sides, bored at the slow progress of the siege, as happened at Winchester in 1141. From the 1130s, if not earlier, as Geoffrey of Monmouth bears witness, it was common for knights to adopt the favours of ladies as a spur to better achievements (usually associated with tiltyard events):

> The knights planned an imitation battle and competed together on horseback, while their womenfolk watched from the top of the city walls and aroused them to passionate excitement by their flirtatious behaviour.[14]

The role of sporting competition was another important aspect of masculine display (as Jeremy Goldberg also discusses in chapter 4).

12. See M. Bennett, 'Violence in eleventh-century Normandy: feud, warfare and politics', in G. Halsall, ed., *Violence and Society in the Early Medieval West* (Woodbridge, 1997), pp.126–40.
13. See R. Barber and J. Barker, *Tournaments* (Woodbridge, 1989), esp. p.23, from which the quote comes.
14. Geoffrey of Monmouth, *History of the Kings of Britain*, trans. L. Thorpe (Harmondsworth, 1980), pt VI, ch.15, p.230.

The main purpose of the tournament in peacetime was to occupy the 'Youth' and to enable them to make money. The epitome of tournament prowess was William Marshal, an Englishman who first made his name at the Le Mans festival in 1167. Through his tournament activities he created both an impressive reputation and a huge fortune in the ensuing decade. He teamed up with another knight and in one ten-month period they captured 103 knights between Pentecost and Lent. William's exploits are recorded in a praise-poem written in the mid-1220s, a decade after his death. The work romanticizes William's career, not least because it is marked by the literary influence of authors like Chrétien de Troyes who wrote romances featuring tournaments and chivalrous behaviour; nonetheless, as both a role-model and in reality, William epitomized masculine values.[15]

Physical presence and dress

Molt le vit bel et dreit et alignie
Alelme esguarde et a mains et a piez
Bien le conut qu'il esteit escuiers

He looked at Alelme's hands and feet, at his handsome face and his well-proportioned body, and recognised him immediately as a squire.
(*Le Couronnement de Louis*, ll. 1839–41)

This passage from *Le Couronnement de Louis* describes the perfect physical form of a *chevalier*, a noble warrior. He should be handsome, tall, strong and well-proportioned. Other texts emphasize that his physique should be that of a horseman: broad-shouldered, slender at the waist and with a good *forcheure* (fork: long legs, well joined at the pelvis). A warrior's physique is distinguished from that of a peasant. The warrior has pale skin, and his eyes, nose and mouth are in proper proportion. In contrast, a non-noble peasant has a dark skin, coarse features and the 'width of a palm' between his eyes. From around 1100, fashion dictated that the hair of warriors should be long and curled outwards. A knight might also be recognized by his dress, which will be of fine quality and well-made.

15. The life and career of William Marshal is an ideal starting point for a study of military masculinity. The poem is entitled: *L'Histoire de Guillaume le Maréchal*, ed., P. Mayer (Paris, 1881–94); David Crouch is producing a new edition and translation into English with an historical background (forthcoming, 1998); for a recent biography see his *William Marshal* (London, 1990).

The tunic, or *bliaut,* was closely fitting to the body, and shoes had long toes, some so long that they had to be tied back to the leg.

The emphasis on physical appearance and dress was uncomplicated in epic literature, yet from another perspective it caused consternation. Ecclesiastical writers were notably very sceptical of such fine dressing, and foppery. The Norman monk, Orderic Vitalis, blamed the notorious rake, Fulk le Rechin (the Irritable), count of Anjou for introducing the elaborate style of shoe with long toes, claiming that it was to hide his deformed feet.[16] But there were other implications for the wearer's virility; when tied back to the shin this style was clearly phallic.

Perhaps the greatest twelfth-century commentator on what makes a Christian warrior – St Bernard of Clairvaux – demanded absolute simplicity from the Knights Templar. He provided these monk-knights with a rule and supported their papal authorisation at the Council of Troyes, 1129. Not only were they denied all extravagance in dress, but they were also instructed to cut the hair on their head short, while eschewing shaving. They were encouraged to be begrimed in the Lord's service. This was in complete contrast to the way in which our secular sources describe knightly style.[17]

It is clear that appearance might be judged in very different ways in texts according to the background and perceptions of the author. Some believed that the fine warrior fashions indicated the virility of the wearer. However, when these fashions were associated with, for example, the court of William Rufus, the second Norman king of England (1087–99), in combination with accusations that he ran a court where homosexuality flourished, then their significance changes. Long hair might be understood to indicate effeminacy or even homosexuality. In a study of the military household of Henry I of England (1100–36), John Prestwich – using the writing of Orderic Vitalis – remarks on the reintroduction of short, 'Puritan' hairstyles by one of William the Conqueror's veterans, Roger de Beaumont. Prestwich connects this with Henry's defeat of his brother, Robert Curthose, duke of Normandy, at the battle of Tinchebrai in 1106, which he calls, perhaps ironically, a 'Round-head victory'.[18]

16. *The Ecclesiastical History of Orderic Vitalis,* ed. and trans., M. Chibnall, 6 vols (Oxford, 1968–80), IV, pp.188–89.

17. See M. Barber, *The New Knighthood: a History of the Order of the Temple* (Cambridge, 1994), pp.42–49, for St Bernard's *De laude novae militiae.* J.M. Upton-Ward, *The Rule of the Temple* (Woodbridge, 1992) is a translation of the detailed regulations governing domestic and military activities of the knights.

18. J.O. Prestwich, 'The military household of the Norman kings', *EHR* xcvi (1981), pp.1–37, esp. pp.29–30, citing *OV,* VI, pp.60–66 (and 90).

Short hair as an indicator of military effectiveness, is however, a twentieth-century prejudice. What Prestwich does not take into account is the impact these 'Norman' hair-styles had on clerical writers when they were first introduced in the early eleventh century. The chronicler, Ralph Glaber, derides the fashions on show at the wedding of the Capetian king, Robert the Pious, to Constance of Arles in 1003, describing the scene as follows:

> men puffed-up with every sort of levity, corrupt in manners and dress, dissolute in their display of arms and overdressed horses, cutting their hair back as far as the middle of the head, shaving their beards like actors, utterly obscene in their style of hose and leggings.[19]

The chronicler blamed the influence of the new queen's Provençal courtiers for introducing such fashions. Yet, as the Bayeux Tapestry shows, such styles were standard Frankish dress by the mid-eleventh century.[20]

Conspicuous consumption

Another aspect of outward display by the noble warrior was his voracious appetite. In the *Chanson de Guillaume*, tragedy and comedy are mingled as the heroes go out to fight invading hordes of Saracens. On Gerard's return, having fought for three days without food, he consumes a shoulder of pork and a bread-cake and downs a gallon of wine in two swallows (ll. 1042–61). William outdoes this feat later in the poem. He eats a loaf of bread and two bread-cakes, a roast peacock and a shoulder of pork, as well as drinking a gallon of wine (ll. 1402–20). The significance of such consumption is explained by William's wife, the converted Saracen Guiborg: '[he] will certainly give his neighbour a hard fight; never will he shamefully run from the battlefield and his lineage will never be shamed by him' (ll. 1,430–32).

In the middle of a battle, Guy, William's young nephew, complains '"I am so hungry I shall die of it. I cannot hold or wield my arms, flourish my lance or control [my horse] Balzan"' (ll. 1,739–41). So William urges him 'to make the enemy his quartermaster' and raid their supplies. This he does, returning to slay three Saracens with three lance-blows, routing them from the field (ll.1,822–42). After the great battle, won at huge cost by the Christians, William

19. Quoted by C.S. Jaeger, *The Origins of Courtliness* (Philadelphia, 1985), p.178.
20. D. Wilson, *The Bayeux Tapestry* (London, 1985), e.g. plates 9–12.

laments that the groaning table prepared for his victorious house-hold will not have justice done to it: 'the dishes filled and overflowing with haunches and shoulders, cakes and dainties. They will not be eaten by the noble mothers' sons who had their heads cut off on the Archamp [battlefield]' (ll. 2,404–7).

Companionship

One of the most distinctive expressions of male military status was the creation of pairs of 'brothers in arms'. The archetypal pair were Roland and Oliver of the *Chanson de Roland* and various other works (see below, chapter 14). Although the oldest version of the *Roland*, as we now possess it, dates from the period 1140–1170, the names are found already paired in the early eleventh century.[21] This is testimony both to the antiquity of the Roland legend and the celebration of companionship between warriors. It is fair to say that this relationship is the most significant and intensely described in the *chanson*. The bond between Roland and Oliver is considerably more emotionally expressed than that between Roland and his fiancée, Aude, Oliver's sister. Aude only appears twice; on the second occasion merely to faint away at the news of Roland's death. Aude is, however, central to the 'homosocial' link between the two men, which is to say the way men form relationships with one another for personal and political advantage. The arranged match is a part of the display of loyalty between Roland and Oliver. Like many friendships, this one began in animosity; Roland attempted to abduct Aude and ended up engaged in jousting with her brother and protector. This, at least, is the story in the prequels to the *Roland* composed at a later date. Sarah Kay has described this as a classic example of the 'suppression of heterosexual for homosocial ties'.[22]

The word 'companion' is used throughout the *Roland* to describe the relationship between Roland and Oliver. The meaning of this relationship becomes clear when the two are dying, and Oliver, who is blinded by exhaustion, strikes his companion with a sword for not having blown the olifant. Roland is bewildered: he and Oliver have argued over his refusal to blow the olifant, but why

21. R. Lejeune, 'La naissance du couple littéraire "Roland et Olivier"', *Mélanges Henri Grégoire, Annuaire de l'Institut de Philologie et d'Histoire Orientales et Slaves* 10 (2 vols, 1950) II, pp.371–401.
22. S. Kay, *The Chansons de Geste in the Age of Romance* (Oxford, 1995).

has his companion struck him without formal defiance ('*desfi*')?[23] This passage demonstrates how much their relationship, although portrayed as one of close mutual affection, is conceived of within the structure of lordship and legality.

When Oliver actually dies, Roland declares that ' "Now you are dead it is a misery that I still live" ' (l. 2,030) and faints in his stirrups. To a modern audience such a depth of passion might seem indicative of a homosexual relationship. Indeed, John Boswell has discussed at length what he perceives as expressions of homosexual desire in mid-twelfth-century literature. He is inclined to believe in a 'golden age' of free expression of physical love between men. His main sources come from the schools of Paris where clever clerics certainly wrote erotic gay verse, but Boswell may have been guilty of reading the social and sexual freedoms of 1970s California back into an earlier period. Clerical moralizers indicate that homosexual behaviour was a part of court culture among young noblemen, and they criticize it. On the rare occasions on which vernacular sources address the issue, they appear to condemn such a relationship as well. There is no doubt that these sources describe homosexual behaviour, but was it considered manly? I suggest that it was not.[24] (See also chapter 13.)

Practically the only poem to explore the issue at all, is the *Roman d'Enéas*, a reworking of Virgil's *Aeneid*. Commentators have identified homoerotic undertones surviving from the original in two episodes: one concerning a pair of Trojans; the other, Enéas himself and his love for the dead Pallas. However, such behaviour is regarded as '*recreant*', and sodomy, treason and cowardice are all linked as unmanly attributes in the same poem (which is discussed in greater detail in chapter 13).[25] The love of Roland and Oliver for each other is far from carnal. Roland does not even cradle the dying Oliver in his arms. The two companions, rather, 'bow

23. *La Chanson de Roland*, ed., F. Whitehead (Oxford, 1978); *The Song of Roland*, trans. D.D.R. Owen (Woodbridge, 1990), ll. 2,000–2.

24. J. Boswell, *Christianity, Social Tolerance and Homosexuality : Gay People in Western Europe from the Beginning of the Christian Era to the Fourteenth Century* (Chicago, 1980). Tosh in 'What should historians do with masculinity?' discusses the impact of the Oscar Wilde case, the creation of the homosexual anti-type (and indeed the word) and homosexual panics of the 1880s, which may influence modern commentators' reading of clerical criticisms. This may explain the misguided attribution of homosexuality to Richard the Lionheart. See J.B. Gillingham, *Richard the Lionheart* (2nd edn, London, 1989), pp.107, 130, 161–2.

25. See R. Cormier, 'Taming the warrior: responding to the charge of sexual deviance in twelfth-century vernacular romance', in M.S. Brownlee, K. Brownlee and S.G. Nicholls, eds, *The New Medievalism* (Baltimore & London, 1991), pp.153–60.

towards each other's breast' (l. 2008) in a formal expression of their
love for each other. In fact, as always, the word love needs to be
glossed; it can mean so many things, and is heavily dependent upon
social and cultural context (as Marianne Ailes and Julian Haseldine
demonstrate below, chapters 13 and 14). What Roland and Oliver
feel for one another might, in modern terms, be called 'respect'.

Another poem, existing in many versions, which explores the
possibilities of male friendship made explicit in its title, is *Ami
et Amile*. 'They are identical in gait, in mouth, face and nose, in
riding and bearing arms, so that you couldn't imagine anyone
finer' (ll. 39–42). They are described as embracing one another so
vigorously that they almost killed one another. Sarah Kay has commented that their friendship is threatened by the possibility of marriage. That the friendship or companionship is a higher prize than
a heterosexual relationship is indicated by the passage involving
Ami's wife, Bellissant. Under cover of darkness she ends up in bed
with Amile, where they are overheard by the traitor, Hardre. He use
this knowledge, not to sleep with Bellissant, but to try to substitute
himself as Amile's companion.[26]

Love and the role of women

Involvement in heterosexual relationships does, however, form a
part of the masculine military character in a number of texts. A
knight's prowess made him sexually attractive to ladies, and rifts
were caused at court if other knights attempted to subvert the relationship between a knight and his lady. For example, this is what is
supposed to have caused William Marshal to have left the court of
his patron, the Young King Henry, in 1182, amidst rumours that he
was romantically attached to Henry's queen. The Lancelot legend
has a similar theme running through it: Lancelot and Guinevere are
attracted to each other, leading to sin and the 'unmanning' of the
warrior hero. Finally, the role of the *losengiers* (malevolent gossips)
in courtly love poetry reveals both the frequency of the attraction
between knights and ladies, and also the tendency of others to
want to disrupt the relationship, as they whispered tales around the
court in order to cause a rift.

Courtly love certainly had a place in defining the masculine
military ideal, and almost all aspects of it have been described,

---

26. Kay, *Chansons*, p.153.

analysed, criticized and reinterpreted according to current literary fashion. Some believe that the origins of the genre lie in odes written by men for boys in Muslim Spain, while others ascribe it to William IX, duke of Aquitaine, noted wit, warrior and crusader, who also wrote (or has attributed to him) some humorous and distinctly heterosexual verse. Stephen Jaeger, however, prefers to ascribe the development of 'courtly culture' not to secular love-lyrics idealizing unattainable relationships between a knight and his lady, but bishops' courts in Ottonian Germany. The 'romance', in terms of both content and genre, came later.[27]

Here is not the place to review the study of courtly literature, but it suffices to say that there was a distinct difference in attitudes to women and to relationships between men and women in the Oxford *Roland* and later *chansons de geste* affected by courtly ideals. Aude's absence from the dramatic narrative of the *Roland* is apparent. Contrast this with the role of Orable/Guiborg in the mid-twelfth-century William of Orange cycle. First she has to be wooed, willingly abducted from her Saracen husband and converted, then she serves as the doughty chatelaine providing the fuel and the moral strength to enable the males for whom she is responsible to carry on the fight.

Women are also shown as playing a role in military activity in the poetic cycle known as the 'epics of revolt'. Some are hapless victims, like Bernier's mother in *Raoul de Cambrai*. She is abbess of the convent burnt down by Raoul, and dies in the flames along with all her nuns. This then confronts Bernier, her illegitimate son, with the dilemma of how he should treat his lord, Raoul, to whom he owes everything, including the knighthood which alone raises his status above that of a landless man. In the end the dilemma is resolved as Bernier kills Raoul, although this provokes a feud, the fans of which are fanned by Alice (Raoul's mother), demonstrating the significance of a woman as a player in the politico-military sphere.[28]

Courage and pride

It is clear from the vernacular literature that courage was a necessary military virtue. Furthermore, as we have already seen, courage

27. Jaeger, *Origins of Courtliness*.
28. *Raoul de Cambrai*, ed., S. Kay, and trans. (Oxford, 1995) and her *Chansons*.

was something that a man might inherit from his lineage. However, courage also had to be tempered by wisdom, as the contrasting attributes of Roland and Oliver make clear. Together, Roland and Oliver make up the perfect *chevalier*. In the line '*Rollant est proz e Oliver est sage*' ('Roland is brave, Oliver is wise') the two essential qualities of a warrior are described: he should be both brave and cunning. This may be compared with the Bayeux Tapestry rubric in which the Norman knights are exhorted to go into battle 'bravely and sensibly' ('*viriliter et sapienter*').[29] This balance is important, for it is Roland's *demesure* – his pride – which leads to his own death and that of his companion and the ten 'Peers of France'. His refusal to blow the olifant, the great ivory hunting-horn, which will recall Charlemagne and the rest of the Christian host, condemns the Franks' rearguard to death. In so doing he fails in his leadership function, since he is *guarant* (leader and security) of his followers. It is Oliver's duty as his *cumpainz* to advise him of the correct course of duty. He even threatens to prevent the proposed marriage to Aude, in his role as companion, because of Roland's refusal to blow the olifant. There is no room in battle for hotheaded and undisciplined behaviour; and Oliver's response is a reflection of this. For, while medieval literature is full of all-out lance attacks, actual warfare revolved around the control of fortifications, and hence was generally slow and attritional in nature. Battle was generally avoided as too risky an outcome, but if it was risked, then the emphasis was on cautious manoeuvre until the last possible moment.[30]

The danger of such reckless behaviour is reiterated in other examples of epic literature. For example, *Raoul de Cambrai* (c.1180) contains repeated examples of unbridled behaviour by the male participants which lead them to their deaths. Pride posed, perhaps, the greatest danger to a man's success in the military sphere. Pride in one's lineage, country, lord and personal prowess were essential buttresses of a man's valour. Yet if it was not properly harnessed it led to disaster. Both the ecclesiastical texts and also secular didactic works preached modesty and *mesure*. It should be said, though, that *orgueil* (pride) was also the Saracen vice. Excessive pride was a sign of unbelief in the True God. Obviously, Saracens fall prey to this by their very nature; but so does Raoul when he defies God. In contrast, 'good Saracens', that is those who convert to Christianity,

---

29. *Roland*, l. 1093; *Bayeux Tapestry*, panels 58–9.
30. See N. Hooper and M. Bennett, *Cambridge Illustrated Atlas of Warfare: The Middle Ages 768–1487* (Cambridge, 1996), pp.8–9 and *passim*.

display all the aspects of *curtesie* (courtliness) one would expect from a Christian knight. Indeed, in the early thirteenth-century work, *L'Ordene de Chevalerie*, it is the Saracen Saladin who instructs the Christian knight, Hue de Tabarie, in true chivalry, knighting him and explaining to him the significance of the ceremony and the obligations it places upon a member of the Order.[31]

In the early part of the *Chanson de Guillaume*, we meet the character Thibault of Bourges. He is a drunkard and afraid to fight the overwhelming number of Saracens, unlike the hero, Vivien. He ascribes Vivien's willingness to fight against the odds as boastful pride, and does not believe that he will carry it through. Before the battle he urges his nephew, Esturmi, to destroy his banner to avoid being identified and does the same himself. Then, when the battle begins:

> As gold separates itself from silver, so all the good men set themselves apart: the cowards fled away with Thibault, all the good knights remained with Vivien; all together they struck straight ahead.
>
> (ll. 328–32)

In his flight, Thibault runs into a corpse hanging from a cross-roads gallows and loses control of his bowels. The poet dwells on the filth defiling the beautiful saddle-cloth of Thibault's horse. He is then unhorsed and disarmed by the young hero, Gerard, who returns to the fray, while Thibault continues his flight on Gerard's hackney (a riding-horse not considered suitable for war). He catches a sheep in the stirrup and drags it after him until finally reaching refuge at Bourges, when only the head is left. This crudely humorous episode illustrates the antithesis of courage. Fear of the enemy, loss of control, emotionally and physically, and its reward, the symbolic trophy identifying his cowardice.[32]

Conclusion

What made a man masculine in the central Middle Ages? How was military prowess a sign of masculinity? The sources which I have examined seem to suggest that the aristocratic warrior of the

31. *Raoul de Cambrai*, ed., Kay; K. Busby, *'Le Romans des Eles' by Raoul Houdenc and 'L'Ordene de Chevalerie'*, (Amsterdam and Philadelphia, 1983). See Tosh 'What should historians do with masculinity?' pp.194–7, for an interesting comparison with the popularity of imperialism c.1900, and the creation of 'negative racial stereotypes' to form the 'Other' against which Christian manhood could be tested.

32. The Thibault episode is contained in ll. 28–404 of the *Chansons de Guillaume*.

period needed to be physically and morally complete (he should display inner perfection by his outer appearance); of the correct age; he had to be well practised in arms, the tools of his trade; and committed to the cause of his lord (whether on earth or in Heaven). He needed to be accepted by his peers, to be able to form close friendship with another man; he could (but need not) be married, too. By the later twelfth century, it was possible to define him in relation to a woman, an adored *domna* (lady), but how much this change is a product of developing literary genres rather than an idea with deep social significance, is a matter of debate. For in this scheme of representation of maleness, military friendship transcends all others. It is worth noting that, in almost all the examples studied, even the archetypes are flawed. That, presumably, is because it is only by exploration of how men fail to live up to model behaviour that they can understand what it is they need to be.

CHAPTER SIX

Images of Effeminate Men: the Case of Byzantine Eunuchs

S.F. TOUGHER

The aims of this chapter are twofold. It will be suggested that a consideration of the portrayal of eunuchs in Byzantine society as effeminate permits deductions about what was thought of as masculine by the same society. It becomes apparent that masculinity, at least for the secular elite, demanded certain physical characteristics (including beards and deep voices) and was displayed through the medium of both heterosexuality and peer group performance. However, it will also be argued that, in contrast, some of the stereotypes of effeminate eunuchs can be exploded, revealing an evident tension between ideal and reality. A closer look at 'effeminate eunuchs' reveals the extent of preconception and prejudice that has shaped their image. This creation of a subordinate masculinity will be shown to be important to the operation of 'hegemonic masculinity' within Byzantium.[1]

Eunuchs and their position in Byzantine society

The Byzantine empire was both renowned for, and distinguished from its western medieval neighbours by, the existence and use of eunuchs.[2] The employment of eunuchs within both the imperial

---

1. For hegemonic masculinity see J. Tosh, 'What should historians do with masculinity? Reflections on nineteenth-century Britain', *HWJ* 38 (1994), pp.179–202, esp. pp.190–92. Note, however, that the concept was formed by R.W. Connell 'in order to explain the gender structure of contemporary societies'.

2. See R. Guilland, 'Les eunuques dans l'empire byzantin. Etude de titulaire et de prosopographie byzantines', *Revue des Etudes Byzantines* 1 (1943), pp.197–238; H. Diner, *Emperors, Angels and Eunuchs. The Thousand Years of the Byzantine Empire*, trans. E. and C. Paul (London, 1938), pp.62–72; S.F. Tougher, 'Byzantine eunuchs: an overview, with special reference to castration and origin', in L. James, ed., *Women, Men and Eunuchs. Gender in Byzantium* (London, 1997), pp.168–84.

household and the imperial administration was particularly marked.[3] This feature is first perceptible in the late third century during the reign of the emperor Diocletian (284–305),[4] and certainly became the norm; only the fourth-century emperor Julian the Apostate (361–363) attempted to dispense with employing eunuchs altogether, and his attempt died with him.[5] The phenomenon of the court eunuch spanned most of the history of the empire, though a tailing off from the thirteenth century has been conjectured as references to eunuchs all but disappear from our sources at that time.[6] At court, eunuchs had a number of positions reserved for them: effectively they could range from humble chamber staff to right-hand man of the emperor. Our knowledge of such positions is particularly good for ninth-century Byzantium, for in 899 a court official named Philotheos produced a work revealing the hierarchy of the imperial court and administration.[7] As well as recording both the eunuch-only offices and the eunuch-only honorific titles, this text also makes it plain that almost all other offices within the imperial administration were open to eunuchs. There were only three exceptions: the positions of quaestor; eparch; and *domestikos* (which itself came in several varieties).[8] Thus the range of offices open to a eunuch exceeded that available to a non-eunuch. Also worthy of note is the fact that eunuchs were not found solely in the imperial service; they could also be found in the households of the elite, but more importantly, as Kathryn Ringrose has reminded us, eunuchs could have independent lives and independent careers, and are found as monks, priests, bishops, singers, actors, prostitutes and teachers.[9] Thus it is clear that eunuchs were prevalent in Byzantine society and that their services were desired and valued.

However, at the same time there was a deep-rooted antipathy towards eunuchs in Byzantine society, which frequently finds expression in the writings of the non-eunuch male elite. The underlying

3. See Guilland's collection of papers on eunuch jobs and titles in *Recherches sur les Institutions Byzantines*, I (Amsterdam, 1967), pp.165–380.

4. See K. Hopkins, *Conquerors and Slaves* (Cambridge, 1972), ch. 4; P. Guyot, *Eunuchen als Sklaven und Freigelassene in der Griechisch-Römischen Antike* (Stuttgart, 1980), pp.130–76; Pádraig Colm Francis, 'Eunuchs and the Roman Imperial Court', MA Thesis (University College, Dublin, 1993).

5. Hopkins, *Conquerors*, p.180.   6. Guilland, 'Les eunuques', p.234.

7. N. Oikonomidès, *Les listes de préséance byzantines des IXe et Xe siècles* (Paris, 1972), pp.65–235.

8. *Ibid.*, pp.303–4, 329–33.

9. K. Ringrose, 'Living in the shadows: eunuchs and gender in Byzantium', in G. Herdt, ed., *Third Sex, Third Gender: Beyond Sexual Dimorphism in Culture and History* (New York, 1994), pp.98–99.

cause of this antipathy seems to be fear of the influence that court eunuchs could have upon the emperor, and perhaps also jealousy of the degree of intimacy between the emperor and his eunuchs.[10] Eunuchs are commonly portrayed as malicious, corrupt, and forces for evil. Such anti-eunuch sentiment can be found throughout the history of the Byzantine empire, but is perhaps most marked in the very period when their prevalence was becoming clear, in late antiquity. The oft-quoted remarks of the fourth-century historian Ammianus Marcellinus can serve as an example of the spleen vented against eunuchs. In Ammianus's experience eunuchs, led by the high chamberlain, Eusebius, were malicious and exerted a pernicious influence over the emperor Constantius II (337–361). Describing the fate of the master of cavalry, Ursicinus, at the hands of the imperial court, Ammianus comments:

> Like a snake bursting with venom which sends out a swarm of its little ones to do mischief when they can scarcely crawl, Eusebius dispatched his subordinates the moment they reached maturity to assail the reputation of the hero [Ursicinus] with malicious suggestions, which their attendance in private gave them the chance of insinuating into the ears of the credulous emperor.[11]

Ammianus despises eunuchs as a group. Commenting on the eunuchs found in the entourage of rich men in Rome he says:

> Anyone who sees ... troops of these maimed creatures must curse the memory of queen Semiramis of old, who was the first to castrate young males, laying violent hands as it were upon nature and wresting her from her ordained course, since it is nature who in our very infancy implants in us the original source of our seed, and points out by a kind of unwritten law the means by which we are to propagate our race.[12]

Even when Ammianus is moved to praise the eunuch Eutherius, who had lent support to another of the historian's heroes, Julian the Apostate (emperor from 361–363), he makes it clear that this was an exceptional case. He states, 'It may perhaps sound incredible, because even if Numa Pompilius or Socrates were to speak well of a eunuch and back their statements with an oath they would be accused of departing from the truth.'[13] For Ammianus eunuchs are nothing but corrupt evil-doers. That such sentiments continued

---

10. Hopkins, *Conquerors*, p.195.

11. Ammianus, XVIII.4.4. This and subsequent quotes from *Ammianus Marcellinus. The Later Roman Empire (A.D. 354–378)*, trans. W. Hamilton (Harmondsworth, 1986).

12. *Ibid.*, XIV.6.17.   13. *Ibid.*, XVI.7.4.

throughout the Byzantine empire is well illustrated by a twelfth-century dialogue written by Theophylact of Ochrid. This dialogue takes the form of a debate between a monk and a eunuch about the character of eunuchs: the monk accuses eunuchs of such characteristics as avarice, maliciousness, ambition, jealousy, deceit and irascibility.[14] What is unusual about this text is that it is concerned to defend eunuchs; Theophylact wrote it for his brother, who was in fact a eunuch, and who was tired of the insults that eunuchs had to bear. Despite the existence of this defence, and indeed because of its existence, it is clear that eunuchs were generally reviled. A Byzantine maxim ran: if you have a eunuch, kill him; if you don't, buy one and kill him.[15]

The physical characteristics of eunuchs

An element in the disgust that Byzantine society felt for eunuchs was the physical condition of such men, and their resultant sexual proclivities. Eunuchs offended Byzantine sensibilities, for although they were men they lacked what contemporaries understood to be masculine characteristics. The noted intellectual and diplomat Leo Choirosphaktes comments in a letter of the early tenth century in a highly derogatory passage that, given the physical nature of a eunuch, it was 'as if he had been born of two women'.[16] The fact, and the effects, of castration meant that eunuchs were deemed to be more feminine than masculine. Some even considered eunuchs a third sex.[17] By examining what it was that made eunuchs effeminate a picture can be built up of what was considered masculine in Byzantium.

It is, perhaps, obvious that the very act of castration meant that eunuchs were no longer wholly male. If masculine attributes can be said to include sexual organs, then eunuchs had an inherent lack of masculinity as they lacked testicles.[18] Ideally, males were created

14. P. Gautier, *Théophylacte d'Achrida. Discours, traités, poésies*, Corpus Fontium Historiae Byzantinae XVI/1 (Thessalonike, 1980), pp.288–331. For further comment on the text see Ringrose, 'Eunuchs and gender', pp.102–7; D. Simon, 'Lobpreis des Eunuchen', *Shriften des Historischen Kollegs Vorträge* 24 (1994), pp.5–27.

15. *Kedrenos*, I. Bekker, ed., *CSHB* (1839), II, p.29.

16. G. Kolias, *Léon Choerosphactès magistre, proconsul et patrice* (Athens, 1939), letter 25, p.121.

17. Ringrose, 'Eunchs and gender'.

18. Francis, 'Eunuchs', pp.3–16; M.S. Kuefler, 'Castration and eunuchism in the middle ages', in V.L. Bullough and J.A. Brundage, eds, *Handbook of Medieval Sexuality* (New York and London, 1996), pp.279–306; Tougher, 'Overview'. Rarely, eunuchs had their penises removed: Ringrose, 'Eunuchs and gender', p.91 and n.21.

eunuchs when they were still young boys, that is, prior to puberty. Our sources also indicate that the physical appearance of the boys selected for castration was an important factor; they should be physically attractive, perhaps indicating that effeminacy was desired rather than purely consequential.[19] Be that as it may, the fact that most eunuchs were created before the onset of puberty resulted in the distinctive physical characteristics of the group.[20] The prevention of puberty had two main physical consequences. First, eunuchs lacked beards, and this made them easy to differentiate from their non-eunuch adult male counterparts. Indeed, Philotheos uses the term 'bearded' to distinguish the non-eunuchs from the eunuchs in the Byzantine hierarchy.[21] It is interesting to note that it was only after the sixth century that the beard as a physical attribute became valued and normative for males in Byzantine society;[22] perhaps it can be hypothesized that the occurrence of this phenomenon was due to the very prevalence of eunuchs within Byzantium, that non-eunuchs felt the need to distinguish themselves from effeminate eunuchs so that they could not possibly be mistaken for one of them.

The second physical consequence was the quality of the voice, which also marked eunuchs out as non-masculine; being unbroken it remained high-pitched. Ammianus describes the eunuch voice as 'childish and reedy'.[23]

Behavioural characteristics of eunuchs

The view of eunuchs as effeminate did not just depend upon their physical appearance; their behaviour also marked them out. Eunuchs were commonly thought to prefer sex with men; the exponent of the anti-eunuch stance in Theophylact's discourse asserts that the majority of eunuchs are homosexual.[24] This concept had a long history; when eunuchs appeared on stage accompanying the ambassador of the king of Persia in the fifth-century BC play *Acharnians* by Aristophanes, this provided the opportunity for an Athenian character to recognise the 'eunuchs' as notorious effeminate

19. See for instance Procopius, *De Bello Gothico* VIII.3.15, trans. H.B. Dewing, *Procopius*, V, Loeb Classical Library (London and Cambridge, Mass., 1962), p.79.
20. For the physical effects of castration see Hopkins, *Conquerors*, pp.193–4; Francis, 'Eunuchs', pp.3–6.
21. Oikonomidès, *Listes*, p.135.9.   22. *ODB*, I, p.274.
23. Ammianus XVIII.4.4.   24. Gautier, *Discours*, p.295.14.

Athenian homosexuals.[25] Eunuchs were also associated with gay sex; in late antiquity Augustine quoted Seneca's remark that 'men have been unsexed to gratify royal lust'.[26] Byzantine monasteries were certainly keen that eunuchs (as well as youths) be kept away from their precincts lest their presence would tempt the monks into sin.[27] The fact that the sixth-century emperor Justinian I (527–565) issued a law punishing homosexuals by castration can only have reinforced the notion that castrated people were homosexual.[28] However, this accusation of homosexuality is not applied consistently or exclusively, for the sexual licence of eunuchs with either men or women is also a common charge; it seems to have been a popular truism that eunuchs were men with women and women with men.[29] Certainly, we do encounter instances where eunuchs are accused of having affairs with women: the case of Constantine the Paphlagonian and the empress Zoe being a tenth-century example.[30] Ironically, however, such behaviour was still read as a sign of the effeminacy of eunuchs; it is their lack of control of their sexual passions that is the core of the charge and this meant that they were acting like women, who were considered to be unable to control their sexual passions.[31] One theory ran that eunuchs were like women because they spent so much time in their company; it was a common perception that eunuchs were mostly employed within women's quarters.[32]

Effeminacy was reflected by eunuchs in other behaviour too. They were perceived as lacking courage and bravery, as being weak and feeble like women. An episode in the chronicle of Theophanes Continuatus runs that when Theodore Krateros, a eunuch at the court of the ninth-century emperor Theophilos (829–842), dared to mock the martial skills of an Arab who was putting on a display in the hippodrome, the emperor turned on him and called him 'effeminate and unmanly' (θηλυδρία καὶ ἄνανδρε).[33] The implica-

25. Aristophanes, *Acharnians*, l. 115–122, trans. Benjamin Bickely Rogers, *Aristophanes*, vol. I, Loeb Classical Library (London and Cambridge, Mass., 1950), p.17.

26. Augustine, *City of God*, VI.10, trans. D.B. Zema and and G.G. Walsh, *The Fathers of the Church*, vol. 8 (Washington DC, 1950), p.332.

27. See for instance *ODB*, II, p.747 and p.946.

28. J. Boswell, *Christianity, Social Tolerance, and Homosexuality: Gay People in Western Europe from the Beginning of the Christian Era to the Fourteenth Century* (Chicago, 1980), p.172.

29. See for instance the comment of Masudi, *The Meadows of Gold. The Abbasids*, trans. P. Lunde and C. Stone (London, 1989), pp.345–6. See also the comments of S. Troianos, 'Kirkliche und weltliche Rechtsquellen zur Homosexualität', *JÖB* 39 (1989), pp.44–5.

30. *Theophanes Continuatus*, I. Bekker, ed., *CSHB* (1838), p.375.15–16.

31. Gautier, *Discours*, pp.293.16–295.3.　　32. *Ibid.*, 293.15–295.6.

33. *Theophanes Continuatus*, p.115.17.

tion was that Theodore, as a eunuch, was in no position to comment on this sphere of activity reserved for real men.

Another perceived lack was that of family; eunuchs were sharply distinct from the rest of secular society as they were not allowed to get married. Further, they could have no children. This lack of a wife, and of children, reinforced the notion that eunuchs were essentially unmasculine.

From this consideration of why eunuchs were thought to be lacking in masculinity, or effeminate, certain characteristics can be deduced that were thought to express societal masculinity. Men should have beards, deep voices, be heterosexual, control their passions, avoid the society of women and spend their time amongst men, display courage and bravery, get married, and have children.[34] Thus we have our images of effeminacy and masculinity, but what of reality? Did all eunuchs really conform to such an image? How extensive is the degree of stereotyping here? When we take a closer look at 'effeminate eunuchs' we begin to see the extent of preconception and prejudice that has shaped their image.

Prejudice and stereotype in attitudes to eunuchs

It is an indisputable fact that eunuchs who were created prior to puberty had the distinct physical characteristics described above: lack of facial hair and high-pitched voices. Yet not all eunuchs were created at the pre-pubertal stage. Such eunuchs tended to be created not for the purposes of trade or in order to partake of a particular career, but as punishment: as real or potential political enemies; as homosexuals; as prisoners of war. Castration as punishment for homosexuals has already been met. Castration of real or potential political enemies can be witnessed when an emperor and his family are usurped. When Leo V (813–820) ousted Michael I (811–813) from power in 813 he not only exiled Michael to a monastery but castrated his sons, so as to prevent them from ever laying claim to the Byzantine throne in the future. The sons of Leo V were to suffer the same fate when their father, in turn, fell in 820.[35] As for the castration of prisoners of war, a case occurred

---

34. Of course not all of these qualities apply to all men, monks and holy men being the obvious exceptions.

35. W. Treadgold, *The Byzantine Revival, 780–842* (Stanford, California, 1988), pp.188–9 and p.224.

in the late 920s when Byzantine troops were captured in Italy.[36]
As Aline Rouselle has noted those who had their testicles removed
after reaching puberty still retained the signs of virility as 'other
male hormones are produced . . . by the suprarenal glands'; post-
pubertal eunuchs could 'feel desire', and 'achieve erection and
ejaculation of seminal fluid from the prostate and the seminal vesi-
cles'.[37] A noted case of post-pubertal castration in the ancient world
was that undergone by the Galli, the worshippers of Cybele, whose
objective had been 'to continue their sexual life, but to remain
infertile'.[38] As we have noted, such eunuchs also existed in the
Byzantine empire; the phenomenon is also explicitly referred to by
Basil of Ancyra. Writing in the fourth century, he advised virgins to
avoid contact with eunuchs, for some of them had only been castrated after puberty and these 'burn with greater and less restrained
desire for sexual union, and . . . not only do they feel this ardour,
but they think they can defile any woman they meet without risk'.[39]
Thus post-pubertal eunuchs retained the physical appearance of
masculinity.

Another supposed effeminate trait of eunuchs was their homosexuality. It has already been seen that this accusation was not consistently applied, as it was also believed that eunuchs surrendered
themselves to their sexual passions and slept with both men and
women. Thus it seems that what eunuchs are really being accused
of is bisexuality. Certainly, there are reported case of eunuchs
having affairs with women, and the incidence of post-pubertal
eunuchs permitted this. A specific example of an active homosexual
eunuch seems rather harder to find. One case is that cited by
Leo Choirosphaktes, the distinguished diplomat of the late ninth
and early tenth centuries, though it is perhaps open to doubt as it
is a deliberate attack on a eunuch. Choirosphaktes had fallen into
disgrace and suffered exile in the aftermath of a two-year embassy
to the Caliphate (905–907), and in a letter to the emperor Leo VI
(886–912) he blames the influence of a eunuch for his fall.[40] This
eunuch was also active in the diplomatic sphere, and Choirosphaktes
asserts that he was both worthless and a homosexual. He states

36. Liudprand, *Antapodosis* IV.9, trans. F.A. Wright, *Liudprand of Cremona. The
Embassy to Constantinople and Other Writings* (London, 1993), p.105.
37. A. Rouselle, *Porneia. On Desire and the Body in Antiquity*, trans. F. Pheasant
(Oxford and New York, 1988), pp.122–3.
38. Rouselle, *Porneia*, pp.122–3. For the Galli see also M.J. Vermaseren, *Cybele and
Attis. The Myth and the Cult* (London, 1977), esp. pp.96–101.
39. Quoted in Rouselle, *Porneia*, p.123.
40. Kolias, *Choerosphactès*, letter 25, pp.120–27.

that the eunuch's sex life was more important to him than any diplomatic mission, and he slept with both Arabs and Iberians. Another case, that of the eunuch Bagoas, has been highlighted by Paul Magdalino, though once again the nature of the evidence is suspect.[41] The story of Bagoas appears in a twelfth-century indictment written by Nikephoros Basilakes. Bagoas was the illegitimate son of a poor fisherman and a Scythian woman, who was put into the care of the fisherman's uncle. This uncle sent Bagoas to school. Magdalino then summarizes: 'On reaching puberty, the young Bagoas, who had inherited his mother's good looks, attracted, and yielded to, the advances of a slightly older schoolmate. In return the boyfriend helped Bagoas with his lessons. Fearful of losing his lover's affections as he grew to manhood, Bagoas had himself castrated in order to keep himself attractive.'[42]

Although some eunuchs may have been homosexual it is a rather different thing to say that all eunuchs had homosexual relationships. However, not all medieval commentators were so short-sighted. Masudi, an Arab who wrote in the tenth century, and who travelled much, seems to have had an interest in eunuchs.[43] Unfortunately, his *Historical Annals*, which included comment on 'eunuchs from the Sudan, the Slavic countries, Byzantium and China', has been lost, but elsewhere he makes the sharp comment that although it was a common belief that eunuchs were men with women and women with men, his opinion was that eunuchs remain men. This seems to acknowledge that eunuchs were as capable as anyone else of having individual sexual preferences.[44]

To say that women and eunuchs were unable to control their sexual passions is another cliché. Further, in the case of eunuchs it is again applied inconsistently, or at least it coexists with a rather different perception of the eunuch state. As Theophylact himself notes in a poem attacking an individual eunuch, it was believed that purity was the natural privilege of eunuchs.[45] The New Testament itself had encouraged such a notion, for 'Jesus had hinted that at least some of his followers were called to be "eunuchs for the kingdom of heaven's sake"'.[46] This simile had been taken literally by some, and some early Christians, including Origen, were

41. P. Magdalino, 'The *Bagoas* of Nikephoros Basilakes: a normative reaction?', in L. Mayali and M.M. Mart, eds, *Of Strangers and Foreigners* (Berkeley, 1993), pp.47–63.

42. Magdalino, '*Bagoas*', p.54.   43. Masudi, *Meadows*, pp.345–6.

44. *Ibid.*   45. Gautier, *Discours*, p.369.4–5.

46. Matthew 19:12; Boswell, *Homosexuality*, p.158.

thus incited to seek their own castration as a guarantee of purity.[47] Certainly, as Theophylact is quick to point out, eunuch clergy, eunuch monks, and eunuch saints existed in Byzantium,[48] and while this is no guarantee of control of passion, it does suggest that it was not thought impossible.

The conception that eunuchs spent most of their time in the company of women has a basis in reality. Eunuchs undoubtedly did have a role as servants and guardians within the women's quarters of imperial and elite households. Eunuchs were felt to be safe to have around women; they would present no sexual danger either because they were all homosexual, or because it was appreciated that if any sexual relations did develop they could never result in an awkward pregnancy. Eunuchs were simply a safer option, as their use by nunneries also demonstrates.[49] The word eunuch itself reflected this role as one etymology of it was 'guardian of the bed' (εὐνή ἔχω).[50] However, this role of serving women was not the only one available to eunuchs, as is clear from the discussion of the roles eunuchs could play; eunuchs in the imperial service were probably just as much, if not more, in the company of the emperor than the empress. The jobs available to eunuchs within the imperial administration also make it evident that eunuchs, like most men, did move in the society of their own sex, rather than in that of women. Nonetheless, one role for which eunuchs were renowned eclipsed all the other possibilities, and eunuchs became forever associated with women.

Despite the perception that eunuchs, like women, lacked strength and courage, one finds numerous instances of eunuchs being appointed to military command, and proving themselves successful. The most famous example is Narses, who served the emperor Justinian I.[51] Originally an imperial treasurer, he played an active role in suppressing the Nika riot of 532, and then in 538 he was set at the head of an army which was sent to Italy to assist the famed general Belisarios. In 550 Narses was commander of the troops in Italy, and he managed to succeed where Belisarius had failed,

47. J.E.L. Oulton and H. Chadwick, *Alexandrian Christianity, The Library of Christian Classics*, vol. II (London, 1954), p.174. See also Justin, *First Apology*, I.29, trans. T.B. Falls, *The Fathers of the Church*, vol. 6 (Washington DC, 1948), p.65, where a Christian shows desire to embrace continence by seeking legal permission to castrate himself.

48. Gautier, *Discours*, pp.319.15–321.7, and pp.327.3–329.8.

49. For the example of the nunnery of Kecharitomene see *ODB*, II, p.1118.

50. P. Noailles and A. Dain, *Les novelles de Léon VI le sage* (Paris, 1944), p.324 n.2.

51. *ODB*, II, p.1438.

bringing the campaign against the Goths to a victorious conclusion. It is interesting to detail here the rest of the story of Theodore Krateros mentioned above. Having been rebuked as effeminate and unmanly by the emperor Theophilos for daring to mock the military and equestrian skills of an Arab, the eunuch then took on the Arab in combat and killed him.[52] That eunuchs were believed to lack manly courage but at the same time might confound such expectations is seen again in George of Pisidia's account of the Persian expedition of the seventh-century emperor Heraclius (610–641). During the sea voyage, when Heraclius's ship crashed onto rocks the other ships in the fleet came to the rescue. George describes the soldiers preparing themselves to cope with this situation and notes that even the eunuchs were to be seen joining in, showing that 'they had not been cut with respect to their masculine nature'.[53] It seems a telling point that the eleventh-century emperor Michael V (1041–2) staffed his personal bodyguard with soldiers who were all youthful Scythian eunuchs.[54]

It is easy enough, then, to challenge the prejudiced perceptions that eunuchs had to face. However, the fact that they could not marry cannot be denied. Quite simply, eunuchs were barred from marriage because they were unable to produce children, which was the aim of Christian marriage. Even the emperor Leo VI, so sympathetic to eunuchs in other areas, could not argue with this. In *Novel* 98 he upholds the law forbidding eunuchs to marry since this contravenes the purpose of marriage – procreation.[55] This brings us to the question of children. Again pre-pubertal eunuchs could not have offspring, but post-pubertal eunuchs could have, for they might have had children prior to their castration. One option that may have been open to eunuchs was adoption. Leo VI in *Novel* 26 ruled that eunuchs should be allowed to adopt.[56] Prior to this ruling, legislation stated that eunuchs were forbidden to adopt on the grounds that what nature has not granted the law cannot supply. However, Leo asserted that it was not nature that had deprived eunuchs of the ability to produce children, but the injustice of men,

52. *Theophanes Continuatus*, pp.115.11–116.8. This reminds one of the case of the eunuch commander Peter the patrician, who surprised the Bulgarians when he took on their general in hand-to-hand fighting and killed him: Ringrose, 'Eunuchs and gender', p.98.

53. George of Pisidia, *De Expeditione Persica*, I. Bekker, ed., *CSHB* (Bonn, 1837), p.11.202–208.

54. Michael Psellos, *Chronographia*, V.15, tr. E.R.A. Sewter, *Michael Psellus. Fourteen Byzantine Rulers* (Harmondsworth, 1966), p.131.

55. Noailles and Dain, *Les novelles*, pp.320–27.   56. *Ibid.*, pp.100–5.

and opined that it was not philanthropic to deprive eunuchs of their only chance of becoming fathers.

Conclusion

From this consideration of the effeminate image of Byzantine eunuchs it is clear that the physical nature of most eunuchs did set them apart from their non-eunuch male counterparts. Further, the laws of society and the laws of nature respectively made it impossible for them to marry and to have children, setting them further apart from the vast majority of non-eunuch male society. However, it is also clear that the effeminate image of eunuchs was also built on prejudice, and certain stereotypes can be identified and exploded. Yet the power of the stereotype was undoubtedly strong and persistent; these were attitudes deeply rooted in Byzantine society. Notably, emperors who made heavy use of eunuchs in their regimes were themselves likely to be characterized as weak and feeble. Indeed, the use and prevalence of eunuchs within Byzantium may even have contributed to the western perception that this empire and its people were essentially effeminate.[57] As a group in Byzantine society, eunuchs were deliberately created: both the physical act of castration and the employment of stereotype were central to this creation. Eunuchs performed invaluable roles within Byzantine society, and their presence also, to some extent, underpinned and determined notions of appropriate masculine characteristics and behaviour among other groups of men. Eunuchs provided the latter with a challenge – both practical and ideological – and, as a result, the manipulation of stereotypes was as important to maintaining the gender imbalance in Byzantine society as the physical act by which eunuchs were created.

57. See for example Liudprand, *De Legatione Constantinopolitana*, ch. 54, trans. Wright, *Liudprand*, pp.202–3.

PART TWO

Lay Men and Church Men: Sources of Tension?

CHAPTER SEVEN

Masculinity in Flux:
Nocturnal Emission and the Limits of
Celibacy in the Early Middle Ages

C. LEYSER

It takes a man six months to bring the nocturnal emission of his semen under control: he must eat two loaves a day, drink as much water as he needs, take three or four hours sleep. He must avoid any idle conversation, and curb feelings of anger. In the final stages, he should cut down on the water, and take up strapping lead plates onto his genitals at night . . .[1]

These, at least, are the recommendations of the fifth-century moral expert, John Cassian, writing in southern Gaul for an audience of ascetics presumably eager for such instruction. Modern readers may find Cassian's prescriptions simply laughable – a comically obsessive regime of sexual self-denial. His contemporaries, however, would have found them unexceptional, the least original thing Cassian had to say. These were, after all, the standard remedies prescribed for any man who, in the opinion of his doctor, was losing too much vital fluid while asleep.[2] What was new was Cassian's desire to move beyond the careful monitoring of nocturnal emission for reasons of health towards its total eradication. Stopping up the involuntary flow of semen at night, Cassian argued, was the outward sign that a man had succeeded in his efforts to live in moral purity. Our own bemusement at this claim ought not to prevent the recognition that, as the western Roman empire disintegrated, Cassian's male

1. Cassian, *Institutiones*, ed., J.-C.Guy, *Sources Chrétiennes* 109 (Paris, 1961), VI.20; *Conlationes*, ed. E. Pichery, 3 vols, *Sources Chrétiennes* 42, 54, 64 (Paris, 1955–59), XII.15. See also *Conl.* XXII. I would like to thank David Brakke, Kate Cooper, Dawn Hadley, and Mark Jenner for their advice on aspects of this chapter.

2. See the summary in D. Brakke, 'The problematization of nocturnal emissions in early Christian Syria, Egypt, and Gaul', *Journal of Early Christian Studies* 3:4 (1995), pp.423–4.

readers were indeed persuaded that such nocturnal exertions in
the pursuit of celibacy represented a sensible course of political
action. As familiar governmental landmarks disappeared, the model
of ascetic masculinity advocated by Cassian and other no less elo-
quent Christian writers offered to male Roman aristocrats a vivid
and compelling idiom in which to redefine the style of their civic
leadership.

The Fathers of the Church, such as Cassian and, in particular,
his contemporary St Augustine, are usually presumed to have fostered a repressed and repressive view of gender and sexuality, with
severe and lasting consequences for western culture. It is not difficult to point to a canon of patristic texts which seem to suggest that
the leading spokesmen for early Christianity experienced sexual
relationships with women, with each other, and with their own
bodies in a 'neurotic' or at best an 'anxious' fashion. The ascetic
teachings of St Paul appear to lead directly to the confessional
pronouncements of Augustine, and from there to the full-blown
monastic and clerical culture of the medieval Church – an institution which encouraged groups of men at one and the same time to
isolate themselves from the sources of their anxiety, and to begin
the apparently all-too successful labour of enforcing their fears on
the rest of the population.

Such a picture of a cloistered, world-denying masculinity tends
to suggest an equal, opposite, and alarmingly carnivalesque view of
the medieval layman. We are tempted to imagine all that the monk
has struggled to repress in himself returning with a vengeance in
the shape of the medieval warlord, who rapes and pillages his way
across the countryside, sating the desires his monastic brother keeps
bottled up. The assumption that 'men who prayed' and 'men who
fought' inhabited different worlds is entrenched by the reminder
routinely issued by medievalists to beware the 'monkish' or clerical
bias of the sources – the implication being that the sexually repressed, bookish men who wrote the texts were ignorant, by accident or design, of life beyond their ascetic horizon.

Such a caricature of the knight and the priest speaks more,
perhaps, to our own pre-Raphaelite yearnings than it does to the
medieval evidence; in many instances (especially where Augustine
is concerned, as we shall see), the texts say the opposite of that
which the stereotypes might lead us to expect. Our interpretive
efforts are only hampered by the easy imputation of sexual guilt to
ancient and medieval Christians – a charge which presumes that
they had modern psyches – while our ready acceptance of ascetic

claims to otherworldly status lends an overly literal credence to a rhetoric that all parties understood to represent a public performance in the here and now.

This chapter interprets the rise of ascetic masculinity in the early Middle Ages not as an introverted discourse of sexual anxiety, but in terms of a fiercely competitive culture of public power, a culture which subsumed the institutional divisions between lay and ecclesiastical estates. In the fifth and sixth centuries – the formative period for the western monastic tradition – monks, priests and laymen inhabited the same moral universe. This is not to say that all men observed the same moral standards, nor that there was universal agreement as to which codes of behaviour were appropriate for which kinds of men. It is rather to suggest that the seemingly arcane model of masculinity set out by the ascetic movement must be understood politically, as an intervention in the post-imperial debate about what entitled a man to exact the respect and obedience of his fellows.

Ascetic masculinity was very flexible. In the last decade of the sixth century, as the sun finally set on the Roman Senate, Pope Gregory the Great, an attentive reader of both Augustine and Cassian, and himself a noted ascetic, succeeded in refining the language of moral authority to the point where it might be used by all those in positions of power, irrespective of their gender or even their commitment to celibacy. It was, paradoxically, this asexual Gregorian model of the 'ruler' which was to speak most directly to the needs of men in early medieval Europe.

Bodily emissions and the body social

There is no reason to regard the abundance of semen in Cassian's texts as a malady. An anthropological approach to his treatment of nocturnal emissions will bypass the question of psychological anxiety, and will seek instead to delineate the social context in which it was relevant for a writer such as Cassian to prescribe a regime for eliminating the unwanted appearance of seminal fluid.[3] In other words, *cui bono?* To whose advantage was it to initiate and sustain

3. An alternative is to seek to refine the psychological model. See e.g. D. Elliott, 'Pollution, illusion, and masculine disarray: nocturnal emissions and the sexuality of the clergy', in J. Schultz *et al.*, eds, *Constructing Medieval Sexuality* (Minneapolis, forthcoming). I am grateful to the author for allowing me to see a typescript of this essay.

this discussion of the outer reaches of male celibacy? From this perspective, the language of bodily purity and pollution represents neither infant trauma nor cultural neurosis, but a set of claims to power and of accusations of infamy.

The pioneer of such an approach is Mary Douglas, whose studies *Purity and Danger* and *Natural Symbols* have inspired a generation of ancient and medieval historians – among many others – to reconsider the meaning of texts where the body features.[4] The body, we now presume, has served as a crucial medium in which to discuss the social order: in texts concerned with bodily purity, if we read them correctly, we may find encrypted messages concerning social relations and the distribution of power. The history of the body, then, so far from being a marginal activity, or so far from overthrowing other, perhaps more traditional, scholarly concerns, generates a fount of new evidence pertaining to the inquiries that historians will always want to conduct.

In *Purity and Danger*, as Mark Jenner has pointed out, Douglas proposes two models of pollution, and both of them may be useful in understanding the meaning of nocturnal emissions.[5] The fundamental premise of both models is that what societies call 'unclean' depends not upon hygienic considerations, but upon social and cultural norms and anomalies. The first, and better-known, paradigm is Douglas's definition of dirt as 'matter out of place'.[6] A society names 'dirty' that which affronts its sense of cosmic order; it very likely invokes images of bodily uncleanness to discuss such challenges to its basic structuring principles. Douglas warns cultural critics to expect that the margins of the body, and the matter that crosses them, will be especially resonant with cultural meaning:

> Any structure of ideas is vulnerable at its margins. We should expect the orifices of the body to symbolize its specially vulnerable points. Matter issuing from them is marginal stuff of the most obvious kind. Spittle, blood, milk, urine, faeces, or tears by simply issuing forth have traversed the boundary of the body.[7]

These excreta are often designated as 'dirty', Douglas suggests, not because of any inherent qualities, but because, having crossed the boundary of the body, they are in the wrong place. Symbolically,

    4. M. Douglas, *Purity and Danger: An Analysis of the Concepts of Pollution and Taboo* (London, 1966); *idem, Natural Symbols: Explorations in Cosmology* (Harmondsworth, 1970).
    5. M. Jenner, 'On *Purity and Danger*', unpublished paper delivered at Oxford University, 1988.
    6. Douglas, *Purity and Danger*, p.40.   7. *Ibid.*, p.121.

they represent a threat to cultural categories established in the social body. As we shall see in a moment, one scholar of early Christianity has recently attempted an analysis of nocturnal emission in precisely these terms, as a bodily symbol for discussing the boundaries of the community in the early Church.

The second model of pollution suggests not dirt as a 'category error', but the more dangerous pollution represented by matter that refuses all categorization. Turning to Jean-Paul Sartre's *Being and Nothingness*, Douglas evokes the terror of the viscous, the matter that knows no place. When a child takes the lid off a jar of honey and inverts the jar, the relation between the child's self and the world threatens to dissolve as the honey drops:

> The viscous is unstable, but it does not flow. It is soft, yielding and compressible. There is no gliding on its surface. Its stickiness is a trap, it clings like a leech: it attacks the boundary between myself and it. Long columns falling off my fingers suggest my own substance flowing into the pool of stickiness.[8]

On phenomenological grounds alone, we might expect this model to be relevant in a discussion of nocturnal emission. A historical demonstration of its usefulness is necessary, however, because as Douglas emphasizes there is no universal experience of bodily emissions. Different cultures treat the same matter in different ways:

> In some, menstrual pollution is feared as a lethal danger; in others not at all ... In some excreta is dangerous, in others it is only a joke ... Each culture has its own special risks and problems. To which particular bodily margins its beliefs attribute power depends upon what situation the body is mirroring.[9]

Purity and Danger thus invites analysis of bodily pollution language in terms of historically specific social structures and and tensions.

Taking up the first of the two models of pollution thus outlined, David Brakke has recently offered to explain the pollution language around nocturnal emissions in early Christianity.[10] As he points out, there has been much recent work on the cultural uses of the female body as icon in the patristic period, with less attention paid to the use of male bodies as a means to 'think with'. Mindful of Douglas's insistence on the particularity of social context, Brakke emphasizes that there was no single Christian tradition on nocturnal emissions: it was not the case that they were always regarded

---

8. *Ibid.*, p.38, referring to Jean-Paul Sartre, *L'Etre et le néant* (Paris, 1943), pp.649ff.
9. Douglas, *Purity and Danger*, p.121.   10. Brakke, 'Problematization'.

as polluting. This caution stated, however, Brakke argues that discussion of nocturnal emission in texts issuing around the Mediterranean from the third to the fifth centuries can be read in terms of a series of debates about the boundaries of the Christian community. Semen emitted at night was a classic instance of 'matter out of place' – it was outside when it should have been inside – and thus it was a natural bodily symbol to consider the issue of who should be inside and who outside the body of the faithful.[11]

The trend of Christian thinking on nocturnal emissions, Brakke finds, reflects the wider history of Christian communities in the Roman empire. In the early Church, Christians were most concerned with distinguishing themselves from Jews in particular and from pagans in general. This involved a strong claim to an inviolable spiritual purity that was on the one hand, distinct from the ritual purity of Judaism, and on the other immune to contamination from the pagan world. Christian leaders taught that a baptized Christian man should not consider himself polluted and abstain from communion simply because he had experienced a nocturnal emission: to do so would be to capitulate to Pharisee or 'worldly' standards of moral integrity. The semen traversing the body's boundary was not held to mean that the Christian had overstepped the line between the purity of his community and the dangerous world outside.[12]

In the fourth and fifth centuries, Brakke records a change in the culture of nocturnal emissions, reflecting the transformation of Christianity from persecuted sect to state religion. In the now Christian Roman empire, it was no longer possible to locate all pollution as outside the community of the faithful, because, in theory at least, there was no 'outside' in the imperial Church. Brakke sees a consequent tendency towards 'introversion': rival groups within the Church now began to layer in claims to moral superiority over and against each other, and individual Christians started to look inside themselves for sources of polluting danger. In the Nile delta, for example, gathered groups of men who had ostentatiously committed themselves to complete renunciation of the financial and sexual transactions in which the rest of the population were involved, and which they perceived to be unclean. These so-called 'monks' – the word in Greek suggesting a life alone and apart – began to insist that, contrary to earlier tradition, nocturnal emissions were, in fact, polluting, because they represented the surrender of the will,

---

11. *Ibid.*, pp.419–22.   12. *Ibid.*, pp.424–33.

under cover of darkness, to the desires of the flesh. A monk who had failed to maintain celibacy in this intimate sense should, indeed, abstain from taking communion. Such was the basic conclusion of an emerging technical literature on the psychology of consent to bodily desire, the overall function of which was to advance the claim of the monks to be the purest Christians.[13]

The articulation of this new monastic standard of sexual purity, however, was not well received by men such as Bishop Athanasius of Alexandria, in whose interests it was to prevent too wide a gulf opening up between the ascetic Christianity of the monks on the one hand, and the less demanding version shared by the rest of the laity. When monks and bishops debated the fine points of the relation between male body and soul, they were, Brakke shows, contending with each other to mark out the moral geography – above all, the place of the monastery – in the Roman imperial Church.[14]

John Cassian, a monk who had travelled in the deserts of Egypt and Syria before settling in Gaul c.415, represents from this perspective the apex of the monastic culture of sexual purity. Building on the work of Michel Foucault, whose unfinished *History of Sexuality* fades out with an essay on Cassian in just this connection,[15] Brakke presents Cassian as the man who perfected the 'introversion' of pollution language initiated by the fourth-century desert fathers. The world outside barely seems to register in Cassian's vision of the monastery as a laboratory of moral purification. We find, therefore, scarcely any discussion of sexual intercourse or masturbation, because the monk is presumed long ago to have surmounted these physical temptations: all eyes are focused instead on cleansing the innermost desires of the monk's heart, as revealed in his ability to reduce, ideally to zero, the incidence of nocturnal emission. Cassian sets up an apparatus of minute scrutiny by spiritual teachers of the moral progress of their disciples; and for Brakke the monastery comes ineluctably to resemble Bentham's Panopticon, famously described by Foucault in *Discipline and Punish*, an environment designed to put humans under microscopic moral supervision.[16]

Brakke identifies a lone voice of protest against this monastic regime of self-scrutiny: that of Augustine of Hippo. Although his very name is a modern synonym for sexual neurosis, careful readers

13. *Ibid.*, pp.433–42.   14. *Ibid.*, pp.442–6.

15. M. Foucault, 'Le combat de chasteté', *Communications* 35 (1982), pp.15–25, trans. A. Forster in P. Ariès and A. Béjin, eds, *Western Sexuality: Practice and Precept in Past and Present Times* (Oxford, 1985), pp.14–25.

16. Brakke, 'Problematization', pp.446–55.

of Augustine will know him to have argued against the grimly ascetic views he is assumed to have held. Like Bishop Athanasius, Augustine's profoundest concern was that the Christian community should not be divided by competition for the moral high ground. The purpose of his theory of human sexuality was to disprove the claims to purity advanced with increasing confidence and sophistication by the monastic movement. For Augustine, nocturnal emissions, like involuntary erections, or unexpected impotence, were a sign of the enfeebled state of the human will after the Fall. To seek to eliminate nocturnal emissions through an ascetic programme like that of Cassian was to address in vain the symptom, and not the cause, of the sinful condition of humanity. The true cause lay in the will, Augustine insisted, and this only divine grace could repair.[17]

Brakke's article typifies the fine work on the history of the body in the ancient world. The danger is, however, that his account, and that of Foucault, may serve to confirm the medievalist stereotype of the monk as a man entirely turned in on himself, severed from the world outside. It was not only bishops such as Athanasius or Augustine who were concerned with the wider social consequences of ascetic claims to purity. Ascetics themselves, refusing easy categorization, addressed themselves to the whole body of the faithful.

John Cassian, viscosity, and power

We may regard nocturnal emission as matter out of place – or alternatively, invoking the other model of pollution suggested by Mary Douglas, we may see seminal fluid as matter that can never stay in place, because its status as matter is disconcertingly viscous. This suggests in turn a different interpretation of the social meaning carried by what it might be more accurate to call wet dreams. Instead of the shape of the community and its boundaries, the flow of semen at night may symbolize the uses of power – its fluidity and control. From this perspective, Cassian's preoccupation with wet dreams represents not the turning inward of a monastic community, but a meticulous bid for public authority on behalf of an ascetic movement which was by no means cloistered.

The philological record suggests that this alternative model of pollution as viscosity is well suited to a discussion of the politics of seminal fluid in the late Roman and early medieval periods. The

---

17. *Ibid.*, pp.455–8. See also R.A. Markus, *The End of Ancient Christianity* (Cambridge, 1990), pp.57–62.

Latin for nocturnal emission is *fluxus*.[18] This already suggests fluidity rather than matter out of place – and what clinches the point, as we shall see, is the appropriately viscous way that *fluxus* changes or expands in its range of meaning across ascetic texts of the period. By the end of the sixth century, in the texts of the ascetic Pope Gregory the Great, we shall see that *fluxus* refers far more often to the flux of desires or the flux of speech than it does to bodily fluids. For Gregory, therefore, talk about *fluxus* in this metaphorical sense is a self-reflexive discussion of the properties of language itself. An ascetic who has control over his 'verbal emission' is a man who can claim to be more trustworthy than his less guarded fellows.

In their preoccupation with flux and its regulation, ascetic writers were making an appeal to received ethical wisdom. Every ancient man – not just a few philosophers – would have understood the consummate need for those who claimed power to demonstrate their physical self-control. As Kate Cooper has described in her recent book, it was in the broadcasting of his 'private' virtue of temperance (*sophrosune*) that a public man might hope to substantiate his claims to the allegiance of his hearers.[19] Above all, a man's chaste – in the sense of properly restrained – sexual relationship with his wife was a guarantee that he would not be tempted by the lust for power to put his own family's interest above the common good. In a symbolic code that remains alarmingly familiar, discussion of a man's sex life stands in for analysis of his financial and political probity.

It is in the context of this moral economy of demonstrable restraint, Cooper argues that we must seek to understand the emergence of celibacy for men and women as the most perfect Christian life. Some Christians seemed to have realized the extraordinary political leverage that the claim to celibacy involved. A celibate man might put himself forward as the ideal civic leader, one who by his renunciation of sexual relations broadcast his complete reliability as a guardian of the civic order. A married man was, by definition, tied to a household: even with the best of intentions he was less free to pursue the public over the private, dynastic interest. He was therefore at a rhetorical disadvantage in the competition

18. The same word is used for menstruation, which suggests that male and female 'flows' could be conceptualized in similar ways (as in, for example, Gregory the Great's letter to Augustine of Canterbury, discussed below).

19. K. Cooper, *The Virgin and the Bride: Idealized Womanhood in Late Antiquity* (Cambridge, Mass., 1996). See also *idem*, 'Insinuations of womanly influence: an aspect of the christianization of the Roman aristocracy', *Journal of Roman Studies* 82 (1992), pp.150–64.

for power with an opponent who had publicly forsworn all sexual relations.[20]

The advocates of celibacy were vociferously persuasive. At the end of the fourth century, in the now Christian empire, a radical ascetic movement sought to press home their shaming of their married peers. In the 380s, men like Jerome managed to obtain a public platform from which to trumpet the virtues of celibacy for both sexes. Jerome had the ear of the bishop of Rome, and accordingly we find for the first time papal edicts insisting upon the celibacy of the clergy. In this context, the language of ascetic purification reads less as introversion, as suggested by Brakke, than as an aggressive claim to moral superiority. The late fourth and early fifth century witnessed a vigorous competition between different types of Christian – and, it should not be forgotten, different types of pagan – for authority in an empire whose political complexion was extremely volatile. Any advantage, however slight, needed to be exploited. It is the context of the high viscosity of power that we might seek to understand the debate over nocturnal emission between monks and bishops.

Cassian's intervention in this political flux was decisive. Precisely through his elaboration of a vocabulary to measure bodily *fluxus*, Cassian ensured the survival of the ascetic movement in the Latin west, and the endurance of celibacy as a valid political ideal.[21] When he arrived in Gaul c.415, the ascetic movement faced liquidation, discredited in the east and the west by its own rhetorical extravagance and political ambition. Cassian was a refugee from the bitter factional dispute among elite Christians known as the Origenist controversy, where best friends became bitterest enemies, and where Cassian had seen both his mentors, Evagrius Pontus and John Chrysostom condemned as heretics. If Cassian hoped for some respite from these troubles in the western Mediterranean, he would have been disappointed. In Gaul, the ascetic party had proved itself an equally fractious and self-serving group. In 408, for example, in the melee of coup and counter coup that followed the barbarian incursions into the province, Cassian's future patron, the bishop of Marseille, had managed to associate himself with the losing Roman general. In the 420s, the pope had cause to rebuke the same bishop

---

20. Cooper, *Virgin and Bride*, pp.1–19.

21. The following paragraphs summarize the argument of C. Leyser, '*Lectio divina, oratio pura*: Rhetoric and the techniques of asceticism in the *Conferences* of John Cassian', in G. Barone *et al.*, eds, *Modelli di santità, modelli di comportamento* (Turin, 1994), pp.79–105.

for publicly rejoicing at the assassination of his rival, the bishop of Arles. These were not men whose reflex was the display of temperance. Cassian's achievement was to teach them a restrained language of public power through ascetic purity, at the centre of which was the control of nocturnal emission.

The regime of scrutiny that Cassian advocated, therefore, was not designed for the private devotional lives of monks behind cloister walls. Cassian wrote as a public advocate for the ascetic movement, describing ascetic practice in language that any educated Roman man could understand, and indeed, carry out in the comfort of his own home. Later readers of Cassian, in particular St Benedict, have assumed that the best place for the implementation of the ascetic arts was the monastery. As a result modern scholars have tended to assume that Cassian was a proto-Benedictine 'monastic' writer. This is an evident anachronism. The dedicatees of Cassian's text include as many bishops as they do monks, and, indeed some monks who went on to become bishops.[22] The larger, unnamed audience whom Cassian had to persuade was composed primarily of men inclined to distrust asceticism. Mindful of these conditions, Cassian was very careful to present asceticism in the most impeccable ancient ethical framework, and crucially, to avoid tying it to any specific institutional structure. While he certainly imagined a regime of scrutiny, Cassian, unlike Bentham, deliberately held back from committing himself to a particular architecture.

Cassian's reluctance to commit to one institutional form related to his abstraction of the problem of moral purity. He saw the real task of ascetic purification as involving the mind rather than the body, as his treatment of nocturnal emissions makes clear. It was impossible to eliminate nocturnal emission altogether, as the male body needed to purge itself of excess moisture: with rare exceptions, the most a man could hope for was to reduce incidence of nocturnal emission to a physiological minimum of once every two to four months.[23] The man who emitted more frequently, however, fell under suspicion of supplementing the physical needs of his body with the desires of the mind. The key issue became, did the monk consent to his emission, or was it truly involuntary?[24]

22. E.g. Honoratus and Eucherius, living on the islands of Lerins and Lero respectively (offshore from modern day Cannes) who went on to become bishops of Arles and of Lyon.

23. Cf. *Inst.* VI.20 (two months), *Conl.* II.23 (four months).

24. *Conl.* XXII, 'On nocturnal illusions' itemizes the possible causes of emissions, focusing in particular on the issue of consent.

In setting out a procedure to adjudicate the purity of a man's thoughts, Cassian called upon a standard philosophical theory of mind (which had been taught to him by his own master Evagrius).[25] According to this view, the key feature of the mind was its 'auto-kinetic' quality: it was constantly in motion, like a millwheel, Cassian said, churning and grinding with thoughts both day and night. It was impossible to stop the movement of the mind. All that a man seeking to establish some ethical direction to his thoughts could do was to determine what kind of material to supply to the mind. He could give either chaff and tares, or good grain – either idle, worldly preoccupations, or edifying, spiritual matter. Everything a man heard or read would then become grist, or otherwise, to his psychic mill. Only at this point in his analysis did Cassian betray his Christian partisanship. A man should not read 'the fables of the poets', he should instead engage in a serious and sustained programme of reading of Scripture, or of spiritual writings such as the works of Cassian.

There were two ways to tell if a man had been sustaining success-ful 'occupation of the mind', as Cassian put it. The first was to listen to what he said: an idler who listened to gossip would only be able to give out the same, whereas the man who had filled himself with good grain would in turn become a fount of spiritual wisdom for others. It was possible, however, to feign pure speech. Cassian also admitted, and could not fully account for, the occasional pos-sibility that a man whose mind was unclean could nonetheless dispense sound moral counsel. The real test, then, came when a man's guard was down, while he slept. Under cover of dark, the pure in heart might receive special intuition into the meaning of the Scriptural passages occupying their attention during the daytime. Those whose concentration had wavered, however, and whose minds had assented to worldly desires were liable to find that their bodies betrayed them through nocturnal emission. An uncontrolled flux of the mind would issue in a surplus bodily *fluxus*.[26]

The effect of Cassian's intervention was to rehabilitate the ascetic movement. No longer was it possible for a pagan senator to accuse ascetics of leading a life of squalor outside the places of human habitation. No longer could Christian bishops complain that monks were simply trying to advertise their spiritual achieve-ments. Cassian had explained that spectacular (or degrading) feats

25. This paragraph summarizes the argument of *Conl.* I and XIV.
26. Cf. *Conl.* XIV.10 (understanding of Scripture), *ibid.* XXII.3 (nocturnal emission).

of renunciation were not the index of moral purity. The key index to the contents of a man's heart was his speech. In so claiming a new mastery of the very ancient art of moral rhetoric, ascetics eventually tightened their grip on public power in the Roman and post-Roman world.

It is commonly assumed that, after 430, the Church in the west had no choice but to implement the dire teachings of Augustine on human sexuality. Not only is this view based on a misreading of what Augustine actually said about sex: it is also founded on an unwarranted estimate of Augustine's authority in the early medi-eval Church. True, all of his readers were unanimous in their lip service to his wisdom – but many of their hearts were far from him. Most ascetics, unsurprisingly, preferred Cassian's sense of the diffi-cult possibility of visible moral progress to Augustine's flat scepti-cism as to ever being able to assess moral progress. Augustine's theories left little room for the politics of moral superiority on which the ascetic movement depended. Cassian's prescriptions, however, were used by Christian leaders to support claims to a purified power inside and outside the cloister. In particular, they were fundamental for the definitive language of moral authority elaborated 150 years later by the first monk to be pope, Gregory the Great.

Gregory the Great and the flux of speech

Gregory the Great is often seen as the quintessential churchman of the Dark Ages, a sickly bishop too weak to rise from his own bed, while all around Europe barbarians roamed free. We imagine him as a survivor, just managing to save the city of Rome from another sacking – at the hands of the Lombards – and to send, as it were, an escape party of monks to the edge of the world in Anglo-Saxon England. What this scenario fails to render, however, is the degree to which Gregory's career followed ancient Mediterranean patterns that Plato, living a millennium earlier, would have recognized.

Gregory was born and raised in a Roman aristocratic, cultured milieu. Having embarked upon a career in public office, in the mid-570s he decided to pursue his ambitions as a celibate rather than as a secular civic leader. This monastic conversion was hardly a withdrawal from the limelight: Gregory was soon appointed papal envoy to the imperial court at Constantinople. His social position, if nothing else, ensured that he would never be far away from executive power, and so far from disowning this condition, Gregory made it his business to study it. His 'medieval' heroism as pope in Dark Age adversity depended upon his thorough assimilation of the classical tradition of the correct moral response to power – tradition mediated in particular by Cassian. What Gregory did was to develop Cassian's analysis of the authority of the moral teacher in order to fashion an enduring model of the Christian philosopher-king, the man who could be trusted with power precisely because, as an otherworldly ascetic, he was not interested in it.

The question of flux and its regulation were, naturally, central to Gregory's discussion of authority. He summarized Cassian's teaching on nocturnal emission in a form that became canonical for the medieval Church. The first to benefit were, perhaps, Englishmen: the occasion for Gregory's pronouncement was an exchange with his missionary disciple in the field, Augustine of Canterbury.[27] Somewhat perplexed by his responsibilities as archbishop to the newly Christian people in Kent, Augustine had asked Gregory for procedural clarification on a number of points, including the very traditional question as to whether a man could receive the eucharist and whether a priest could celebrate it after a nocturnal emission. Gregory's answer was that everything depended on the reason for the sleeper's emission: 'Sometimes it happens through gluttony, sometimes through the natural superfluity or weakness, sometimes through the thoughts.'[28] The first two cases were not sufficiently polluting to cause concern: only if the mind of the sleeper consented to the evil thought of sin was the emission reason enough to forbid reception or celebration of the eucharist.[29] As a bodily infirmity seminal *fluxus* was not, in itself, contaminating, Gregory insisted. Pollution resided in the mind.

The letter to Augustine of Canterbury is the only place in his extensive corpus where Gregory considers the issue of bodily pollution through nocturnal emission. Elsewhere, the flux that interested Gregory was the metaphorical flux of desire, and above all, of speech. We have seen that Cassian, while proposing a man's speech as an index to the contents of his heart, wanted also to retain some kind of physical measure of moral purity. In extending the range of

27. Gregory's reply to Augustine is found in *HE*, I,27.   28. *Ibid.*
29. Gregory's response to Augustine on this point follows from his previous answer to the question of whether menstruating women can receive communion. Gregory recognized that menstruation, like emission, was a sign that fallen humanity did not have complete control of its bodily functions – but the 'natural overflowing' of menstruation 'cannot be reckoned a crime'; *ibid.*

Cassian's discussion, Gregory almost entirely abandoned this physical dimension, devoting instead all his energies to answering the
problem Cassian had not been able to solve: how could one safely
distinguish speakers of true spiritual wisdom from purveyors of empty
falsehoods?

The problem of rhetorical authenticity seems to have preoccupied Gregory from the start of his career as an ascetic. His first
work, the *Morals on Job,* is an enormous homiletic commentary on
the book of Job, which he began while in Constantinople at the
request of his entourage, a mixed group of clerics, monks, and rich
laywomen. The basic moral of the story, for Gregory, was Job's
unwavering capacity to endure the temptations of both suffering
and success. He presented Job as a man who perceived that the
moral truth of any situation always lay behind its worldly appearance, and whose speech was securely grounded in this spiritual
insight. Job's comforters, by contrast, while their advice may have
contained a grain of wisdom, were not to be trusted as speakers,
because they made no real effort of ethical discernment. 'You only
set in order speeches to upbraid, and you speak words against the
winds' (Job 6:26), Job rebuked his friends. Gregory's comment was:

> To speak words to the wind is to talk idly . . . and while we neglect to
> guard against idle words, we are frequently brought to mischievous
> ones . . . and sometimes the tongue even breaks out into open re-
> vilings. Hence it is well said by Solomon, 'He that lets out water is a
> beginner of brawls' (Prov. 17:14). For to let out water is to let the
> tongue loose in the flux of speech.[30]

Speech was always dangerous. Even the pure in heart could not
hope to control the fluidity of discourse:

> For the human mind is like water: when enclosed, it is collected on
> high . . . but when let loose, it comes to nought . . . The mind is, as it
> were, drawn down in so many streams the moment it lets itself out in
> superfluous words from the strict enclosure of silence.

This was not, however, to argue that a cloistered silence was the
ideal spiritual state: speech was also necessary:

> It should be known that when we withhold from speech by an excess
> of fear . . . we are subject to a mischievous degree of much talking in
> the heart. Our thoughts become the more hot within, the more the
> violent keeping of indiscreet silence confines them.

---

30. This passage and those following are from *Moralia in Job* 7.37.57–61. The
translation is adapted from *Morals on the Book of Job,* 3 vols. (Oxford, 1844), I, 410ff.

The answer Gregory proposed was the maintenance of a judicious rhetorical self-restraint:

> The tongue must be carefully kept under great control . . . to prevent it running loose on the one hand, and going slack through being too tightly bound . . . Thus does Solomon say, there is a time for speaking and a time for silence.

Gregory's articulation of an ideal of rhetorical temperance as the mark of a well-qualified ruler is, perhaps, the third term in a long development of moral language. In the ancient city, the sexual temperance of a married man was the guarantee of his good intentions towards the city. In the texts of fourth- and fifth-century Christian ascetics, such as Cassian, the celibate man replaces the husband as the emblem of moral self-control. In Gregory's world, however, sex is no longer part of the equation: the epitome of moral authority proposed by Gregory is the man who has tamed his tongue in the daytime, not his penis at night. The 'ruler' Gregory describes in his handbook on *Pastoral Care* could be anyone in any kind of position of responsibility, clerical or otherwise. Through its very asexual character, Gregory's language of authority, paradoxically, sets the seal on the appropriation by Christian celibates of the ancient ethical tradition of moral guidance. By the late sixth century, it was no longer necessary for male ascetics to flaunt their sexual self-control in order to convince as civic leaders.

In view of his towering later influence, the irony is that Gregory's own tenure of power was far from secure.[31] The minute attention he devoted to the workings and the language of authority point to the uncertainty of his position in Rome. His problems were not only the advance of the Lombards outside the gates, nor the streams of refugees looking to St Peter for protection: his most dangerous enemies lay within the Lateran and Vatican Palaces themselves, in the shape of the established Roman clergy. The city's priests formed a tight and jealous corporation, whose traditional procedures and career structures had been disrupted by the rise to power of Gregory and his ascetic companions. After Gregory's death, an open conflict between his disciples and the clergy ensued for a generation, with the clergy emerging as the winners, and the monks confined to liturgical duty in the Roman basilicas. In this embattled context, of which Gregory was fully aware, he, like Job, could not afford a word out of place.

---

31. See P. Llewellyn, 'The Roman Church in the seventh century: the legacy of Gregory I', *JEccH* 25 (1974), pp.363–80.

Conclusion: Gregorian masculinity in medieval Europe

Hotly contested in Rome, Pope Gregory's authority as a moral teacher was accepted across the breadth of the Roman world, from Alexandria and Constantinople to Whitby, where the first *Life* of Gregory was produced c.700. Before the end of the seventh century, excerpted versions of his works, (in particular the *Morals on Job*), were circulating in Visigothic Spain and in Ireland.[32] When therefore, two hundred years later, Alfred of Wessex translated Gregory's *Pastoral Care* into English, he was not only demonstrating his exceptional prowess as a literate warrior – he was also attempting to invoke a language of rulership that had acquired classic status among western aristocracies. As Janet Nelson and Ross Balzaretti demonstrate elsewhere in this volume, a Gregorian discourse of power provided a shared frame of reference for the men of the sword and of the cloth in Carolingian Europe. In this sense, the four centuries from Gregory's death until the millennium constitute the era of what we might call 'Gregorian masculinity'.

The age of Gregory VII in many ways brought an end to the epoch of his earlier namesake. The moral universe in which clergy and laity cohabited seems to have exploded in the white heat of the reform movement. Instead of measuring the flow of each other's seed or words, men now accused each other of adultery, incest, sodomy, genital torture.[33] A lurid rhetoric of sexual danger was used by the new Gregorians to demand, notoriously, that the ranks of the priesthood be uncontaminated by any kind of association with their lay brethren. The upshot, as Robert Swanson argues in this volume, may have been to mark out the celibate clergy as a 'third gender', irretrievably disengaged (at least in theory) from the sexual and property transactions that continued to define the lives of laymen. The paradox remains, however, that, for all the polarizing force of their polemic, both the reformers and their opponents appealed to the texts of the Fathers – the moral language of the past – to justify their claims and to discredit those of their enemies. However the story of social and religious revolution

32. For a recent assessment of Gregory's influence in these terms, see Peter Brown, *The Rise of Western Christendom* (London, 1996), esp. pp.133–66.

33. C. Leyser, 'The rhetoric of sodomy in Peter Damian's *Book of* Gomorrah', *Romanic Review* 86 (1995), pp.191–211; and 'Custom, truth, and gender in eleventh-century reform', in R.N. Swanson, ed., *Gender and the Christian Religion*, Studies in Church History 34 (1998), pp.75–91.

in the eleventh century is told, we must recognize the period's rhetoric of gender – and specifically the model of masculine self-control invoked by all parties – to be an ancient, inherited language, whose authority remained as volatile as it was universally acknowledged. Of this point, there is no better illustration than the assumption of the name 'Gregory' by Archdeacon Hildebrand in 1073, as he strove to present himself as a man who could be trusted.

CHAPTER EIGHT

Monks, Secular Men and Masculinity, c. 900

J.L. NELSON

Christianity has often seemed a very comfortable religion, applying flattering unction to souls. The Church universal has adapted well to diverse environments. It has rendered unto Caesar, leaving in decent obscurity those biblical passages that expressed misgivings about worldly power. Adaptive strategies included picking up pre-Christian customs and reusing them: *peregrinatio pro Christo* (becoming an exile for Christ's sake) continued older forms of political exiling; child oblation was in some respects a revamped version of aristocratic fostering, whereby young nobles were customarily brought up away from their natal homes in the households of great men; convents of royal and noble women solved their families' problem of limiting the supply-side of the marriage-market, while at the same time affirming the perfect match of moral with biological nobility; noble warriors' swords and helmets were adorned no longer with lucky swastikas but with Christian symbols and invocations.[1]

And yet . . . a smoothly operating functionalism is not the whole story of early medieval christendom. Ever since the serving soldier St Martin had thrown down his weapons, while being prepared

1. For some varieties of adaptation, see V.J. Flint, *The Rise of Magic in Medieval Europe* (Princeton, 1991); T. Charles-Edwards, 'The social background to Irish *peregrinatio*', *Celtica* 11 (1976), pp.43–59; P. Wormald, 'The age of Bede', in J. Campbell, ed., *The Anglo-Saxons* (London, 1982), esp. p.89; J.L. Nelson, 'Parents, children and the Church in the earlier Middle Ages', in D. Wood, ed., *The Church and Childhood*, Studies in Church History 31 (1994), p.109; M. De Jong, *In Samuel's Image. Child Oblation in the Early Middle Ages* (Amsterdam, 1996); K. Leyser, *Rule and Conflict in an Early Medieval Society* (London, 1979); J. Backhouse, D. Turner and L. Webster, *The Golden Age of Anglo-Saxon Art* (London, 1984), no. 14, pp.34, 101–3; L. Webster and J. Backhouse, *The Making of England. Anglo-Saxon Art and Culture AD600–900* (London, 1991), pp.59–60. I am grateful to Dawn Hadley for her editorial skills. My thanks for comments on this chapter go to Sarah Hamilton, Stuart Airlie, David Bates and Michael Kennedy.

121

to fight in the front rank without them (no coward he), some Christians had worried about the morality of shedding blood in warfare. Ever since St Ambrose had imposed penance on the emperor Theodosius for sanctioning a minor massacre, some churchmen had worried about the dangers of excessive collaboration with the powers that were, and even, occasionally, about state violence.[2] Ever since St Aidan had wept when King Oswine threw himself before him, promising never again to criticize what the bishop might do with any royal alms, the sight of a humble king had alarmed some thinking souls, for it raised the spectre of conflicting goods.[3] Ever since the Church, while approving marriage as a Christian state, had endorsed celibacy as the means and the sign of openness to the Holy Spirit, and then required this of its professionals, some lay Christians had been, on the one hand, attracted to this higher form of spiritual life, and, on the other, made anxious by the needs of the body, the attractions of sex, the social requirement of procreation.[4] Marriage itself could thus become problematic.

For most people, marriage was the site where gendered difference became and remained most central, and most visible, in their lives. I say 'gendered' advisedly, because I do not just refer to sexual difference, fundamental as that is, but to socially constructed and therefore historically conditioned difference. I say 'visible' advisedly: I am talking about expectations of public conduct, of roles and rules, of what it meant socially to be man or woman. Historians should perhaps have paid more attention than they have to how masculinity was successively *re*constructed in the early Middle Ages. There is quite a large body of work, especially from North America, on women's history in this period which, valuable as it is, has not dealt with gender, hence has not looked at masculinity.[5] Recently, in another part of the wood, research has focused on the writings of

2. C. Stancliffe, *Saint Martin and his Hagiographer* (Oxford, 1983), p.149, also comments on the attitudes of saint and biographer to blood-shedding at pp.124, 138–48; S.M. Hamilton, 'The penance of Robert the Pious', *EME* 6 (1997), pp.189–200; J.L. Nelson, 'Violence in the Carolingian world and the ritualization of ninth-century Frankish warfare', in G. Halsall, ed., *Violence and Society in the Early Medieval West* (Woodbridge, 1997), pp.90–107.

3. *HE*, III, 14; J.M. Wallace-Hadrill, *Early Germanic Kingship in England and on the Continent* (Oxford, 1971), pp.85–6.

4. J. Bugge, *Virginitas. An Essay in the History of a Medieval Ideal* (The Hague, 1976); P. Brown, *The Body and Society. Men, Women and Sexual Renunciation in Early Christianity* (Princeton, 1989), esp. pp.400–8, 416–27; D. Elliott, *Spiritual Marriage. Sexual Abstinence in Medieval Wedlock* (Princeton, 1993).

5. J.L. Nelson, 'Family, gender, sexuality in the Middle Ages', in M. Bentley, ed., *Companion to Historiography* (London, 1997), pp.153–76.

ascetic men in Late Antiquity, their very evident concerns over their own sexuality, and the significance of these as responses to changing forms of power in a Christian world (see above, chapter 7). Taking this line of enquiry further into the early Middle Ages is one of my objectives here. But I also want to shift from an exclusive focus on monks to consider as well men who remained in the world of *res saeculares*, secular things. How did secular men conceive and express their masculinity? How did they experience this subjectively? What difference did it make when a warrior aristocracy became a Christian elite? In many times and places, gendered difference could be seen as straightforwardly supporting the political order. Sometimes, in circumstances of particular social stress, things were far from straightforward and, for the individuals living through those times, far from comfortable, as gender identity came under pressure, and had to be rethought and redefined. The sixteenth-century Reformation constituted one such case.[6] In this chapter, I suggest that the second half of the ninth century marked another. During it, the working-out of an earlier reformation in changed circumstances produced a sharpened consciousness, on the part of at least some male members of the elite, of existing social arrangements as disfunctional, and of themselves as subjected to dissonant social messages and conflicting imperatives. Seldom do the scarce and, above all, ecclesiastical sources of the earlier Middle Ages reveal much of the interiority of the lives of secular men. I argue that, in a small number of cases from the later decades of the ninth century, faint traces may be retrievable. Given the nature of the evidence, it is hard – and perhaps pointless to try – wholly to disentangle the experiences of monks and laymen: that very entanglement constitutes a starting-point.

Odo of Cluny and Gerald of Aurillac

I begin with a monk: Odo of Cluny.[7] Odo was a monastic biographer in the sense of being a monk who wrote biography. Yet he chose as his subject a man who was not a monk; and he wrote for audiences

---

6. L. Roper, *The Holy Household: Women and Morals in Reformation Augsberg* (Oxford, 1989).

7. This paper is greatly indebted to S. Airlie, 'The anxiety of sanctity. St Gerald of Aurillac and his maker', *JEccH* 43 (1992), pp.372–95. The broader context is illuminated by P. Wormald, 'Æthelwold and his continental counterparts', in B. Yorke, ed., *Bishop Æthelwold: his Career and Influence* (Woodbridge, 1988), pp.13–42.

that would include not only monks but secular men, laymen. Monks' writing of biography, like so much else about Carolingian monasticism, could be an interaction with the world rather than a symptom of hermetic sealing-off from it. My inquiry is unavoidably concerned with some varieties of that interaction, and the differing readings of masculinity they entailed.

Like Notker of St-Gall, who inserted into his *Gesta Karoli* a little panegyric of Louis the German (the work was dedicated to Louis the German's son Charles the Fat),[8] Odo held up as a model for his readers and hearers a man whose life had been lived out in the *res publica terrena*. Yet unlike Notker's exemplar of *potentia*, Odo's subject was not a king but a *potens laicus*, a lay man of power; and while Louis the German had practised with success 'the very things without which the *res publica terrena* cannot carry on, namely, marriage and the use of arms', Notker was not claiming sanctity for King Louis, hence not addressing a problem of incompatibility between *potentia* and holiness. For Odo the hagiographer, however, that problem was so crucial as to require the casting of his holy man, Gerald of Aurillac, in a new mould.

Odo's Gerald was a layman who was unable to live comfortably with the two fundamentals of the *res publica terrena*: marriage and the use of arms. Gerald's discomfort was, in Odo's view, the prerequisite of his sanctity. Establishing that Gerald had indeed performed miracles involved the relatively easy task of convincing sceptics. Another potential target-audience posed a much harder challenge: 'Some men, trying to excuse their sins, praise him without making a necessary prior distinction: they say that he was a *potens et dives* – a powerful man and a wealthy one – and lived with physical pleasures, and was *et utique, sanctus* – holy, just the same' (I, preface, 640–1).[9] This proposition challenged a scale of values that placed sanctity far above wealth and pleasure. It also blurred the distinction between heavenly and earthly things. It raised a problem of cognition. Odo's task was to insist on, to underscore, the disjunction between two ways of life: the profane, characterized by the practice of arms and of sexual relations, and the holy, typified by renunciation of precisely those things. Two cadres, both manned

8. *Gesta Karoli* II, 10, ed. H.F. Haefele, *MGH Scriptores rerum germanicarum in usum scholarum* (hereafter *SRG*) new ser. xii, (Berlin, 1959), p.66.

9. The English translation by G. Sitwell, *St Odo of Cluny* (London, 1958), pp.89–180, should be used with some caution. References are given in the text to the *Vita Geraldi* in the form of the volume number, the section and the column(s) as they appear in *PL*.

by those whom the world called noble, were thus radically distinguished by their ways of life. For Notker, it had been possible for
the earthly *res publica* and the heavenly one to meet: Charles the
Fat's *adventus* was hailed at St Gall. A Carolingian commentator on
the Rule of Benedict prescribed such reception-rituals not only for
kings but, in modified form, for queens (regality went some way
towards obliterating sex) and also for great men, whose presence
in the monastery was, it seems, not thought *per se* to defile the
immaculate ones within.[10] Odo, by contrast, wondered how Gerald,
acknowledging the *ius armatae militiae*, could remain 'untainted
by the saeculum [secular world]' – *immaculatus ab hoc saeculo* (I, 7,
646). Or again, how could Gerald carry out his obligations *in saeculi
negotio* yet keep himself from defilement – *a stupro?* (I, 10, 649).
Monks, free of the defiling business of the earthly *res publica*, could
aspire to holiness. Gerald was not a monk (though he wished to be
one) (II, 8, col. 675). Yet Odo wished to claim that he was holy: that
despite his having been *in saeculo potens*, hence with ample opportunity for pride, he had held power humbly (I, 42, 668). Such sanctity
was *novitas* indeed (II, preface, 669).[11]

Odo's concerns had much to do with his own life. The Vikings'
ravaging of Tours in 903 had been traumatic for the young
tourangeau: he made sense of it in terms of divine punishment on
St Martin's community for their lax ways.[12] Discipline was the answer
for them. It was also the answer for laymen. Gerald provided Odo
with a model of a *disciplinatus vivendi modus* (I, preface, 640): a
model urgently needed, for the chronological passage of Odo's life
had been matched by a spatial shift from the Loire valley, where
some kind of royal authority persisted, to Aquitaine: a region teem-
ing in the early tenth century with new kinds of power of question-
able authority. Gerald himself, says Odo, had 'usurped' his comital
title (I, 32, 661).[13] Odo wrote the *Life of Gerald* in part precisely to
correct and warn lay *potentes* who, according to Odo, were claiming
in Gerald a sanctification of secular power and wealth, without
further qualification (I, preface, 642). Such a misconception, and
on the part of such people, had to be corrected: for them the

---

10. P. Willmes, *Der Herrscher-Adventus im Kloster des Frühmittelalters* (Munich, 1976),
pp.62–70, 178.

11. '*Nam laico homini multa licent quae monacho non licent*' ('for many things are
permitted for a layman which are not so for a monk').

12. *Vita S.Odonis* II, 12, *PL* 133, col. 67.

13. For the regional context, see J. Schneider, 'Aspects de la société dans l'Aquitaine
carolingienne d'après la *Vita Geraldi Auriliacensis*', *Comptes rendus de l'Académie des
Inscriptions et Belles-Lettres* (Paris, 1973), pp.8–19.

corrupting nature of secular power had to be reasserted. Yet, after all, Gerald was holy. Odo himself had doubted Gerald's sanctity, he says, because of its *novitas* (I, preface, 639). Writing the *Life* was a hard task indeed. But it was also an opportunity to confront again the ambiguities of power in the *saeculum*, to reconsider the forms of accommodation that the ninth-century Carolingian Church had evolved. If Gerald had not existed, Odo might have had to invent him.

Of Notker's 'things without which . . .', Odo found the use of arms in a sense less problematic to deal with than marriage. The modern historiography of the *Vita Geraldi*, in focusing on the difficulties Odo encountered in the attempt 'to incorporate [secular aristocrats'] occupational hazards into a model of sanctity', has, however, been largely concerned with the issue of lay violence.[14] It is no coincidence that there has been scholarly dispute over the extent to which Odo sought, or achieved, a legitimation of Christian warfare. In my view, Stuart Airlie is right to discern something 'bizarre', 'a whiff of the absurd', in Odo's depiction of Gerald urging his men to fight only with the flat of their swords and with the butts of their spears.[15] For the framework assumed by earlier Carolingian churchmen – Alcuin, Jonas, Sedulius, Hincmar – and the layman Nithard too, was that of a functioning state: the shedding of blood might be justified, when authorized by the king for the common good, or while on 'public expedition', undertaken in self-defence.[16] But Odo wrote in and for a changed world. His public were the *pagenses* of Aurillac, and more broadly, the *potentes* of the Auvergne and the Limousin. It was hard to link their power with royal authority. In these parts by the 920s, *regalis potentia* of the kind appreciated by Notker in late ninth-century Alemannia had faded: stripped of that qualifying adjective 'royal', the power of the powerful was a naked tautology.

Yet, however difficult it was to square even Gerald's paradoxically pacifist form of fighting with *religio*, however delicate Odo's balancing-act on legitimizing violence, marriage was, for Odo, an even more problematic element in the life of a secular aristocrat who aspired to be a man of God. The use of arms was incorporated, if somewhat awkwardly, into Odo's image of Gerald. Marriage could not be. In the late eighth century and the first half of the ninth, the

14. Airlie, 'Anxiety', p.374. Airlie, however, also comments perceptively, if briefly, on the issue of sexuality in the *Life*.

15. *Ibid.*, pp.375–6, with reference to *Vita Geraldi* I, 8, cols. 646–7.

16. Nelson, 'Violence', pp.91–4.

authors of 'mirrors for laymen' offered lay *potentes* an apparently
straightforward, and 'attractive', inclusion of family life within the
model of moral public service.[17] But the accommodation had been
rather less comfortable than some modern commentators have
alleged. Jonas of Orleans in his *de Institutione laicali* offered lay *potentes*
the prolific patriarchs of Israel as role models: Job, David, and
Tobias, whose story he cited twice.[18] Jonas explained how Tobias's
intended bride Sarah had had seven bridegrooms in succession:
each had died on the marriage-night, killed by a demon. Tobias
succeeded where they failed: he drove off the demon by magic, and
the couple then prayed together before lying down for the night.
Following Augustine, Jonas of Orleans interpreted the demon as
lust, Tobias's achievement as lust-free intercourse. Tobias, with the
other patriarchs, combined fecund marriage with chastity.[19] Hincmar
of Rheims, blessing a Carolingian princess and her bridegroom in
in 856, in the first extant full marriage-rite, asked God 'to make
them worthy, by their unstained marriage-bed, to be joined in the
company of the holy patriarchs'.[20] In the *Life of Gerald*, Odo presents
Gerald's father in far more reserved fashion as following the patriarchal path by choosing 'to make himself chaste precisely in marriage (*in ipso coniugio sese castificari*)'. Gerald's father had required
two angelic visitations on a single night before he was able to stay
awake long enough to engender the future saint (I, 2–3, 643–4).
Dhuoda, a Frankish aristocrat who wrote a *Manual* of advice for her
fifteen-year-old son, assured him that the *doctores*, the teachers of
the Church, 'had not refused to join the marriage-bed to the things
that are holy (*nuptiarum sacris iungere thorum*)'. Dhuoda saw the
patriarchs as 'serving God in the marriage-bed (*in thoro conjugatorum
militantes*)'.[21] But even this, the most frankly positive view of sexual
activity to be found in a Frankish writer (Dhuoda looked forward
to the proliferation of the family-line), did not really constitute a

17. Earlier commentaries on these sources in my view smooth over some painfully
rough edges: an exhilarating review of these texts and their context is J. Smith,
'Gender and ideology in the earlier Middle Ages', in R.N. Swanson, ed., *Gender and
the Christian Religion*, Studies in Church History 34 (1998), pp.51–73.

18. The Vulgate Book of Tobias (Tobit) was relegated to the Apocrypha, hence is
absent from the Authorized Version. It is included in *The New English Bible* (Oxford,
1970), pp.540–68.

19. Jonas, *de Institutione laicali* II, 2, and 9, *PL* 106, cols. 171 and 185.

20. *Ordo* of Judith, *Ordines Coronationis Franciae. Texts and Ordines for the Coronation
of Frankish and French Kings and Queens in the Middle Ages*, ed., R.A. Jackson, vol. 1
(Philadelpha, 1995), prayer no. 3, pp.76–7; cf also prayers nos. 5, p.77, and p.11, p.79.

21. Dhuoda, *Liber Manualis* IV, 6, trans. P. Riché, *Dhuoda, Manuel pour mon fils*,
Sources chrétiennes 225 (Paris, 1975), p.228.

whole-hearted endorsement, certainly not an explanation, of sexual relations within marriage. It comes at the close of a chapter that begins with the 'titillation of the pricking of the flesh', and continues with a citation of the Vulgate (Apocryphal) Book of Ecclesiasticus (Sirach), 23: 6: '*Aufer a me ventris concupiscentias et concubitus concupiscentiae ne apprehendant me* . . . (Take away from me the desires of the belly and the couplings of desire, lest they overwhelm me)', but substitutes the Augustinian term *libido* for *venter*. If Augustine's shadow loomed over Dhuoda when she advised her teenage son on chastity, it was, more surprisingly, given the absence of reference to monks or monasteries anywhere in the *Manual*, the Benedictine Rule that inspired her recommendations about frequent private prayer. Wallace-Hadrill was right to see this programme of spiritual exercises as one that 'might have strained a monk'.[22]

Odo's treatment of Gerald's sexuality is crucially relevant to the problem of power and pollution. Odo begins by self-consciously distancing his saint-hero from precisely that trait of the patriarchs which, for the ninth-century mirror-authors including Dhuoda, had warranted sexual activity within marriage: their fathering of many offspring. 'The things which Job and David and Tobias did, and through which they were blessed, were not the things Gerald can be shown to have done' (I, preface, 642).[23] While Odo elsewhere cited Job and David as prototypes of Gerald's humility and justice, the patriarchs had to be clearly differentiated, as model progenitors, from the celibate Gerald. For him, according to Odo, chastity meant total abstinence. Even when a politically advantageous marriage was pressed on him, Odo says, Gerald rejected it 'because of his love of chastity' (I, 34, 662–3).[24] The passage continues:

> How great was his abhorrence of fleshly filth may be reckoned from this, that he could not suffer a nocturnal illusion without suffering grief. For whenever this misfortune of humanity happened to him when he was asleep, his body-servant brought him a change of clothes, ever kept ready for this purpose, and a towel and a tub of water. That cultivator of internal purity so shunned the pollution of his body

22. J.M. Wallace-Hadrill, *The Frankish Church* (Oxford, 1983), p.286, though without mention of Dhuoda's citations of the Rule.
23. On Odo's use of the model of Job (but without comment on Tobias), see F. Lotter, 'Das Idealbild adliger Laienfrömmigkeit in den Anfängen Clunys: Odos *Vita* des Grafen Gerald von Aurillac', in W. Lourdaux and D. Verhelst, eds, *Benedictine Culture 750–1050* (Louvain, 1983), pp.76–95, at p.85.
24. Airlie, 'Anxiety', p.390, wonders why Odo 'did not use a St Alexis-type model of heroic chastity within marriage'. On that theme, see now Elliott, *Spiritual Marriage*. But for a possible explanation for its absence in Gerald's *Life*, see below, p.139.

that he washed away what had happened to him while asleep not only with a bath but with tears. This action may seem foolish (*stultum*) to those whose filthy mind reeks with the foul stink of vice. Such men pollute themselves whether naturally or deliberately, but they do not think fit to wash away their filth.

Here Odo picks up a long-standing monastic preoccupation: involuntary nocturnal emission had been a recurrent theme in the *Collationes* which Odo wrote for monks, following directly on from John Cassian's work of the same title, but also, at least in part, for lay *potentes*.[25] Carolingian penitentials may have extended this monastic concern to a wider, lay, audience; for their strictures concerning nocturnal emissions were evidently not directed only at monks and clergy.[26] A particular, and peculiarly masculine kind of self-control, once the badge of the cloistered ascetic, constituting his claim to moral superiority, could now be represented as the mark of the superior layman. This special virtue required a prior internalizing of sexual anxiety and guilt. It would also be subjected, in the layman's case, to continual testing as, in the run of secular life, potential objects of desire presented themselves to the eyes, those 'windows of sin'.[27]

The onset of the testing-time belonged to a particular stage of a boy's development. Odo identified it precisely in describing 'how stern Gerald showed himself to the adolescents [in his entourage], how he used to say that this was a very dangerous age (*valde periculosum tempus*) – the time when every adolescent puts off the voice and appearance of his mother, and begins to assume his father's voice and face: [this was the time] when anyone who made strenuous efforts to preserve himself would find, through that, that he would easily be able to overcome the incentives of the flesh

25. For close thematic links between the *Collationes* and the *Vita Geraldi*, and *potentes* as the intended audience of both works, see Lotter, 'Idealbild', pp.86–9.

26. See P.J. Payer, *Sex and the Penitentials* (Toronto, 1984), pp.49–52, 92. An influential source was Gregory the Great's ninth response to Augustine of Canterbury, *HE* I, 27 (cf. chapter 7, above, p.116). Body and clothes should be washed with water, and guilt washed away with tears: *Vita Geraldi* I, 24, col. 663: '*non solum balneis quin etiam lacrimis abluerit*'.

27. Dhuoda, *Manuel* IV, 6. Biblical sources are Matthew 5: 28; Job 31: 1; Ecclesiasticus 9: 8–9; Jeremiah 9: 21; but a further influence is surely Gregory the Great's *Moralia in Job*, XXI, ii, 4–7, ed. M. Adriaen, *Corpus Christianorum*, Series Latina 145, 3 vols (Turnhout, 1979), II, pp.1065–9, commenting at length on Job 31: 1. Dhuoda cites or echoes the *Moralia* at least a further seventeen times. Gregory's reading of Job 31: 1 is also drawn on by Odo, *Vita Geraldi* I, 9, col. 647: Odo wrote an Epitome of the *Moralia*, and his works, unsurprisingly, are shot through with Gregorian reminiscences.

(*incentiva carnis*)' (I, 15, 652). In the *Collationes*, written some years earlier, Odo described what could happen when strenuous efforts were not made. 'A certain hermit told his young acolyte (*filius suus*) of many virtues; and then about an idea which the Devil had put into his head: that whenever a man was titillated by lust, by rubbing his penis he should eject his semen, just as he might blow snot out of his nose.' Later when the hermit died, the young companion saw him being handed over to demons. The young man despaired: 'O, who can hope to be saved when this man perished!' An angel appeared, to defuse the question by demonstrating that no injustice had been done in this case: 'don't worry, this man did achieve much, but that one vice which the Apostle calls uncleanness made everything else filthy'.[28]

The theme of training in masculine self-control was relevant to monks and laymen alike. It brings us up sharp against the problem of historicity in Odo's *Life of Gerald*, a problem common to all hagiography,[29] but compounded in this case by the very obvious autobiographical element in Odo's work, and by the fact that we know of Gerald only through Odo's *Life* of him. Who was troubled by the demands of power in the *saeculum* – Gerald, or Odo? Both Odo, according to what purports to be his own account incorporated in John of Salerno's *Vita Odonis*, and Gerald, in Odo's presentation of him, had experienced a particular kind of personal crisis. Both had been the subject of very clear parental expectations. That was hardly surprising in a society where children expected parental direction. The crisis, in each case, resulted from change in those directions. Odo himself, according to his biographer, had originally been destined by his father for a clerical career – but the father had then changed his mind and began to draw his son away from the ecclesiastical *ordo*, and apply him to *militaria exercitia*, especially hunting. The lad was not a success in his new métier and experienced increased anxiety.[30] When he was fifteen, which was,

28. *Collationes* II, 26, *PL* 133, col. 570. The references to Rom. 1: 24, and I Thess. 4: 7, are followed by a citation from Isaiah 1: 15: '. . . *et cum multiplicaveritis orationem, non exaudiam, manus enim vestrae sanguine plenae sunt*' ('. . . and when you make many prayers, I will not hear: for your hands are full of blood'). The association of semen and blood is noteworthy.

29. See P. Fouracre, 'Merovingian history and Merovingian hagiography', *Past and Present* 127 (1990), pp.3–38, and also P. Fouracre and R.A. Gerberding, *Late Merovingian France. History and Hagiography 640–720* (Manchester, 1996), pp.33–52.

30. *Vita S.Odonis* I, 8, 47: '*totam venationem meam vertebat in fatigationem . . . rediebam moerens sine omni affectu et fatigatione confossus*' ('[this] turned all my hunting into anxiety . . . I used to return, wretched, struck down with all kinds of weakness and anxiety)'. Compare the psychological sense of *fatigué* in modern French.

though the biographer does not say so, the age of *adolescentia*, and of Frankish legal maturity, with marriage clearly on the horizon, Odo was attending the Christmas vigil in the presence of the canons of St-Martin, Tours, when he suddenly felt impelled to go and stand in their midst. A terrible headache struck him, and for the next two years he suffered so much pain that his father changed his mind again and Odo after all received the tonsure and joined the canons of St-Martin.[31]

Compare Gerald's experience as described by Odo: Gerald's parents had him trained in '*saecularia exercitia*', notably hunting, '*sicut nobilibus pueris mos est*' (I, 4, 645). He became ill with a chronic skin disease, which sounds like an infantile version of Job's boils, and is regarded by Odo as a serious illness (*pustulae* echoes Leviticus 13: 2 where the context is leprosy). Gerald's parents therefore changed their plans and applied the boy to *litterarum studia*, 'by which, if he should be less apt for the needs of the *saeculum*, he would be made suitable for ecclesiastical office'. As he grew older, however, Gerald's illness got better, and his parents changed their minds again, and set him to military *exercitia* after all. Gerald's experience is thus the mirror-image of Odo's: both sets of parents change their minds twice over, and both sons' chronic illness seems to preclude a secular career. The likely effect of all this on the boys concerned, assuming an element of historicity in these accounts (and remember that the audience for the *Vita Geraldi* included many who had known Gerald) would have been to create insecurity as to both parental intentions and personal prospects, and, further, to cause some difficulty in adapting to the career eventually determined for each of them. A crisis of identity is not too strong a description of each boy's adolescent experience – a crisis rendered the more acute when fathers changed their minds. Manhood, masculinity, was presented to each boy in radically different, indeed contradictory, forms. Anxiety centred in both cases on the essential activites of the noble man's life in the *saeculum*: training for the use of arms, and the sexual activity that produced noble heirs.

In Gerald's case the anxiety remained. It was not only that he refused to wear splendid clothing. 'Furthermore, the leather strap (*reminiculum*) by which he was in the habit of keeping his sword hung at his side, he managed to keep on using for twenty years and more: he did not take the trouble even to change it or get a new one. What can I say about his belt or fine belt-fittings (*balteum vel*

---

31. *Ibid.* I, 9, col. 47.

ambitiosa cinctoria) when not only did he not wear any gold but could not even bear to own any?' (I, 16, 653). The belt quite literally highlighted a man's social identity: without his belt a man was unmanned. The gold-adorned sword-belt and harness marked out the noble office-holder.[32] These, the very signs of his rank and of his masculinity at the same time, were precisely what Gerald refused to use or even have. A sword without a proper strap was pretty much like a sword without a haft: it represented incompleteness, uselessness.[33]

Gerald's anxiety had another aspect too. As a young man, he tried to seduce the daughter of one of his own tenants, and had the girl brought to his room: 'at that moment she suddenly appeared to him no longer attractive but loathsome and hideous' (I, 9, 647–9). Temptation receded. Gerald's sudden vision of 'reality' is reminiscent of Odo's advice in the *Collationes*: to see, as it were with X-ray eyes, beneath the skin of women, nothing but a bag of shit (*saccum stercoris*).[34] Some time later in his life, Gerald underwent a temptation that was similar but different. He was offered marriage to the sister of his lord and patron Duke William of Aquitaine. Gerald refused, clinging to chastity (I, 34, 662).[35] It is at this point in the *Life* that Odo recounted the story of Gerald's wet dreams and his obsessive washing that seemed so foolish to the filthy-minded.

Anxious young men: aristocratic masculinity in crisis

There are some further contemporary cases of anxious young men who were Gerald's contemporaries. First is that of Wolo, recounted in Ekkehard's monastic history of St-Gall.[36] This lad, offered as a child to the monastery, could not adapt to the cloistered life. He was '*inquietus*' (restless, anxious) et *vagus*, given to 'wandering' among the mountains. The abbot made allowances for his strong will: 'St Gall

---

32. K. Leyser, *Communications and Power in Early Medieval Europe*, ed., T. Reuter, 2 vols (London, 1995), I, pp.55–7.

33. Cf. Gerhard, *Vita S. Oudalrici* c.3, *MGH Scriptores IV*, p.38, with the comment of Leyser, *Communications*, I, p.86.

34. *Collationes* II, 9, col. 556.

35. That Gerald never did marry seems indicated by the inheritance claims of his nephew: see below p.139. The internal coherence of this story suggests to me that Odo's account of Gerald's rejection of marriage rests on fact.

36. Ekkehard IV, *Casus Sancti Galli* c.43, ed. H.F. Haefele (Darmstadt, 1980), pp.96–9. Ekkehard wrote in the mid-eleventh century, but this story purports to come from the late ninth. Wolo's fate was possibly suicide: Nelson, 'Parents', pp.113–14.

only recruited boys of free birth and the more noble used to stray from the path more often [than the rest]'. The abbot tried to remedy the situation with words and with beatings (*verbis verberibusque*). The boy's parents, 'concerned for the boy', came to the monastery, and thanks to their advice Wolo improved for a bit. But the improvement was temporary. Not long after, the boy fell from (threw himself from?) the monastery bell-tower, and died, but not before he had had time to request that he be carried, not to the infirmary, but to the altar of the Virgins, where the dying boy assured the abbot that 'however wicked I was in other ways, I never slept with a woman'. Wolo's last desperate thoughts were about his own sexuality.

Second, the case of Rigramnus, a noble Frankish boy from Le Mans.[37] This is a story about choice between, not lay and religious lives as such, but between the ascetic monastic life and the life of a canon, which was here depicted as no different from that of a noble layman. Rigramnus's uncle wanted to dedicate him to the life of a secular cleric so that he might eventually become a cathedral canon; but the boy suffered from terrible stomach pains. Finally, he confessed that his now-dead father had previously dedicated him to the monastic life. The uncle was furious: 'how could you prefer the life of pigs in a vegetable-garden? what about the joys of hunting? what about the voluptuous touch of women?' The boy for a while stuck to his monastic preference; but finally, when his uncle lay dying, he agreed to become a canon. Interesting here is, once again, the description of physical symptoms of anxiety: the pain of the boy's dilemma, caught between conflicting duties to father and uncle. Interesting too is the emphasis on diet as a sign, one with strongly gendered connotations too. Canons hunt and eat meat like men: pigs, but also monks and nuns – and women generally? – eat vegetables.[38]

The third, and in some ways best-documented, case is that of a prince, Charles, son of Louis the German. Charles was welcomed to St-Gall as emperor in 883. His future had not always looked so bright. He was born probably in 839, a youngest son. Nothing is known about his childhood. Had his father died in his forties instead of at seventy, Charles's brothers might well have thought

37. *Narratio de monacho Cenomanensi ad canonicam vitam et habitum converso, PL* 129, cols. 1263–8. David Ganz kindly drew my attention to this interesting text. Cf. Nelson, 'Parents', p.113.

38. Interestingly, Odo thought it necessary to defend Gerald against the criticism that he regularly ate meat: *Vita Geraldi* II, preface, col. 669: he was after all a layman, not a monk. For evidence that the diet of the St-Gall monks sometimes included meat, see *Casus S. Galli* c.105, p.212.

of tonsuring the boy: fraternal rivalry was as potent a source of conflict within royal families as filial impatience.[39] Perhaps Louis himself had thoughts of offering Charles to the Church. As it was, in 862 Louis the German gave Charles Alemannia as a sub-kingdom and arranged his marriage to a noble lady, Richardis.[40] Charles's career for the next decade or so is poorly documented. It seems clear, though, that the marriage produced no children. Charles, like his brothers, rebelled more than once against his father. On 26 January 873, at an assembly in his father's palace of Frankfurt, Charles suddenly 'leaped up and said that he wished to abandon the world and would not touch his wife in carnal intercourse. He took his sword from its belt and let it fall to the ground. As he tried to undo his sword-belt and take off his princely clothing, he began to shake violently . . .'.[41] Hincmar of Rheims, describing this event in the *Annals of St-Bertin*, attributed Charles's problems to diabolical possession, and his subsequent cure to the intercession of the saints ('Charles's father ordered him to be led about from one sacred place of holy martyrs to another so that their merits and prayers might free him from the demon and he might recover his sanity (*ad sanam mentem redire*)'). It is worth stressing that in this case, there can be absolutely no question of literary invention: the *Annals of Fulda* report the same episode, though with some different emphases (they add, for instance, that '[Charles's father] and all who were with him were appalled, and wept . . .').[42] Charles, son of Louis, really did perform an extraordinary act of role rejection. To be precise, he rejected the tokens of secular masculinity, the sword and the belt, and at the same time spelled out to his father and the assembled aristocracy the further implication that he could no longer do service in the marriage-bed.[43]

39. R. Schieffer, 'Väter und Söhne im Karolingerhause', *Beiträge zur Geschichte des Regnum Francorum*, Beihefte der Francia, Band 22 (Paris, 1990), pp.149–64; J.L. Nelson, *Charles the Bald* (London, 1992), pp.71–4. See also chapter 3, above.

40. *MGH Diplomata regum Germaniae* I, ed. P. Kehr (Berlin, 1937), no. 108, pp.155–6. For Louis the German's provision of his son's morning-gift, see J.L. Nelson, 'A tale of two princes: politics, text and ideology in a Carolingian annal', *Studies in Medieval and Renaissance History* 10 (1988), pp.116–17.

41. *The Annals of St-Bertin*, trans. J.L. Nelson (Manchester, 1991), p.182. The exact date is supplied by the Annals of Fulda, see next note.

42. *The Annals of Fulda*, trans. T. Reuter (Manchester, 1992), pp.69–70.

43. Behind at least some ecclesiastical interpretations of the belt was Job 12: 18, '*Balteum regum* [*Dominus*] *dissolvit et praecingit fune renes eorum*' ('[The Lord] looseth the belt of kings, and girdeth their loins with a rope'). Cf. the commentary of Gregory I, *Moralia in Job* XI, xiii, 21, ed. Adriaen, 2, p.597: '*Qui membrorum suorum motus bene regere sciunt, non immerito reges vocantur* (Those who know how to rule well the movements of their members are not undeservedly called kings).'

What made Charles, suddenly, at the age of thirty-three, reject the life of a prince? Both contemporary annalists suggest he felt guilt at rebelling against his father (almost a necessary condition of being a Carolingian's son). Did Charles interpret his childless marriage as a heavenly sign, indicating a monastic path? His wife was later to claim that he had never slept with her.[44] Charles was devoted all his adult life to the Alemannian monasteries of Reichenau and St-Gall, and surely numbered monks among his confidants. He had a reputation for piety, though perhaps no more so than other Carolingians. He suffered from terrible headaches in the last year or so of his life,[45] and these, together with the 873 episode, have given rise to the suggestion, unsustainable in my view, that he was epileptic. When he eventually ruled in his own right as king, then emperor (876–887), Charles shouldered an excruciatingly difficult job with some success. He also produced an illegitimate son, Bernard, whom contemporaries expected to succeed him.[46] Charles, as man and as Carolingian, faced some dilemmas inherent in the potentially contradictory requirements of the roles and rules governing his existence.

Fourth and last, in the same time-frame but across the Channel in a West Saxon court profoundly influenced by Carolingian models, there is the case of Alfred. He too was a youngest son. His father seems to have wanted to secure some kind of subkingdom for him (this I take to have been the purpose of sending the boy to Rome to receive some kind of papal blessing);[47] but when Alfred was left fatherless at the age of nine, his older brother(s) may well have proposed a monastic vocation for him. Such a plan could only have been encouraged if Alfred was an ailing child.[48] In fact he remained in secular life; but we have no idea where Alfred lived between 858 and 868 and what sort of future was mapped out for

44. Regino of Prüm, *Chronicon* 887, ed. F. Kurze, *MGH SRG* (Hannover, 1890), p.127.

45. *s.a.* 886 (main text), 887 (Bavarian continuation), pp.105, 115, *Annals of Fulda,* pp.101, 113 with n.2, 114.

46. *Ibid.,* 885 (main text), *Annals of Fulda,* pp.98–9 with n.7.

47. See J.L. Nelson, 'The Franks and the English in the ninth century reconsidered', in P. Szarmach and J. Rosenthal, eds, *Preservation and Transmission of Anglo-Saxon Culture,* Studies in Medieval Culture 40 (1998); see also my revised views on the genesis of royal anointings in Wessex, in J.L. Nelson, *Politics and Ritual in Early Medieval Europe* (London, 1986), chs 15 and 16; and S. Keynes, 'Anglo-Saxon entries in the "Liber Vitae" of Brescia', in J. Roberts and J.L. Nelson, eds, *Alfred the Wise. Essays in Honour of Janet Bately* (Woodbridge, 1997), pp.99–119, at 107–14.

48. Asser, *Alfred the Great. Asser's Life of King Alfred and Other Contemporary Sources,* trans. S. Keynes and M. Lapidge (Harmondsworth, 1983), c.74, p.89.

him. In 868 he married. And, according to his biographer Asser, in chapter 74 of the *Life*, at the wedding feast, in the midst of vast assemblage of persons, men and women, he was suddenly struck down by a terrible pain. No-one knew at first what was the matter; the doctors could offer no diagnosis. Some people suspected witchcraft practised by some of those present.[49] Alfred recovered; and soldiered on – as everyone knows. But he suffered all his life thereafter from painful illness itself or from fear that another attack of it might strike. Asser explained that this tribulation was heaven-sent in response to a request from Alfred himself: God had responded with an illness that would ensure Alfred's humility while not rendering him useless and contemptible for heavenly and worldly affairs (*inutilis et despectus . . . in divinis et humanis rebus*).[50] The implications of both adjectives are equally significant: one refers to the performance of a job, the other to reputation. Alfred knew what depended on how he performed in the eyes not only of God but of men. As king he must be effective, and be seen to be so.[51] He apparently did not think that those whose approval he sought would be unfavourably impressed by the knowledge that he suffered from chronic illness. To put matters more bluntly, the court audience for whom Asser wrote was perfectly well aware that the king was afflicted, from time to time, by debilitating pain. What they had to be persuaded of, and this was the purpose of chapter 74, was that since the illness (unlike blindness[52] or leprosy) put no blemish on Alfred's outward appearance and afflicted him infrequently, it did not impair his regular performance; but more important still, Asser told his audience the illness had been imposed by God, at Alfred's own request.[53]

Asser's story may have impressed contemporaries: it does not impress Professor Alfred Smyth. Indeed, contempt is just the

49. *Ibid.* For modern medical views on Alfred's condition, see G. Craig, 'Alfred the Great: a diagnosis', *Journal of the Royal Society of Medicine* 84 (1991), pp.303–5.

50. *Asser, Alfred*, c.74, p.89. The phrase is repeated in the last sentence of c.74, p.90. Cf. Dhuoda, *Manuel* V, 2, p. 272, which could be read as linking *inutilitas* in this sense with sin and punishment.

51. A. Scharer, 'The writing of history at King Alfred's court', *EME* 5 (2) (1996), p.187, n.62.

52. Cf. the temporary blindness by which Gerald was afflicted after the episode with the girl, and the blindness that struck him for the last seven years of his life, testing him through suffering like Job: *Vita Geraldi* I, 10, col. 649, III, 2, col. 690. See further below p.137.

53. The point was made briefly by J.L. Nelson, 'Wealth and wisdom: the politics of Alfred the Great', in J. Rosenthal, ed. *Kings and Kingship* Acta XI (Binghamton, NY, 1986 for 1984), p.45, and more amply and effectively, by Scharer, 'Writing', pp.187–9.

reaction Smyth evinces when confronted by a 'neurotic invalid'.[54]
Smyth's choice of language seems vividly to express his own revul-
sion, as he re-presents for us what he insists is Asser's 'depressive',
'obsessive', 'sickly', 'fanatical' Alfred suffering from illness that
was 'ghastly', 'gruesomely mysterious', 'repulsive', 'crippling', worst
of all perhaps, 'self-inflicted'. Asser's chapter 74, Smyth says, 'is in
conflict with much of what we know about Alfred from contemporary sources'. Smyth thus pits (the *Anglo-Saxon Chronicle*'s) 'macho
warrior' against (Asser's) 'pious "wimp"'. And such a wimp, Smyth
says, 'could never have . . . won the support of his battle-hardened
warriors'.[55]

Among other traits which, Smyth claims, mark Asser's *Life of
Alfred* as inauthentic, a work of later monastic fantasy, one of the
most damning is its alleged dependence on Odo's *Life of Gerald
of Aurillac*. The resemblances between these two *Lives* are indeed
interesting.[56] In principle, one might have been amongst the other's
models. But to confirm any such hypothesis, the manuscript traditions of both would need to be examined, and alternative possibilities weighed. Smyth fails to address the *Life of Gerald*'s transmission
in a small number of exclusively French manuscripts, and the
absence of any evidence for its ever being known in England. More
seriously, he does not consider the possibility that the two *Lives* are
similar because they draw on similar traditions, come from similar
monastically influenced milieux. Asser's Alfred, like Odo's Gerald
and John's Odo, was a marked man – marked by the divine. These
authors, but also their subjects, were familar with the biblical story
of Job, and with Gregory the Great's reflections on his own physical
sufferings in light of Job's.[57] They were familiar, too, with St Paul's
understanding of divine/paternal discipline as a form of love: 'For
whom the Lord loveth, he chastiseth, and scourgeth every son whom
he receiveth'.[58] The suffering of Asser's Alfred was a heavenly gift
to save him from pride. Like contemporary Carolingians, Asser's

54. For this, and what follows, see A. Smyth, *King Alfred The Great* (Oxford, 1995),
pp.199–216.

55. *Ibid.*, pp.203–4.

56. Smyth, though he never says as much, is not the first to have noticed them:
Patrick Wormald's lecture at the Anglo-American Conference of Historians in 1985
is acknowledged in Nelson, 'Tale of two princes', p.140, n.103; see also Wormald,
'Æthelwold', pp.19–21. Cf. Smyth, *King Alfred*, pp.205–10, 213, 214, 273–4.

57. Gregory, prefatory letter to the *Moralia in Job*, ed., M. Adriaen, CCSL 145
(Turnhout, 1979), p.6, quoted by Scharer, 'Writing', p.188.

58. Heb. 12: 5–6 (echoing Prov. 3: 11–12): cited by Gregory (see previous note),
and repeatedly by Odo in the *Collationes* and in the *Vita Geraldi* (and once by Dhuoda,
Manuel V, 8, p.280). Cf. Nelson, 'Parents', pp.86, 95.

Alfred fitted the model of the servant of God who suffered and therefore triumphed.[59] Why should warriors, battle-hardened no doubt but also pious, not have admired, even identified with, this Alfred? Asser, and, perhaps still more important, Alfred himself in his own writings, depicts a West Saxon court geared to the inculcation of both secular and spiritual wisdom.[60]

In the end, what makes Smyth's reading of Asser and his rejection of the *Life*'s authenticity *en bloc* (he argues that it was a forgery made c.1000 at the monastery of Ramsey) fundamentally unconvincing is his failure to take into account this whole Christian world of sense and meaning, and a context wider than the single other case of Gerald. Those two, but also the other young men whose cases I have considered, are depicted as having difficulty in living out an assigned role, a difficulty which became embodied in anxiety about masculinity. In five out of the six cases there were acute physical symptoms: headaches, stomach pains, skin disease. In two cases, the sword/sword-belt became the symbolic object of rejection. In all cases, sexual activity did. Yet how could a man remain a man – especially, a noble man – without weapons and, above all, marriage? How else could he perform the seminally important role of progenitor, continuator of the *progenies*, the descent-line?

Text and social reality

Until now I have kept open, just, the possibility that all we have confronted so far are exercises in monastically inspired rhetoric. If I were a literary scholar, I might leave it there. But I am a historian, and I want to go on, now, to suggest that these texts give access to real men – I mean, men who once really lived. 'The good historian is like the fairy-tale giant: he knows that wherever he catches the scent of human flesh, there his quarry lies.'[61] In Gerald and Odo, in Alfred, Charles, Rigramnus and Wolo, human scent is unmistakable. I myself would prefer to think in terms of commemoration: of the historian's' craft involving the attempt not only to reconstruct the social memory of past generations but to recover and remember

59. R. Deshman, 'The exalted servant: the ruler-theology of the prayer-book of Charles the Bald', *Viator* 11 (1980), pp.385–417; N. Staubach, *Rex christianus. Hofkultur und Herrschaftspropaganda im Reich Karls des Kahlen*. Teil II: *Die Grundlegung der 'religion royale'* (Cologne-Weimar-Vienna 1993).
60. J.L. Nelson, 'The political ideas of Alfred of Wessex', in A. Duggan, ed., *Kings and Kingship in Medieval Europe* (London, 1993), pp.125–58.
61. M. Bloch, *The Historian's Craft* (English trans., Manchester, 1954), p.26.

something, however little, of individual flesh-and-blood men who lived and suffered. And so, perhaps a shade optimistically, and certainly sailing close to the methodological wind, I take these texts to preserve vestiges of the similar concerns and similar conduct of elite laymen who were contemporaries, formed by similar value-systems, and subject to similar social and mental pressures.

All these young men were born to prospects of secular power. Yet for all, those prospects were uncertain. Indeterminate succession and at least an element of partible inheritance within royal and noble families compounded the uncertainties produced, in any case, by personal accidents of sickness and mortality and sterility, and by conflicts of lordship and loyalty within and between kingdoms. Monastic oblation could create, as well as solve, problems for the oblate himself and for those who offered him. Individuals were trained to subordinate their interests to those of their close kin, to suppress individual desires, to align their wills with lordly interests, and, still more unremittingly, with family strategies as determined by parents or elder brothers or uncles, or even nephews. Elders regularly coerced the young. The transmission or acquisition of political authority was a delicate and dangerous business, a trade-off between such competing pressures. It often involved the use, or the threat, of force, and the requiring, or the withholding, of marriage; it was liable, therefore, to evoke feelings of confusion, guilt and resentment. In the cases of Alfred and Charles, we have enough evidence to know something of the play of family politics. In Gerald's case, we have only the *Life* to go on. Yet we know that Odo wrote for, among others, *potentes* involved in such relationships, who had known Gerald as a neighbour, ally or competitor, and, like him, no doubt, known tension and violent conflict as part of family life. For Gerald, celibacy ensured there would be no conflict between him and any son. But he had nephews, his sister's sons, one of them destined to inherit many of Gerald's lands in the Auvergne.[62] The foundation of the monastery of Aurillac required that nephew's agreement, and was at the expense of part of his inheritance. No wonder there were headaches for Aurillac after the uncle's death. Had Gerald decided to forego marriage and sons as part of a family compact? Had Charles, for a while at least, practised celibacy within marriage for similar reasons? His younger West Saxon contemporary, King Athelstan, seems deliberately to have renounced paternity in the interests of collaterals, in that

---

62. *Vita Geraldi*, The will of Gerald, col. 672, and IV, 11, col. 702.

case, half-brothers.[63] Nepotism, the succession of a chosen nephew, whether a brother's or a sister's son, in aristocratic as well as royal families, may sometimes have been the preferred prophylactic against the fragmentation of family holdings.[64] It was one thing for an elderly man like Charlemagne in 811, with a tribe of children and grandchildren, to consider the possibility of *voluntaria saecularium rerum carentia* (abandoning the world);[65] quite another thing for a man in the prime of youth to contemplate celibacy, still more complex and problematic if such a man, instead of withdrawing to a monastery, remained *in saeculo*, as four of the six young men in these case histories did. The price in psychological terms was high, even if he went on to overcome his scruples about service in the marriage-bed. The familial, specifically paternal, pressures brought to bear, especially if the young man was treated as mad or diabolically possessed (as Charles the Fat and Alfred were), were heavy indeed.

The case studies belong in the wider context of the Church's evolving challenge, and response, to the lay world. The Church could never have imposed its ideology or its material interests on wholly reluctant *potentes laici*. If pollution clung to the twin necessities of power in the *saeculum*, that was not only because churchmen clung grimly to patristic tradition: the powerful laymen also had their use for rules and institutions that would contain excesses both of violence and of progeny, would contain the boys themselves. It seems unsurprising that many fathers (and mothers) imposed the celibate life on their sons without apparent conflict or excessive pain. It is no more surprising that some young laymen, and perhaps more than the scant surviving evidence hints at, should have recoiled from these necessities – but recoiled just as sharply when paternal strategy changed, as inevitably it sometimes did. That has implications for the reliability of the biographical data in Odo's *Life of Gerald*. In the setting I have sketched, Gerald's subjection to his father's changing will, and his later attitudes to sexuality and marriage, are at least plausible. What we might have been tempted to dismiss as Odo's transference of his own experiences should perhaps be understood as a parallel instance of a wider phenomenon: Odo recognized in Gerald a fellow-sufferer. *Omnis filius flagellatur . . .*

63. A point made by Michael Wood in an unpublished paper.
64. The variability of family strategies, and the need for an analysis that includes gender, are incisively discussed by P. Stafford, '*La mutation familiale*: a suitable case for caution', in J. Hill and M. Swann, eds, *The Community, the Family and the Saint. Patterns of Power in Early Medieval Europe* (Leeds, 1998).
65. Einhard, *Vita Karoli* c.33, ed. O. Holder-Egger, MGH *SRG* (Hanover, 1911), p.39.

What the Church offered, notably from the later ninth century onwards, were means of decontamination, an internalizing of discipline which could help individuals cope with the roles and reversals imposed on them, and to make some sense of the suffering they encountered. Thanks in part to the Church's efforts, the tenth-century powerful could feel themselves members of an *ordo*, having a profession of their own.[66] Not only did they clearly regard their power as authorized and purposeful (their charters show that): they glimpsed holiness through their oblated sons, immaculate lambs, at St-Gall, at Cluny.[67] Alongside the *castella*, symbiotically linked, were the *castra Dei*.

For in the ninth and tenth centuries, there was a new preoccupation with monastic purity, and, at the same time, there were new kinds of positive attitude to secular power. Alongside the warlike king (and he did not vanish), a peace-loving and humble king was being constructed: *potentia* remodelled by *religio*. The philosopher-ruler lived again in Francia, and in Wessex. This entailed some rethinking of the way kingship had hitherto been gendered. Alongside, but sometimes obscuring 'masculine' justice were 'feminine' mercy and gentleness; David gave way to Solomon.[68] Being on the receiving end, so to speak, of the Carolingian Renaissance surely affected the inner life of young elite males. It inculcated the values of 'effective administrators (in the manner of the old Colonial District Officers rather than the modern bureaucrat) of their counties or other territories'.[69] If 'talents limited to fighting' were no longer sufficient to secure success at court, new talents, new learning skills were developed. What *pueri* heard and read imposed duties in the world, yet drove some – only a few are documented – to contemplate, then agonize over, abandoning the world. Gerald and some of his generation (I include Alfred advisedly), and also Odo's generation that followed, were impaled on this dilemma. Whether brought up in external schools of monasteries or bishops, or at home by pious mothers and their clerical assistants and confessors, some boys learned to appreciate the ambiguities of the *saeculum*, to

66. G. Duby, *The Three Orders: Feudal Society Imagined*, trans., A. Goldhammer (Chicago, 1980), esp. pp.97–9.

67. D. Iogna-Prat, *Agni Immaculati. Recherches sur les sources hagiographiques relatives à saint Maieul de Cluny* (Paris, 1988); B. Rosenwein, *To be the Neighbour of Saint Peter: the Social Meaning of Cluny's Property* (Ithaca, 1989).

68. Cf. J.L. Nelson, 'Kings with justice, kings without justice: an early medieval paradox', *Settimane* 43 (1997), pp.796–823.

69. D. Bullough, '*Aula renovata*: the court before the Aachen palace', *Proceedings of the British Academy* 71 (1985), pp.267–301.

sense the dangers of power, and to know guilt as well as shame, often to make use of books, to pray privately, to practise self-defence against the Devil's assaults.[70] Arguably, such experiences became more likely for noble boys born and brought up in the decades after c.820 than they had been for earlier generations. Carolingian reform thus impacted on masculinity. Gerald, Odo, Alfred, Charles III had inner lives that were complicated; they suffered much, as did their contemporaries Rigramnus and Wolo. While they lived they surely offered food for thought to those who knew them and watched them in action. In the context of this volume, they inspire some concluding reflections. However scarce and intractable early medieval evidence may be, however indispensable literary criticism of texts, the recovering of individual lives and experiences through and beyond the texts must remain the historian's quest. If lay masculinity was not homogenous in the Carolingian period, this resulted from continual contact and interaction between monastic and secular worlds. The 'hairy nobleman' depicted in the Sacramentary of Gellone, c.800, whom Michael Wallace-Hadrill (with a hint of irony) found 'repulsively realistic',[71] may not have seemed repulsive to his peers, or to his mother or his wife, and in any event ought not to signify repulsiveness as the paradigm of early medieval elite manhood. The notion of warrior and wimp as mutually exclusive categories may be as positively unhelpful for understanding ninth-century masculinity as I think it is for the late twentieth century, for then, as now, men were offered competing, even conflicting, models of manliness, and learned somehow to live with dissonance.

---

70. Manuscript evidence suggests that private prayer and private penance were becoming increasingly widely used by and for elite laymen in the course of the ninth and tenth centuries: see S.M. Hamilton, 'The Practice of Penance c.900–c.1050', unpublished Ph.D. thesis (University of London, 1997), esp. chs. 7 and 9.

71. Wallace-Hadrill, *The Frankish Church*, p.178.

CHAPTER NINE

Men and Sex in Tenth-century Italy

R. BALZARETTI

It is popularly believed that the Middle Ages was a time of 'sexual repression'. Consider the following sentence from George Rattray Taylor's pioneering study *Sex in History*, published in 1953:

> The Church never succeeded in obtaining universal acceptance of its sexual regulations, but in time it became able to enforce sexual abstinence on a scale sufficient to produce a rich crop of mental disease. It is hardly too much to say that mediaeval Europe came to resemble a vast insane asylum.[1]

This could only have been written in the wake of the late nine-teenth-century discovery of the science of sex, sexology, and the researches of its most famous exponent, Freud.[2] Since that time the enormous outpouring of psychological and medical research into sexual behaviour has produced results which, on first reading, present historians with serious methodological problems. Put simply, debates have raged between 'essentialists', who believe in the genetic innateness of sexual identity and 'constructionists', who argue that people choose their sexual behaviours depending on the contexts in which they find themselves. Essentialism forbids historians to look for sexual variations between cultures of otherwise great dis-similarity, as all humans are assumed to approach sex and sexuality in preconditioned ways. In this vision a homosexual is always a homosexual, whether in second-century Rome, ninth-century Frankia or twentieth-century London. Conversely, constructionism allows so many variations that the object of study is liable to disappear.

---

1. G. Rattray Taylor, *Sex in History* (London, 1953), p.19. My thanks go to Dawn Hadley, Trish Skinner and my final year 'Body and Sexuality' students for helpful comments on this chapter.
2. G. Hekma, 'A history of sexology: social and historical aspects of sexuality', in J. Bremmer, ed., *From Sappho to De Sade. Moments in the History of Sexuality* (London, 1989), pp.173–193.

Sexual identities are consciously changeable: one can begin life homosexual and choose to end up heterosexual.[3] The area was greatly complicated by the work of Foucault, his followers and critics, who argued that linguistic categories common in the west such as sexuality, homosexuality and heterosexuality are no more than products of the modern western desire to put the experience of sex into words: other societies may have imagined matters very differently. The more recent emergence of gender studies has further complicated research into human sexual behaviour. Do apparently fundamental biological distinctions between men and women determine distinctive male and female behaviours? Or are masculinity and femininity also primarily constructed categories? It is this contentious context which provides the starting point for my research into the attitudes of tenth-century men towards sex.

The recent outpouring of research into sexuality has not been widely taken up by serious historians of the Middle Ages. There is only one reference to sexuality in all 1,082 pages of the otherwise comprehensive *New Cambridge Medieval History* covering the eighth and ninth centuries.[4] It is not shocking therefore to learn that male sexuality is completely foreign territory to historians of early medieval Italy. This lack of research is not due to an absence of evidence of sexual activity and opinions about it, although such material is comparatively rare. Nor is it the case that an interest in sex is a twentieth-century habit unknown to early medieval people. Rather it stems from the conventions of modern historical writing, embodied in its desire to be properly academic, and its understanding that where there is sex there are always women and never men. In particular, it is the relationship between sexuality and masculinity which has been least researched and it is to this debate that this chapter contributes.

The main evidence for the argument advanced in this chapter is provided by a few didactic texts, both historical and theological, written by three bishops in the course of the tenth century. This is, admittedly, a limited sample on which to base a discussion of sexuality in a complex society, and in these circumstances it is important to be explicit about my methodology. I shall be taking a sequence

---

3. For reasons of space the characterization is crude. For further discussion see R. Balzaretti, 'Michel Foucault, homosexuality and the Middle Ages', *Renaissance and Modern Studies* 37 (1994), pp.1–12 and D.F. Greenberg, *The Construction of Homosexuality* (Chicago, 1988), pp.482–99.

4. *New Cambridge Medieval History*, vol. II, ed. R. McKitterick (Cambridge, 1995), at p.667.

of snapshots primarily from Ratherius of Verona's *Praeloquia* and numerous other polemical works directed at the Veronese clergy, Atto of Vercelli's *Capitulare* and *Polypticon* and Liutprand of Cremona's *Historia Ottonis*. These texts need to be read in comparison with those of earlier periods (see chapters 7 and 8, above), to assess from whom our authors may have borrowed ideas, and later periods (chapter 10, below), to understand how influential these texts were. Once this is done, it becomes clear that in northern Italy the political, social and cultural ramifications of sex were discussed at length in the tenth century; but only by a tiny number of clergy. Perhaps their most interesting conclusion was that irregular sexual union, involving men as well as women, should be blamed for political corruption and crisis. Or, put in another way, the violence of the times was just reward for an improperly sexual masculinity.

The evidence found in all these texts is by no means as one-sided as a superficial reading of modern accounts might indicate. When Ratherius, Atto and Liutprand became bishops of important north Italian sees they envisaged their pastoral role as encompassing the production of written commentary on the moral state of contemporary society. Such commentaries were pointless unless clearly recognizable by the men who were the intended readers of, and listeners to, the tirades. If, as seems to have been the case, it was men's sexual behaviour which provoked their most profound criticisms, it is important to realize that the interpretation of these texts which currently dominates focuses on what they have to say about women. Historians such as Jon Sutherland, Suzanne Wemple and Philippe Buc have taken the time to uncover misogynistic representations of women's sexuality in these authors, mostly Liutprand. However, they have failed to appreciate that these distasteful views are voiced precisely because of unease with male promiscuity and a growing concern with the need for clerical celibacy. The emphasis on male sexuality was expounded in an overtly political context: sexual behaviour was adduced and judged as part of an examination of a person's public persona, and as a statement of his suitability for office-holding, both clerical and lay. It may surprise some to find out that this episcopal unease does not seem to have met with agreement in all quarters, especially not among the north Italian clergy.

The disturbed bishop: Ratherius of Verona

The voluminous output of Ratherius of Verona (c.888–974), the most prolific author of his day, provides an absorbing beginning to a discussion of men's sexuality in this period.[5] Ratherius is particularly interesting to read as he had a consuming interest in himself; although it often seems like extreme arrogance to us, as we try to cope with his overcomplex prose, it was a stance well received by educated contemporaries north of the Alps. Ratherius was a monk from Lobbes in Lotharingia who became bishop in Liège, and later Verona. He had a voracious mind and wrote on every subject imaginable at that time. Once he arrived in Italy his literary output increased, mostly as a result of his intense desire, as a foreigner, to resist the rapid social changes he observed there. While the Po plain had been a land of cities for many centuries, in the course of the tenth century these cities began to diverge more than ever from the social control of the old-established aristocratic elites. Cinzio Violante, in a classic study published in 1953, analysed Milan, the most dynamic of all these cities. He found that in the course of the later ninth and early tenth centuries 'new men' appeared with specialized occupations as notaries, judges, merchants, artisans, who developed close links with local churches and sometimes entered the religious life, while remaining married to their wives.[6] Similar patterns can be seen in cities such as Pavia, Bergamo, Brescia, Cremona and Verona, and it was in precisely this area that justifications for clerical marriage continued to be voiced until well into the eleventh century. The need for clerical celibacy was at the heart of the furious Patarine debates and inspired Peter Damian (b. 1007) in his fight to end moral corruption within the Milanese Church. The link was hardly coincidental and had to be broken.

Like Peter Damian, Ratherius was essentially a monastic writer. His many works show him to have been fondest of Augustine of Hippo, Benedict of Nursia and Gregory the Great, themselves instrumental in fostering the celibate monastic life. He took a predictably dim view of sex and indeed the justification of much of his huge output is his personal shock at the low moral state of the Italian bishops and their clergy. Throughout the period (935–968) of his literary output Ratherius' views on sex and the clergy appear to have developed hardly at all. In Book 2 of his *Praeloquia*, his earliest work outlining the moral duties of all Christians, written when imprisoned in Como and Pavia by King Hugh of Provence, he expounds the classic Augustinian position that sex should be contained within marriage solely for the purposes of procreation or the avoidance of fornication, citing the latter's *De Bono Conjugiali*

---

5. P.L. Reid, *The Complete Works of Ratherius of Verona* (Michigan, 1991).
6. C. Violante, *La Società milanese nell'età precommunale* (Bari, 1953).

and St Paul. Of these options, marriage for procreation is a positive good whereas marriage to avoid promiscuous or irregular sexual union is allowable, but obviously not faultless. On the latter he is very clear:

> that is, to prevent a man who cannot control his lust from sinning through adultery or any forbidden desires or – what is incomparably worse – from being driven to unnatural acts (*contra naturam*) in any way; for it is on account of these that 'it is better to marry than to burn' – that is, to be consumed up to the point of release (*usque ad eliquationem*) or unlawful (*illicitum*) or unclean ejaculation (*immundissmum fluxum*) and not to be restrained by any love of God or fear of hell.[7]

Ratherius reveals in this passage the classic monastic distaste for bodily fluids, in this instance semen, which he perceived as dirty (see above, chapter 7). All men, not just monks, are supposed to be able to control these bodily urges by sheer force of mind, subjecting their flesh to the soul, and the soul to God. In this they contrast with soft, passive, irrational women who will inevitably find such control much more difficult. Nevertheless, women must still aim to overcome 'the mad passions of vice and pleasure' (*insanos vitiorum voluptatumque*).[8] As important as this typically (deliberately?) simplistic gender divide, is the explicit link between permitted behaviour and forbidden deviance. Ratherius does not explain what he means by *contra naturam*, but in most authors of this period it means sexual acts between men, usually anal penetration. Note that in Ratherius' characterization these acts are open to all men and that, therefore, this view represents something rather different from modern notions of 'innate homosexuality', based largely on overriding same-sex desire.[9] Nevertheless, this is a very interesting configuration because men are defined sexually by their relations with both women and other men, pre-empting similar constructions of masculinity in the west at a later date.[10] Ratherius, like Augustine, regards male responsibility in sexual matters as important:

> But whatever is forbidden to women is clearly forbidden to men also, as reason shows, as far as relates to their contract: and it is quite abhorrent if what the stronger sex demands of the weaker, it does not, when overcome and enslaved by lust, allow to the weaker.[11]

7. Part II, 5 (Reid, *Ratherius of Verona*, pp.65–66).   8. Part II, 3 (*ibid.*, p.64).

9. J. Boswell, *The Marriage of Likeness. Same-Sex Unions in Pre-Modern Europe* (London, 1995), pp.xix–xxx.

10. Especially 'sex-role' theories outlined by R.W. Connell, *Masculinities* (Cambridge, 1995), pp.21–6.

11. Part II, 7 (Reid, *Ratherius of Verona*, p.69).

These remarks were directed at the lay population only, and Ratherius offers no real surprises. Augustine's vision of marital sexual relations comes through intact.

Ratherius reserves his main criticisms for the male clergy, particularly as he becomes acquainted with his own Veronese clergy in the 950s and 960s. It soon becomes clear that he is quite disturbed by what he has found. Clerical marriage and various other forms of union are the norm and there is resistance to any observance of canon law on these questions. His opinions are clearest in a text known as 'On the Contempt of the Canons' (*De Contemptu Canonum*), written in November 963 and addressed to Bishop Hubert of Parma. In this work he castigates clerical abuses of many sorts but, as ever, reserves his greatest vitriol for sexual sins. In a passage on corrupt priests (which takes its lead from Gregory's *Pastoral Care* and clearly owes much to other Late Antique monastic authors such as John Cassian) he emphasizes that even thinking about sex is wrong for male clerics:

> if he is so crushed by wantonness (*lascivia*) of the genitals that, even though he does not practise it in action, yet he never abandons it in his thoughts and is never at rest, in the manner of one with swollen testicles (*ponderosus*): how does this man presume to offer his bread to the Lord, who daily hears that he is prohibited by Him to whom it ought to be offered?[12]

Such a man is guilty of two linked grave sins: pride (*superbia*) by opposing God and lust (*luxuria*) by refusing God's commandments.[13] He believes that it is the pleasure of sex which explains why even those who ought to know better disobey God, something which even he in his old age can understand. Italian clerics are more guilty than others because they use aphrodisiacs (*pigmenta*) and wine to enhance their sexual abilities. He even cites the case of a cleric who boasted that he had masturbated to orgasm having just recited the morning office:

> I learned recently that a certain person (he told it to others with his own lips – for shame) in almost the very hour in which he most wretchedly sung the offices . . . was so burned up with this deadly fire that to his own damnation in lust and wantonness he caused 'the pleasure that scratches the itch within' to be stimulated to the point of obscene discharge (*vice reciproca voluptatem obsceni fluxus ad ungnem*).[14]

12. Chapter 1, 19 (*ibid.*, p.369).   13. Chapter 1, 21 (*ibid.*, p.371).
14. Chapter 2, 3 (*ibid.*, p.376).

Here, although he has to explain the act longwindedly because he seems unable to use the Latin word for masturbation (*masturbor*), he is still extremely provocative for a bishop in both the explicitness of his language and the subjects he is prepared to write about (and, paradoxically, to think about himself). The exaggerated language surely reveals the deep fears he himself has about all these matters.

From the *Praeloquia* and *De Contemptu Canonum* it is quite clear that Ratherius held the view, earlier developed at length by Augustine, that physical sexual urges were very difficult to resist mentally and therefore needed to be confined by legal rules: continent marriage for lay people and celibate confinement for clerics. He gives the impression, surely intended, that the Italian clergy of his day were constantly thinking about sex, whether with women, with themselves or with other men. Further details come to light from his letters to his own clergy on these subjects, which I turn to next.

Ratherius was worried about the pollution of religious ritual by clerical marriage. This is clear from chapter five of the *Synodica* (Lent 966): 'But where are those who daily celebrate the Mass, daily make the Pasch – that is eat the flesh of the Lamb and drink his blood – and yet frequently beget sons and daughters by adulterous intercourse (not to mention the rest) . . .'.[15] In chapter six he quotes the *Admonitio Synodialis*: 'First we urge that your life and habits be beyond reproach, that your cell be close to the church, and that you keep no women in it.'[16] In chapter eleven he worries about incest.[17] In the *Itinerarium* (December 966) he compares canonical disobedience with physical sickness (chapter three) and in chapter five accuses his clergy of being adulterers and bigamists: 'If I were to expel from the clergy those with many wives, whom would I leave in the church except boys? If I were to cast out the bastards, whom of these boys would I permit in the choir?'[18] In chapter fifteen he is back with the law: 'For it is clear that every illegal coition is either fornication or adultery. No law allows marriage to ministers of the altar.'[19] It clear from chapter one of this text that Ratherius had encountered arguments in favour of chaste clerical marriage. Not all the clergy shared his extreme approach.

The ideas of Ratherius' opponents can perhaps be grasped by reading carefully between and beyond the lines of his writings. Apparently, they married and wished to stay married. Did all these

15. *Ibid.*, p.447.   16. *Ibid.*, p.448.   17. *Ibid.*, p.450.
18. *Ibid.*, pp.470, 472.   19. *Ibid.*, p.480.

clerics marry deliberately in defiance of the canonical laws of the Church? This is certainly possible, although it may have been the result of the simple ignorance of church law, with which Ratherius liked to characterize them. Yet, as Heinrich Fichtenau has argued, it is much more likely that clerics married in order to keep church property from being exclusively under the control of lay families.[20] Married clerics were not simply mimicking lay customs but rather trying to preserve landed property, the lifeblood of the Church, which they understood to be in the direct ownership of God and the saints, not themselves. Only if clerics had children could they transmit their property to sons and daughters who were themselves committed to continuing Church traditions. For ordinary priests this must have seemed the common-sense option in a violent world.

Ratherius encountered other, more subtle, objections. In his *Discordia* (a letter written to Otto I's Italian chancellor Ambrose in April 968) he hints that one of the reasons why so many clerics had sexual relationships with women was to avoid being accused of similar relationships with men:

> They openly and habitually keep women, which was forbidden in the Nicene Synod, and they hold so lightly the respect of God and man, and even belittle the very fear of hell, that they think that it not only *may* but even *must* mean that anyone who refuses to keep a woman must be engaging in that foulest sin which the apostle mentions in his Epistle to the Romans.' (my italics)[21]

In this sentence Ratherius clearly has sins *contra naturam* in mind once more. He uses a Latinized Greek word for these men, *arsenoquiter*, who are compared directly with adulterers (and vice versa). Men who had sex with men clearly existed, both real and imagined, and constituted the group who least conformed to the sexual code expounded by Ratherius. The most interesting aspect of this passage is the suggestion, popular with many modern western heterosexual men, that any man who is not in a sexual relationship with a woman is somehow not a proper man and therefore likely to be homosexual.[22] This implies a type of male sexual behaviour which, ironically, is not masculine because it does not conform to societal expectations of masculine behaviour. This notion may

20. H. Fichtenau, *Living in the Tenth Century* (Chicago, 1991; original German 1984), p.115.

21. Chapter 1 (Reid, *Ratherius of Verona*, p.492).

22. A. Hunter, 'Same door, different closet: a heterosexual sissy's coming-out party', in S. Wilkinson and S. Kitzinger, eds, *Heterosexuality*, (London, 1993), pp.152–5.

well have existed amongst the north Italian laity, from whom all clergy were necessarily drawn. It is a passage which allows us to glimpse the sexual fears of the Veronese clergy and the part these may have played in the construction of their masculine identities.

The worried bishop: Atto of Vercelli

According to the contemporary chronicler Andrew of Bergamo, when Berengar of Friuli attacked Bergamo in 876 the men of the district fled to the city or the mountains with their wives and concubines (*cum uxuribus et paramentum*).[23] Andrew does not comment unfavourably on this, although he was a priest in the city. Indeed, his offhand remark suggests that by no means all sexual relationships were regulated by marriage alone by this date. The desirability of marriage was itself still in dispute in some circles. In Ravenna, at the other end of the Po valley, Agnellus, another priest, writing his history of the archbishops of Ravenna in the 840s, felt moved, in the course of a moralistic reworking of Paul the Deacon's tale of Queen Rosamond who murdered her husband Alboin in 572, to explain that wives were the ruin of all men, particularly married clerics, who made up the bulk of his audience. He did so in language which suggests that he was wary of marriage for the laity also.[24] Two such fleeting glimpses of priestly opinions on marriage and concubinage introduce an issue which was to preoccupy Atto, bishop of Vercelli, until his death in 960: what type of marriage was best suited to his own, apparently unstable, society?

Initially Atto wrote in the Carolingian tradition. He used the biblical commentaries of the controversial Spaniard Claudius, bishop at nearby Turin (died c.840), and repeated Claudius' views on clerical marriage in instructions to priests in his own diocese. After he became bishop in 924 (or 925) he wrote several tracts criticizing his contemporaries, notably *De pressuris ecclesiasticis* in the 940s and the *Polypticon* in the 950s. Like Ratherius, Atto's direct influence over his audience was small, if the few manuscripts which survive of these works is anything to go by.[25] His first works, traditional biblical commentaries in five epistles, represent the wholesale adoption of conventional Frankish ideas on marriage and sex. Married clergy

---

23. *Historia* chapter 20, MGH, *Scriptores Rerum Langobardicarum et Italicarum saec. vi–ix*, ed. G. Waitz (Berlin, 1878).

24. J. Pizarro, *Writing Ravenna. The Liber Pontificalis of Agnellus of Ravenna* (Michigan, 1995), pp.125–6, 137–40.

25. S. Wemple, *Atto of Vercelli* (Rome, 1979), pp.185–90.

had to renounce their wives and, if they refused, should be spurned by their fellow priests and, in extreme cases, excommunicated. In common with Ratherius, Atto uses inflammatory words to describe the women with whom these clerics live so publicly. They were nothing less than whores. While, at a pinch, a priest might live with his nearest female relative, the clear implication is that these men should live in all-male celibate communities.

As typical examples of the exegetical method of dealing with male sexual behaviour Atto's epistles are worth more detailed examination. An example of this literary technique is his commentary on St Paul's famous passage about sexual relations 'against nature'.[26] His arguments about natural and unnatural sexual union were borrowed directly from Claudius of Turin, who relied in turn on John Chrysostom. Claudius, although regarded as a heretic by the Carolingian theologians Dungal and Jonas of Orleans, was still highly valued for his biblical commentaries and Atto's exegetical approach was very similar to his. He was discussing Paul's famous Epistle to the Romans 1: 26–27 as transmitted by Jerome's Vulgate. Atto's comments begin with verse 26: 'For this cause God gave them up unto vile passions (*in passiones ignominiae*): for their women changed the natural use into that which is against nature (*contra naturam*).' Atto wrote:

> Here the Apostle avoided the obscene thing by periphrasis (i.e. circumlocution). But as is known, this place has been explained by various teachers. However, let it be understood in the manner demonstrated by the Apostle, when he added: 'And likewise also the men, leaving the natural use of the woman, burned in their lust one toward another, men with men working unseemliness, and receiving in themselves that recompense of their error which was due.'

Atto now proceeds to a longer exegesis:

> For when he said *similarly*, he evidently showed that just as men might work (*operare*) obscenely with men, so women might seize women with obscene desire. Having noted that which is not said, they changed from the conjugal use, which is natural; for whosoever mixes his member with those members which God created for procreating offspring, even if these be the members of a prostitute, the use is natural, however illicit the sexual act is; whoever joins with those members which God did not create for procreating children, even if these are the wife's members, this is not natural use. And so the Apostle said . . . [he repeats Romans 1: 27 at this point] . . . They burned, he said, that is they were alight with the ardour of incredible lust.

26. *Epistola Ad Rom.* 141D–142A, *PL* 134.

Later in this passage Atto, in time-honoured fashion, explicitly links the sexual sin *contra naturam* with the inhabitants of Sodom and Gomorrah.

The first thing to notice is Atto's refusal to name the forbidden acts clearly. His expansion of Paul is so euphemistic that it is not immediately obvious that he is referring to anal sex, and possibly oral sex. The universality of Atto's interpretation is, by contrast, very clear. Anyone, male or female, married or not, can engage in sins against nature in what we should term both heterosexual and homosexual contexts.

In contrast to Ratherius, Atto's views on clerical celibacy and concubinage developed over the next twenty years, eventually coming close to the severe approach of some eleventh-century reformers. Whilst he did not accuse errant clerics of heresy, as Peter Damian was to do, he developed quite a distinctive line in his *Capitulare*. Injunctions against concubinage were stronger, and guilty clerics were threatened with excommunication, a punishment also destined for those who shielded them. In Atto's overall moral scheme marriage for the laity was just about acceptable for the purposes of reproduction but not lust.[27] He did not adopt the softer Augustinian line that mutual fidelity, companionship and love of children were the positive benefits of marriage, preferring to praise virginity and continence for all. For clerics it was far better to be without a wife (*sine uxore*) as the married were inevitably too involved in worldly matters to serve God.

Putting the worries of Atto alongside the disquiet of Ratherius we find that the sexual behaviour of men, both ecclesiastical and lay, is an important theme in their work. Why was this? Distaste for sex, derived from Apostolic and monastic teaching, was a contributory factor. Both bishops feared for the salvation of mankind if God's laws were being broken. Particularly awful was clerical resistance to the laws of the Church, especially priests' refusal to give up marriage. While this was in part genuine pastoral concern, it may well be that there was more to it. Episcopal interest in ecclesiastical property should not be ruled out. In the wake of continuing political instability much Church land was undoubtedly under the control of lay people, especially those families who had sons or daughters in the Church. Charter collections from Milan, Bergamo, Verona and elsewhere reveal quite clearly the complexity of ownership at this time. How were the bishops to get this property back? Kings

---

27. *Epistola Ad. Cor.* 350A, *PL* 134.

and their agents were wrapped up in continual political infighting and were not really in a position to help. Even Otto I could not help Ratherius to resist successfully the interests of the powerful, married, cathedral clergy. So both Atto and Ratherius developed a different tactic: they tried to shame these men with accusations of sexual promiscuity and deviance and to terrify them with promises of eternal damnation. Their linking of men, sex, property and politics was quite deliberate. This was an attitude which found its most interesting advocate in Liutprand of Cremona, the principal historian of tenth-century Italy.

The gossiping bishop: Liutprand of Cremona

It is a nice irony that the best evidence for male sexual behaviour in this period comes from the historical and not the exegetical writings of clerics. By far the most explicit of these is Liutprand of Cremona, the tenth-century writer above all others who uses sexual imagery to serious historical purposes. He does not express distaste for sex quite as Ratherius does, probably because he was not a monastic writer. This in part explains why sex could fill the pages of his historical works. Unlike Ratherius and Atto, he clearly regarded sexual behaviour as a necessary part of being human, more or less from an Augustinian perspective. He understood that lust motivated people and that an analysis of their lust could be used to explain their political actions, however extreme. As one of the great historical writers of the medieval period his choice of subject matter and how he wrote about it was part of his reaction to history as a genre. He knew well that people love to read about the sexual doings of others as much as they would be horrified to read about their own. He could not know that the more prudish of his twentieth-century male readers would have found his interest in sex surprising, even shocking, while revelling in his portraits of lewd women, thirsting for power.

Liutprand's *Liber de rebus gestis Ottonis* (Book of the deeds of Otto, often known as *Historia Ottonis*, The History of Otto's Reign) is a short text written in a simple style in 964–5 at the point when Liutprand became bishop of Cremona.[28] It was intended to justify

28. *Liutprandi Opera*, ed. J. Becker, *MGH, Scriptores Rerum Germanicarum* (Hannover, 1915). English translation by F.A. Wright, *The Works of Liutprand of Cremona* (London, 1930), reprd. with an introduction by J.J. Norwich as *The Embassy to Constantinople and Other Writings* (London, 1993).

Otto I's political claims over the pope, in the person of John XII; an analysis of this work demonstrates rather well the simplistic way in which commentators have taken it too much at face value. Jon Sutherland in his biography of the bishop argued that: '. . . it showed his devotion to actions (or to pragmatic issues) with little heed to philosophical problems lying behind them'.[29] This is unfair. Given the context surrounding its production, Liutprand had little choice but to go over in some detail the political events surrounding the attempted deposition of Pope John, who was just eighteen when he became pope in December 955. If, in comparison with other writers, Liutprand grossly exaggerated Otto's probity and John's wickedness, this was surely with philosophical intent: the good should triumph over the wicked.

Let us observe how Liutprand proceeds to destroy the pope's political and religious reputation with a series of accusations about his sexual behaviour. He employs tactics similar to those used in *Antapodosis* (The Book of Revenge) with regard to the women of the Italian Carolingian line; the same purpose is served by a remarkable elision of political crisis and corrupt sexual morality, which harks back to Louis the Pious and Judith, and Lothar and Theutberga.

The first instance of John's sexual misbehaviour (chapter four) is openly acknowledged by Liutprand to be gossip from the mouths of the Roman populace, juicy and slanderous hearsay evidence of the most racy sort. According to Liutprand John had sex with the widow of his own vassal Rainerius '. . . a woman with whom John has been so blindly in love (*quam caeco captus igne*) that he has made her governor (*praefectam*: note the female form of the word) of so many cities and given to her the golden crosses and cups that are the sacred possessions of St Peter himself'. This woman was followed by Stephana, 'his father's mistress who recently conceived a child by him and died of an effusion of blood'. As a result, John turned the Lateran into a brothel:

'Witness again the absence of all women (*mulierum*) here save Romans: they fear to come and pray at the thresholds of the holy apostles, for they have heard how John a little time ago took women pilgrims by force to his bed, wives, widows and virgins alike (*coniugatas, viduas, virgines, vi oppressisse*).' 'Witness the women he keeps, some of them fine ladies who, as the poet says, are as thin as reeds by dieting, others everyday buxom wenches (*Testes sunt non solum iuncearum*

29. J. Sutherland, *Liudprand of Cremona: Bishop, Diplomat, Historian* (Spoleto, 1988), p.111.

curatura, sed et cotidianarum mulieres formarum). It is all the same to
him whether they walk the pavement or ride in a carriage and pair.

John's personal moral decay is directly linked with his failure to
maintain church buildings (clearly symbolic as well as actual) and
with political deceit (John was negotiating with Adalbert, marquis
of Tuscany, having earlier come to an agreement with Otto not to
do so).

With few words Liutprand links sex with political power, reproduction, death and violence. He does not do this unwittingly.
If again we read between the lines, the specific accusations made
here allow us to determine quite easily what moral code Liutprand
thought upright men should espouse. Of course we have to be careful. We are dealing with the pope (rather than the papal office)
and not with lay society, and we know that Liutprand was deliberately exaggerating. He has two main accusations: John has multiple
sexual partners drawn from all social ranks, not just the wealthy
(repeated in chapter nineteen); and he has partners of precisely
those men to whom John should have been loyal (his vassal, his
father). These were two unpardonable violations of the sanctity of
the *familia*, the world of those close to you. By implication then,
an upright man should be sexually loyal to one partner, his legitimate wife. As we shall see, Liutprand is very keen on the constancy
of marriage.

Liutprand has several sub-themes, of which the most important
is age. In chapter fifteen John is accused of providing a poor example to the young ('But how many chaste youths by his example
have become unchaste?'). Yet in chapters five and six he implies
strongly that sexual transgression by young men was expected when
Otto remarks that, 'he is only a boy, and will soon alter if good men
set him an example' and 'that it was not surprising if in the heat of
youth he had hitherto indulged in childish follies; but now the time
had come when he would fain live in a different fashion'. Liutprand
allows these remarks even though John was in orders before he
became pope. This expectation of sexual activity on the part of
young men did not excuse it. If we forget for a moment that John
was the pope we have a young unmarried man involved with married, probably older, women, which must still have seemed an
inversion of the natural order. It recalls a chapter of the Lombard
laws (King Liutprand's edict 129, dated 733) which suggests the
sexual vulnerability of young males (*puerolus parvolus*) to adult
women (*mulieres*) who might seduce (*copolabant*) them into marriage.

From this law it is clear that women's sexuality, when it is not properly channelled towards reproduction, is feared. One might add that for Bishop Liutprand male sexuality posed exactly the same problem, because it *was* the same problem.

It was up to fathers to keep control of their children, male and female. Pope John no longer had a father because Alberic, his natural father, died in 954. As pope he did not even have a spiritual father who could correct him. Liutprand saw this gap and filled it with Otto. The emphasis on John's sexual misconduct may have had the fairly subtle literary purpose of allowing Otto to be portrayed as John's father figure. In chapter five Otto says:

> Then let us address some words of fatherly admonition to the lord pope. His sense of shame, if not his own wishes, will soon effect a change in him for the better. Perchance if he is forced into good ways, he will be ashamed to get out of them again.

Aged forty-three when John became pope at eighteen, Otto was in fact old enough to be John's father. John's imaginary filial disobedience should have shamed him, an attitude which is shot through with the morality of Ratherius and Atto, though it is open to question whether the young man saw things in the same light. Anyway he soon died, predictably enough when having sex (chapter twenty), which satisfied Liutprand's moral sense from all points of view.

Liutprand's polemical exposition of Otto's activities in Italy reveals a great deal about contemporary attitudes to male sexual reputation and is far from being the superficial, gossipy nonsense most historians believe it to be. In it Liutprand propounds the view that the workings of human history, in this instance contemporary history, conditioned by sin, were best understood through analyses of the sexual activities which first gave rise to that sin. Adam and Eve were never far from the minds of tenth-century writers. That one's enemies behaved badly in sexual matters and one's friends did not, simply proved the influence of the Devil on the world. Once this is clear, Liutprand's emphasis on sexual politics can no longer be regarded as aberrant.

Conclusions

Masculinity, like sexuality, was a concept foreign to the Latin language in which all three of our authors wrote and probably thought. We must not expect, therefore, to find fully formed discussions of either notion in these or any other Latin text. However, in my view, Ratherius, Atto and Liutprand had formulated some ideas which we can best approach via our own words 'masculine' and 'sexual'. Their views on sex are easier to grasp because of the pervasiveness of the Christian tradition in western thinking. They had worked out a moral stance in which the sexual behaviour of men, both clerical and lay, was quite as important as that of women for the maintenance of right order in the world and a reasonable chance of eternal salvation. This moral scheme was built upon monogamous heterosexual marriage for everyone except the clergy. In their characterization of marriage, Ratherius, Atto and Liutprand thus approach the hegemonic, male-dominated heterosexuality of more modern times in which all men are presumed to want monogamous sexual relationships with women. Men who do not are not properly masculine. However, their conceptualizations allowed for one, perhaps surprising, transgression: all men could be tempted by sex with other men and had to guard against it. Let us recall here the defence of Ratherius' clergy: they wanted to be married to *avoid* being accused of sex with men. These clerics desired to be part of 'compulsory heterosexuality', to be part of the masculine world of real men from which their celibate selves would be excluded. Whether this stance on sexuality, worked out in the course of debates on clerical marriage, constitutes a distinctive concept of masculinity is problematic. I feel that in one respect it does. Fluid sexual desires had to be curbed by all men and women, clerical, monastic or lay. What distinguished men from women, in the eyes of these three bishops, was that they thought them to have a more realistic chance of controlling their desires and behaving responsibly in sexual relationships than the opposite sex. Sexual self-control, marital fidelity and procreative responsibility were more likely to be achieved by men because men's physicality did not predominate over their mental faculties to the extent that women's did. This gender-specific sexual existence was replicated at the level of the body politic: political instability, including dissent within the Church, was directly related to a lack of sexual control on the part of some men. Whether it was adultery, sex *contra naturam* or clerical marriage did not in the end matter.

For these reasons the sexual behaviour of men was easily of as much interest to those male ecclesiastics who wrote about Italian society in the tenth century as it had been in Frankish contexts in the ninth and was to be everywhere in the eleventh. That they preferred to explain the sexual behaviour of men obliquely with stories whose main subjects were women merely places them within a tradition of clerical writing in Italy which, perhaps more than elsewhere, looked to marriage as the only context for sex. Marriage had always been a surprisingly controversial arrangement. If, in the cases examined here, clerical authors argued that the clergy should not marry and that marriage, although important for lay people who could not be celibate, was inferior to virginity and continence, historians have to face the problem that the surviving sources most probably do not represent the full range of contemporary views on this question. We have to imagine that dissenting views were held by those bishops, clergy and monks who were not authors and that some of these, since they practised it in their own lives, must have argued in favour of clerical marriage. It was against this context that the fierce views of the eleventh-century reformers were directed. As all authors envisaged sex with reference to marriage in some form or other we have had to do the same. However, we must not distort our understanding of tenth-century marriage and sex by concentrating disproportionately on what male clerical authors had to say about women and sex. While there is no doubt that they railed against women on many occasions, neither is there doubt that shrewd women could indeed, as Liutprand showed, exploit adulterous relationships because men were sexual beings too, however much the bishops tried to deny it.

Angels Incarnate: Clergy and Masculinity from Gregorian Reform to Reformation[1]

R.N. SWANSON

The historiography of medieval gender rarely praises the Church. An oppressive patriarchy and virulent misogyny are easily blamed on Christianity and a male priesthood. The charges are not entirely untrue, but they may oversimplify: the real situation was perhaps more complicated, as appears when considering the clergy in the period between the Gregorian reform and the start of the Reformation. Those clerics were certainly 'male', but were they 'men'? The medieval clergy challenge many assumptions about gendered identities, especially the blunt equation of body and gender. If masculinity is defined by the threefold activities of 'impregnating women, protecting dependents, and serving as provider to one's family',[2] then the medieval clergy as unworldy celibates were not meant to be masculine. What 'gender' did they then have? The question immediately challenges historians. The norm is to refer to two genders – or to none. Men and women present an obvious polarity whose opposition allows an immediate and automatic allocation to one or the other. Yet the temptation to see 'sex' and 'gender' as equivalent, and to assume that where there are only two sexes there can only be two genders, imposes a false simplicity on the issues.

1. Much of this discussion is necessarily speculative. The attempt to develop a coherent argument within a limited space omits numerous nuances and qualifications, ignoring the many local and chronological evolutions in medieval western Christianity which affect the overall picture. The reactions and relationships discussed here are somewhat idealized and homogenized; reality would vary considerably, with the relative awareness of the prescriptions by the various parties, and with the value those parties attached to individual elements of the equations in their own particular circumstances.

2. V.L. Bullough, 'On being a male in the middle ages', in C.A. Lees, ed., *Medieval Masculinities: Regarding Men in the Middle Ages* (Minneapolis, 1994), p.34.

Recent discussion of the existence of 'third sexes' or 'third genders' can be extended back in time to the Middle Ages, and to the medieval clergy in particular.[3] As a construct distinct from biological sex, such a third gender arguably did exist in the medieval west, among the religious. As a construct, deliberately but artificially (perhaps ideologically) formulated, this 'third gender' raises numerous questions, particularly with regard to the secular clergy, those priests who served in the parishes and were meant to be the main link between humanity and God. Arguably, the ambivalence of the clergy's status in its fully developed form separates them from the generality of 'men'; yet there are signs of significant tension between a societal concept of 'masculinity' and the constructed 'third gender' of the clergy which, for want of a better term, is here called 'emasculinity'.

A tripartite categorization of medieval humanity seems to be validated by the insufficiency of the blunt masculine/feminine, male/female division. A recent examination of medieval masculinity argues that the period offers 'many examples of cross-gender behavior among medieval women, but almost none among medieval men'. This, however, assumes that to cross gender means 'performing in the role of the opposite sex'.[4] If emasculinity provides a third gender, the synonymity of sex and gender evaporates: emasculinity means that *all* clergy (or, specifically, all members of religious orders, and secular clergy above the rank of subdeacon) engaged in 'cross-gender behavior'. Yet, although legally committed to their new gender, many of these men found the demands too great. The medieval *Herrenfrage* – 'the men question' – is certainly about the status of masculinity, and men's struggle to control women in the period.[5] It is, however, also about the status of emasculinity, and the constant tension between the wish that priests be angels, and their urge to be men.

The medieval Church in the eleventh and twelfth centuries

The starting point for analysis of these tensions is the major transition associated with the Gregorian reform of the eleventh and twelfth

3. G. Herdt, ed., *Third Sex, Third Gender: Beyond Sexual Dimorphism in Culture and History* (New York, 1994), although with virtually no medieval content.

4. Bullough, 'On being a male', p.34.

5. J.A. McNamara, 'The *Herrenfrage*: the restructuring of the gender system, 1050–1150', in Lees, ed., *Medieval Masculinities*, pp.3–29. The 'men question' cannot be confined within these date limits.

centuries.[6] This complex movement had two results of immediate importance: the sacerdotalization of monasticism, as it became increasingly normal for monks to advance to priesthood; and the monachization of priesthood, in the search to impose chastity and celibacy on the clergy in general. The sometimes violent resistance to the demand that clerics set aside their wives shows that this was not a universally popular shift (see above, chapter 9). Sometimes the ideal was imposed almost as a commercial transaction. Thus, in a financial agreement between the French monastery of La Trinité of Vendôme and the parish priest of Mazé of c.1050–1070, made following the parish's transfer to the abbey, the priest was required to renounce his wife and accept an obligation to chastity.[7]

The insistence on clerical celibacy was driven by two different concerns. One was bluntly practical, to prevent the alienation of church property through descent, perhaps also to prevent the creation of a hereditary priestly caste. The other was ideological, requiring that those dealing with sacramental matters be unsullied. This demand for the formal renunciation of sexual status may have meant – in fact or theory – a renunciation of gendered status as then identified. Contemporaries treated it in those terms: the chronicler Lambert of Hersfeld records that married clergy vociferously spurned the opportunity to become angels.[8] The language here is important, for the link with the angels marks a hierarchical progression. In the transition there is almost the creation of a genderless status, not necessarily limited to erstwhile men. The so-called 'double houses' of monks and nuns of the twelfth century fit into the pattern here, reflecting the equally ungendered status which became an ideal for nuns. Ideal and reality did not always cohabit, as is shown by the tale of the nun of Watton (Yorkshire), who became pregnant by a monk of the house.[9] Formally double houses did not last long. Moreover, despite the double houses, emasculinity might not actually be something attainable by both sexes. If the renunciation of gendered sexuality was a hierarchical shift, a step up the Ladder of Creation, the rungs may have differed for men and

6. A.L. Barstow, *Married Priests and the Reforming Papacy: The Eleventh-Century Debates*, Texts and Studies in Religion, 12 (New York and Toronto, 1982).

7. P.D. Johnson, *Prayer, Patronage and Power: The Abbey of La Trinité, Vendôme, 1032–1187* (New York and London, 1981), p.161.

8. H.C. Lea, *History of Sacerdotal Celibacy in the Christian Church* 2 vols (3rd edn, London, 1907), I, p.271.

9. G. Constable, 'Ailred of Rievaulx and the nun of Watton: an episode in the early history of the Gilbertine Order', in D. Baker, ed., *Medieval Women*, Studies in Church History: Subsidia, 1 (Oxford, 1978), pp.206–9, 222.

women. Jerome's assertion that when a woman 'wishes to serve Christ more than the world, then she will cease to be a woman and will be called a man'[10] initiated a tradition of female 'virility' associated particularly (but not exclusively) with the adoption of a rigid regular life. Men might be similarly converted, but for them the progression was perhaps felt to be into the ranks of the angels.

The demand that married secular clergy abandon contemporary ideas of masculinity, to which a male sexual identity was fundamental, was perhaps matched by changes in monasticism. The twelfth century possibly saw the abandonment of a specifically religious 'masculinity', one tied to monasticism as a life of battle and athleticism. This may be reflected in changing attitudes to Christ, as the Cross of Victory became a Cross of Humiliation; it is also suggested by the transition which placed monks (and perhaps eventually, by extension, priests) among the *pauperes*, the impotent.[11] Among the evolutions in twelfth-century monasticism, the end to oblation introduced profound changes:[12] it removed the earlier coherence of monastic masculinity; new inmates now had to reject secular masculinity to achieve their angelic status.

A final twist to such evolutions came with the rehabilitation of marriage which occurred around 1200, and perhaps compounded the tension between masculinity and emasculinity. Some thirteenth-century sermons contrast marriage as an *ordo* with the *ordines* of the regular religious life, occasionally to the latter's disadvantage.[13] By insisting that marriage had been instituted by God in Eden (suggesting that prelapsarian sexuality was sinless, and masculinity and femininity the original gender roles) while religious orders were merely human institutions (sometimes, like the mendicants, only recently established), the validity of the search for angelic perfection was implicitly undermined. Male progenitive activity was also validated, producing a contrast in which clerical renunciation could almost be depicted as an avoidance of divine precepts.

The transformation of the Gregorian reform – in which the attack on clerical marriage was but one element – eventually led to

10. Quoted in Bullough, 'On being a male', p.32, from Jerome, *Commentary on Ephesians*, *PL* 26, bk. 16, col. 56.

11. R.I. Moore, *The Formation of a Persecuting Society: Power and Deviance in Western Europe, 950–1250* (Oxford, 1987), pp.102–4.

12. J.H. Lynch, *Simoniacal Entry into Religious Orders from 1000 to 1260: a Social, Economic and Legal Study* (Columbus, Oh., 1976), pp.36–50, 56–60.

13. N. Bériou *et al.*, *Modern Questions about Medieval Sermons: Essays on Marriage, Death, History and Sanctity*, Società internazionale per lo studio del medioevo latino, 11 (Spoleto, 1994), pp.72–4, 139.

the construction of a highly demanding definition of priestly status. Theological developments added additional baggage and nuances. The outcome was an ideal proclaimed, for example, in the fifteenth-century English play of *Everyman*:

> . . . priesthood exceedeth all other thing . . .
> God hath to them more power given
> Than to any angel that is in heaven . . .
> No remedy we find under God
> But all only priesthood.
> . . . God gave priests that dignity,
> And setteth them in his stead among us to be;
> Thus be they above angels in degree.[14]

The perfection which this required was set out in William Melton's sermon to ordinands at York c.1510: a priest should be 'blameless . . . , sober, elegant, prudent, chaste, hospitable, a teacher, not a drunkard, not violent, but restrained, not involved in disputes, not avaricious'.[15] If the question of masculinity is invoked here, priesthood does seem to be a status which transcends gender and gender roles as applied to the contemporary laity, marking a progression beyond masculinity. Priesthood becomes almost divine, especially through its mediation of the sacraments – particularly the eucharist – and through the notion of the priest as a Christ-substitute. This identity should not be pushed too far: a key point in practice was that the priest was all too often too obviously human; which was clearly part of the problem. Issues of priestly 'pollution' raised during the Gregorian reform movement persisted for centuries, and in the same terms, precisely because of the status ascribed to the priest.

The gender of the clergy

The clergy's continuing humanity nevertheless challenges the practicality of assigning them a status as a 'third gender'. That clerics had renounced sexual masculinity placed them in an ambivalent position, and the renunciation itself imposed severe strains. Some dealt with them, and maintained their emasculinity; others, quite

---

14. *Everyman*, in *Everyman and Medieval Miracle Plays*, ed., A.C. Cawley (2nd edn, London, 1974), p.228, ll. 732, 735–6, 745–9.

15. William de Melton, *Sermo exhortatorius cancellarii Eboracensis hiis qui ad sacros ordines petunt promoveri* (London, c.1510), sig. Aviii[r].

clearly, did not (see below, chapter 11, for examples of the latter). A fundamental difficulty remained: whatever gender they may have sought to adopt, physically they remained male. Many doubtless remained emotionally masculine. Their lay counterparts still perceived them as both – while perhaps thinking that they ought to be neither.

This ambiguous and ambivalent gendering of the clergy was problematic. Their continuing maleness laid them open to charges of being sexual, or maintaining a sexuality which besmirched their priesthood. While few challenged the doctrine that sacraments were valid simply because the ritual had been correctly performed, and regardless of the personal moral state of the celebrant, much could still be made of the unworthiness of a priest who handled God immediately after handling his mistress. Awareness of priests' maleness is obvious in the pervasive search for evidence of lascivious clerics. Prominent among the inhabitants of Purgatory, in a nun's vision supposedly experienced in 1422, are those regular and secular clergy (male and female) who had not maintained their chastity.[16] Priests therefore thundered against their fellows for not maintaining their chastity – and in the process berated all sexual sins which could be linked to masculinity.

The non-ecclesiastical response to the putative abolition of sexual identity in ordination remains to be judged. It seems evident, however, that there were problems. Recent discussion of attitudes to hermaphrodites has emphasized the insistence on the choice of a polarized sexual identity in such cases: although physically both male and female, only a single active sexual identity could be adopted, with no sign of tolerance of an 'in-between' status.[17] Priests, physically male, would be expected to be masculine by gender.

That insistence on priestly masculinity was perhaps reinforced by the Church itself, through the theology of the Incarnation. The Word did not become simply 'flesh', it became a man. There was, as priestly status became more defined, a paradox. The God-man who was the unique receptacle of two natures was represented by individuals who, when asserting their priestly status, were denatured. Or were they? Physically, indeed, there was a clear insistence on maleness: just as Christ was humanly perfect, so should a priest

16. M.P. Harley, *A Revelation of Purgatory by an Unknown Fifteenth-Century Woman Visionary*, Studies in Women and Religion, 18 (Lewiston and Queenston, 1985), pp.60, 69–74.

17. M. Rubin, 'The person in the form: medieval challenges to bodily "order"', in S. Kay and M. Rubin, eds, *Framing Medieval Bodies* (Manchester, 1994), pp.101–6.

be. Physical deformity was unacceptable, at least at ordination. While the decrepitude of old age would unavoidably take its toll, prospective priests, or those injured after ordination, needed a dispensation from bodily imperfections to receive orders or continue to officiate. Even minor defects were enough to raise doubts; *castrati* were presumably unacceptable (but see above, chapter 6, for the Byzantine situation).

The tension of persistent maleness, of masculinity, is just as pervasive. Among the clergy as a whole, it was perhaps most overt in the emphatically male emasculinity of the military orders – reflected not only in their fighting, but in the moral failings (real or alleged) associated with the Templars and the Iberian orders.[18] It was perhaps no accident that the Iberian orders were the first to be absolved from their vows of chastity. For many of the men sacrificed to a clerical career this lingering masculinity proved irresistible, sometimes provoking self-doubt, even 'a form of "self-hatred" '.[19] For others, and for the moralists, that lingering masculinity and its attendant sexuality threatened the stability and status of those who would be emasculine. Hence the need to preclude temptation, with rules about priests sharing their houses with women, and limitations even on their sight of women in confession.[20]

This fear of being proved male affects interpretations of 'clerical misogyny'. The words may be 'anti-women', but is what they say actually what they mean? Are these sentiments instead directed primarily against the perceived threat to clerical aspirations to angelic status? While clerical misogyny's virulence and incorporation into cultural norms cannot be denied, it can also be seen as a gendered response to a threat, to an awareness that emasculinity was fragile, and prone to violation. That awareness made sexuality itself threatening. From that perception, extremist misogynistic writings become statements of fear: essentially, all women are rapists. Yet the real rapist remains male: the danger is not posed by women, but by the clerics' suppressed masculinity. Here 'woman' is objectified: she is not Eve, but the apple. The doubly seductive role of Eve *and* serpent is played by masculinity. Yet without totally

18. M. Barber, *The New Knighthood: a History of the Order of the Templars* (Cambridge, 1994), pp.227–8, 301–2.

19. B. Scribner, 'Anticlericalism and the cities', in P.A. Dykema and H.A. Oberman, eds, *Anticlericalism in Late Medieval and Early Modern Europe*, Studies in Medieval and Reformation Thought, 51 (Leiden, New York, and Köln, 1993), pp.153–4.

20. P. Marshall, *The Catholic Priesthood and the English Reformation* (Oxford, 1994), pp.23–4; P. Heath, *The English Parish Clergy on the Eve of the Reformation* (London, 1969), p.106.

abandoning masculinity as both a sexual and a gendered status, it would be almost impossible to eliminate the temptation.

The threat, however, came not only from women. Although perhaps less vociferous in their denunciations, commentators condemned the sexual challenges of masturbation and sodomy – the latter perhaps particularly because it was assumed that men deprived of female sex would turn their attentions to their own.[21] Moreover, clerics were unavoidably part of their contemporary societies; they would generally accept and be affected by the contemporary construction of masculinity and its associated attitudes – of which they were often the articulators.

The lay response to the gender status of the clergy

While the clergy faced dilemmas about their gendered status, their renunciation of masculinity although still visibly male complicated their relationships with lay males. The twelfth century's search for the emasculation of both sexes challenged the societal view of gender. Religious women still fitted into the traditional trinity of female life-styles (virgins, married, widows), but religious men became extraneous to contemporary gender constructions. The insistence on chastity (as opposed to virginity) meant a denial of sexuality and a rejection of the generative power/reproductive claims of masculinity. Although 'married to the church', such marriage could not be equated with the nun's status as 'bride of Christ'. Yet clerics' assertions of their moral superiority directly challenged the non-clerical life-style; their existence outside the normal social systems challenged established social patterns, perhaps particularly threatening familial and household relationships between men and women as rulers and subjects. Unsurprisingly, they generated responses which might be called 'anti-clericalism'. Such anti-clericalism could be considered as gendered: hostility to the clergy is often voiced in tones similar to those of medieval misogyny.

Such anti-clerical attitudes may have been fostered by the clergy's visibility, and by the links between visible appearance, gender, and gendered expectations. At its most basic, this is a matter of hair-styles and clothing. In a world of symbolism, symbols matter, but

21. T.N. Tentler, *Sin and Confession on the Eve of the Reformation* (Princeton, N.J., 1977), pp.91–3; V.L. Bullough, 'The sin against nature and homosexuality', in V.L. Bullough and J. Brundage, eds, *Sexual Practices and the Medieval Church* (Buffalo, N.Y., 1982), pp.64–6.

may convey 'wrong' meanings (an issue discussed in Chapters 5 and 8 above). The function of the tonsure, and of clerical garb, was precisely to separate clerics from laity, but gave different messages. While 'first tonsure' was perhaps almost a normal rite of passage for many boys, the full tonsure as a mark of clerical status emphasized the separation. Its visibility encouraged its use as a determinant of status in judicial processes dealing with 'criminous clerks' in England (before a reading test made external appearance less important). Clerical clothing, disconcertingly, was like female clothing in cut, making clerics quasi-transvestites. This is exemplified by Richard Rolle's final breach with 'the real world' when he adopted the status of a hermit in fourteenth-century England. Although he was not entering a formal order, he proclaimed his changed state by a change of clothing – using one of his sister's dresses to make a habit. Such ambiguity might well influence onlookers, as might clerical riding practices. Clerics, abandoning masculinity, also abandoned horses – in theory. Like women, they rode mules. Like women, they rode side-saddle. Both might be taken to indicate the neutering, the emasculating, of the cleric. Here, however, as in many other spheres, norms were not static or universal. Awareness of the norms, willingness to adhere to them, and reactions to failure to do so, would vary across time and space. Widespread ignorance of the rules, or even so basic a problem as a shortage of mules, would also affect reactions. On the other hand, a gendered response to mule-riding would be inappropriate in Iberia, where mules were the normal mount even for gentlemen until the late fifteenth century. Only then was horse-riding encouraged, to improve preparedness for war; only priests and ecclesiastics were to retain mules. Until then, the denigration of clerics as mule-riders could not occur, but if 'clerically' dressed they presumably still rode side-saddle and so incurred some comment.

The issue of visibility also appears in attacks on clerics' failure to be non-masculine. A frequent complaint was against clerics who carried weapons, with numerous episcopal and other prohibitions on the practice (see below, chapter 11). On the other hand, William Melton's assertion c.1510 that 'the weapons of priests are prayers and tears' raises an affinity with the intercessory mercy-inducing role often ascribed to women.[22] Just as common were tirades against what might be considered 'clerical transvestism', the wearing of clothes which were male rather than clerical. These were again

---

22. Melton, *Sermo exhortatorius*, sig. Avii^v.

commonplace, but their precise value is not clear. Some of the problems may have been accidental: if clerics inherited good-quality clothing, or acquired it as mortuaries (funeral gifts), they could only be expected to wear it. A distinction may be needed between simply wearing too much finery, and wearing the latest male fashions – those pointed shoes and excessively short tunics which brought Avignon into such disrepute in the fourteenth century.

Other features of priestly status could also make clerics objects of masculine comment. If 'clerical poverty' meant being ranked with the *pauperes* in the widest sense of the term – the impotent – then these men who renounced power but, perhaps all too often, still wielded it, remained chimaeras. More significant would be the clergy's dependence on patronage in their careers. Priesthood's monachization in the Gregorian reform was actually a compromise with the laity, occurring in conjunction with major changes in inheritance patterns across much of Europe. Celibate and non-hereditary priests could be more effectively integrated into lay family strategies, become pawns in patterns of landholding and patronage, and offer a way to resolve tensions in these changing inheritance systems. Such a resolution precluded the predatory competition for wives and inheritances which is a feature of 'youthful' existence in the twelfth and thirteenth centuries. The link with family strategies was an important force throughout the Middle Ages, as clerics worked with (or were used by) their kin to exploit ecclesiastical resources and advance family fortunes, making entry to the priesthood acceptance of a career rather than a vocation, with ordination patterns responding to demographic and economic changes in late medieval society. Priests as protégés, as servants, were subject to control, and were unable to claim the independence sought in the Gregorian reform. William Melton's York sermon again asserts the ideal: all those who hoped for advancement from contacts, or contracts, were to consider themselves tantamount to simoniacs, and unsuitable for ordination. But the very perception of the Church as a career structure, in which patronage and connection were essential ingredients for any advancement (let alone success) would not encourage attitudes of respect and submission among the laity themselves.

Indeed, the priestly abandonment of masculinity had serious personal consequences because of its social context: 'Failing at these [masculine] tasks [of impregnating, protecting, and providing] leads not only to challenges to one's masculinity, but also to fear of being labeled as showing feminine weakness . . . Males who fail to perform as males have their manhood questioned.'[23] Clerics faced that risk; but a greater danger was that other males would still see them as males, with a closet masculinity. It has been argued that for women in a female environment, 'patriarchal gender stereotypes can quickly lose their importance because the visible reference for all stereotyped behaviour – men – is absent'.[24] If that is so, if men are 'the visible reference for all stereotyped behaviour' – presumably including male behaviour as well as female – they can never attain the same freedom as women, save by a formal act of rejection. All their behaviour, in all circumstances (except perhaps the solitary) is stereotypical, because men can never be absent from themselves. A tension between desire and stereotype perhaps imposed its own momentum and restrictions on the spiritual evolutions of those who adopted the clerical life. Moreover, lay men's awareness of the freedom which women (and by extension the emasculine) sought might encourage attempts to limit that freedom out of jealousy, or alienation from the religion which women and the emasculine shared.

Although physically (and therefore still sexually) male, the clergy had adopted a status which can be considered liminal with regard to that inherited masculinity. Such liminality in itself threatened lay masculinity, because of the privileged status which women often granted to the clergy. As in modern cases of gender liminality,[25] affinities developed between the clergy and women which were not necessarily sexual. The collusion between clerics and women to civilize and Christianize medieval lay men could easily be interpreted as a conspiracy against male control over the family and domestic life: the clergy could be attacked as having too close attachments to women, encouraging their spirituality and acts of charity without reference to their husbands, thereby undermining lay male power. Lodovico Ariosto commented in his fifth *Satire* (written in 1521) that if his wife 'wished to attend more than one mass a day I should be displeased, and I would have it suffice if she confessed herself once or twice a year. I should not wish her to have business with those asses who bear no burdens, or to be making tarts and repasts every day for her confessor.'[26] Apart from

---

23. Bullough, 'On being a male', p.34.

24. U. Wiethaus, 'In search of medieval women's friendships: Hildegard of Bingen's letters to her female contemporaries', in U. Wiethaus, ed., *Maps of Flesh and Light: the Religious Experience of Medieval Women Mystics* (Syracuse, NY, 1993), p.96.

25. The Polynesian *mahu*, as described in N. Besnier, 'Polynesian gender liminality through time and space', in Herdt, ed., *Third Sex, Third Gender*, pp.285–328, 554–67.

26. *The Satires of Ludovico Ariosto: a Renaissance Autobiography*, trans. P. DeÇa Wiggins (Athens, Oh., 1976), p.135 (original text at p.134, ll. 196–201).

insisting that clergy should not disrupt family life, lay men could also respond with accusations of sexuality: the clergy's masculinity might emerge from the closet, and produce bastards. Clerical sexuality as a threat to domestic male dominance heightened the tension between masculinity and emasculinity, with the continued threat of clerical sexuality available for use as an anticlerical weapon by the threatened males. The clergy's reputation for sexuality – and the assumption that the accusations would stick – meant that rape charges could be an effective weapon against the clergy when the real basis of a dispute was completely different. English cases of the fourteenth and fifteenth centuries suggest that rape was a charge frequently levied, and perhaps frequently believed, no matter how unlikely or incredible the circumstances.

The belief that the clergy remained sexual and masculine was often fully justified: they could then be condemned for falling short of expectations. Indeed, in sexual matters, the clergy might be viewed as aggressors, because they were physically male. The nuances are complicated by the fact that most anti-clerical works which reproduce the stereotype of the randy cleric were actually written by males, both clerical and non-clerical. From a lay standpoint such literature becomes a gendered response to the fact of the putative third gender; from the clerical standpoint it challenges those clerics who did not maintain the ideal (and might also be a male rather than emasculine reaction).[27]

In addition to the danger of clerical sexual advances, lay male authority might be challenged in other ways. Clerical idealists who really believed in their emasculinity, and in its benefits, not unnaturally sought adherents and followers. The advancement of emasculinity transformed the threat posed by clerical activity from that of the importation of cuckoo offspring, to the dissolution of lineage and household. Chastity, and the renunciation of family bonds, threatened patriarchy, patrilinearity, and patrimony, especially if male renunciation was encouraged. Giovanni Dominici's success in attracting men and women to the regular life in early fifteenth-century Venice was supposedly rewarded with no fewer than seven assassination attempts by outraged relatives of the converts. Hostility to the mendicant orders found voice in allegations

---

27. On anti-clericalism see Scribner, 'Anticlericalism and the cities'; S.H. Hendrix, 'Considering the clergy's side: a multilateral view of anticlericalism', in Dykema and Oberman, eds, *Anticlericalism*, pp.456–7; Marshall, *Catholic Priesthood*, pp.155–6; R.L. Storey, 'Malicious indictments of clergy in the fifteenth century', in M.J. Franklin and C. Harper-Bill, eds, *Medieval Ecclesiastical Studies in Honour of Dorothy M. Owen* (Woodbridge, 1995), pp.222–38.

that they enticed young boys to join them, resulting in England in a Statute against the practice.[28]

While the laity (and the ecclesiastical authorities) might want them to be angels, the clerics (especially those ordained to a career rather than a vocation) often failed in their obligations. The aspiration to moral probity and meeting the ideal appears frequently in wills, and cases where the late-medieval laity retained control over the appointment and dismissal of priests, notably with regard to chantries. Yet the clergy would persist in drinking and fornicating, in shattering expectations. The charges of the burgesses of Saltash (Cornwall) – presumably lay males – against their vicar in c.1405, in which he was identified as a litigious drunkard who failed to teach, ignored his sacramental responsibilities, and scandalized his parishioners, are almost an inversion of the model advanced by William Melton in the following century, as already quoted.[29]

One outcome of this imbalance between ideal and reality of priestly behaviour was a challenge to spiritual values: a quasi-donatism which questioned the validity of actions performed by a priest who remained male. In the late eleventh century, the papacy had encouraged lay action in its struggle to impose celibacy by urging lay boycotts of the ministrations of married or concubinary priests. It was a short step to deny the validity of the sacraments they performed – even though that was formal heresy. Hints of such views appear across the centuries.

Lay male responses to the priest's ambivalent gender status seem to focus on two main areas. In both hostility – perhaps 'anti-clericalism' – almost becomes a variant of misogyny. First, there is the basic question of sexuality and power. Clergy, by their very status, were denied marriage. Accordingly, they could not participate in that system of relationships which provided 'the connective tissue of late medieval society'.[30] Yet their maleness threatened that tissue. It can be no accident that in many tales of marital battles the wife's sexual adventures are with a priest. If such tales reflect men's own sense of lack of control over women, as 'men's ways of coping with their worries about being outflanked by female mobility', and that 'Male order would like to have women fixed in the place

---

28. D.E. Bornstein, *The Bianchi of 1399: Popular Devotion in Late Medieval Italy* (Ithaca and London, 1993), p.181.

29. R.N. Swanson, *Catholic England: Faith, Belief, and Observance before the Reformation* (Manchester, 1993), p.261; for Melton, above, at n.15.

30. J.A. Brundage, *Law, Sex, and Christian Society in Medieval Europe* (Chicago and London, 1987), p.497.

defined for them by men',[31] then the priests' activities in these tales surely ought to evoke the same responses. That search for control culminates in tales where the cuckolded husband gains revenge by castrating the errant cleric – a forced imposition of emasculinity, which technically also denied the priest the exercise of his orders. The classic 'real-life' instance of this response is, of course, Peter Abelard in the twelfth century.

The second type of clergy-directed 'misogyny' derives from confession, and the associated priestly power to grant absolution. A feature of late medieval reform movements is an attack on sacramental auricular confession. By contrast, a major clerical concern was always to affirm their power to receive confessions, against the challenges of friars and others whose integration into local society was less intense – and whose power to disrupt it was accordingly less immediate. Apart from its other strands, this can be seen as part of the battle over confession as a form of 'social control',[32] but other interpretations are possible. The central issue is power, power of knowledge. The paradigm anti-feminist text, the *Roman de la Rose*, written in the thirteenth century, warns against confiding secrets to women: 'No one born of a mother, if he's not drunk or mad, should reveal to a woman something that should be kept quiet, if he does not want to hear it from another person.'[33] This fear of breach of confidence, 'fear of [a woman's] power as a knowing subject' has been seen as part of 'the character of misogyny'.[34] With little change in wording, the same strictures, the same fear, transferred to the knowledge gained through confession, becomes part of 'the character of anticlericalism'.

The fear of clerical masculinity produced paradoxical responses. At one extreme, clerical sexuality was vehemently denounced: sexual slander of the period commonly focused on clerical concubines and their offspring. Moreover, clerical concubinage was rooted out by vigilant hierarchs, and denounced at visitations by lay juries. On the other hand, clerical marriage continued in reality: in many

31. M. Chinca, 'The body in some Middle High German *Mären*: taming and maiming', in Kay and Rubin, eds, *Framing Medieval Bodies*, p.191.
32. T.N. Tentler, 'The summa for confessors as an instrument of social control', in C. Trinkaus and H.A. Oberman, eds, *The Pursuit of Holiness in Late Medieval and Renaissance Religion: Papers from the University of Michigan Conference*, Studies in Medieval and Reformation Thought, 10 (Leiden, 1974), pp.103–26; L.E. Boyle, 'The summa for confessors as a genre and its religious intent', *ibid.*, pp.126–30.
33. D. Poirion, *Le Roman de la Rose*, Guillaume de Loris and Jean de Meun, eds (Paris, 1974), p.440, ll. 16349–53.
34. S. Kay, 'Women's body of knowledge: epistemology and misogyny in the *Romance of the Rose*', in Kay and Rubin, eds, *Framing Medieval Bodies*, p.216.

places it was considered better for the priest to have a steady concubine than to be promiscuous among his parishioners – or rather,
among the wives and daughters of his male parishioners. Indeed,
parish priests might be required to take a concubine as part of
the condition of their employment – something condemned, for
instance, at the Synod of Valladolid in 1322, and elsewhere. There is
a clear ambiguity in the lay reaction here, which may be a regional-
ized response as well. When English clergy were eventually allowed
to marry, their wives – like their concubines in earlier days – often
became objects of derision.

Perhaps there was a generational or life cycle element to these
attitudes. For men, old age brought the waning of sexual and physical powers. Accordingly, a progression to an emasculated post-sexual
life might be considered natural and acceptable. Spiritual and chaste
marriages were not uncommon, but would normally follow years
of procreation. Likewise, men would move beyond masculinity to
spirituality by terminating marriages (with their wives' consent) to
become anchorites, hermits, or priests. Priestly chastity, adopted early
in life, disrupted that sense of progress, imposing abnormal and
unnatural strains, which were then resented. Some men seeking
spirituality with maturity possibly also felt that marriage prevented
them from attaining that objective – Guillaume Saignet's tract against
clerical celibacy written in 1417–18 may contain a hint of such a
stance.[35]

The clergy's response to the ambiguity of their gender

For the clergy, meanwhile, the search for a new gender could leave
them in a state of gender limbo. While some in the early stages
kept their options open about their eventual choice of masculinity
or emasculinity, it was after ordination that precise identity could
become problematic. Some secular clerics sought to define their

---

35. For discussion of the debate about clerical celibacy see S. Ozment, *The Age of
Reform, 1250–1550: An Intellectual and Religious History of Late Medieval and Reformation
Europe* (New Haven and London, 1980), pp.381–91; J.K. Yost, 'The Reformation
defense of clerical marriage in the reigns of Henry VIII and Edward VI', *Church
History* 50 (1981), pp.152–65; H.L. Parish, ' "By this mark you shall know him":
clerical celibacy and Antichrist in English Reformation polemic', in R.N. Swanson,
ed., *The Church Retrospective, Studies in Church History* 33 (1997), pp.253–66.

status more clearly, by a stricter renunciation of sexuality with formal monastic vows. Thus, in 1340, the rector of Church Mottram (Shropshire), renounced his benefice to enter a religious order. Others reaffirmed their sexuality in marriage, abandoning the claim to emasculinity. This particularly produced several prominent changes of status, perhaps most extreme in cases of high-born individuals who exchanged clerical for knightly status to publicize (and perhaps to assure) their changed social position. But people lower down the scale also made the changes. In 1339 another Shropshire incumbent, the vicar of Alderley, had resigned his benefice to marry a daughter of Sir John Davenport. In the next century, a collusive plea of pre-contract of marriage brought by a priest overrode his orders and restored his lay masculinity. Even members of religious orders are found rejecting their status in favour of marriage.

Such formal readeptions of masculinity were presumably considered better than the informal returns evident in visitation complaints and court records. The acknowledgement that priestly celibacy was primarily a matter of discipline rather than doctrine meant that it was always open to debate. Celibacy's dangers and demands were recognized by many, within and outside the ecclesiastical establishment; and no sooner was it being enforced than writers argued emphatically against it. Among them, in the early fourteenth century, was William Durant the Younger, the great canonist. While insistent that under the current dispensation clerics should remain bound to chastity – fulfilment of the implicit vow of ordination was apparently his main concern – he was clearly not convinced, at a utilitarian level, that celibacy was beneficial. Too many clerics could not remain chaste; accordingly they became sinners, while their offspring – not responsible for the sins of their fathers – faced discrimination. As celibacy was a matter of discipline rather than faith, Durant argued for the adoption of the more liberal approach of the Orthodox Church. His call was repeated by others in the fourteenth and fifteenth centuries, until it became overwhelming in some areas in the sixteenth.[36]

Nor was it only the Orthodox who argued for clerical marriage. Those rejecting the Church also rejected the demands of priestly celibacy. Notable here were the Lollards in fifteenth-century England. They denied any requirement of celibacy, for both male and

36. C. Fasolt, *Council and Hierarchy: The Political Thought of William Durant the Younger* (Cambridge, 1991), pp.187–8, 238.

female religious; while at least one priest who became a heretic, William White, emphasized his rebellion by marrying.[37]

Conclusion

At this point, late medieval societal changes must be integrated into the picture. There are signs of increasing patriarchy in the fifteenth and early sixteenth centuries. Male control and assertiveness seem to have increased, and female independence declined. In particular, men were increasing their control within the family, to the extent that 'Reformation Europe . . . may be described as the heyday of the patriarchal nuclear family'.[38] This shift towards a more definite patriarchy was not specific to Protestantism. Protestantism, after all, grew out of Catholicism, and the trend towards patriarchy had originated within the latter, as the developing cult of Joseph indicates. In such circumstances, the oddity and artificiality of emasculinity perhaps became increasingly obvious, provoking more insistent calls for change. The challenge to square the circle could only be resolved by a radical change in the concept of priesthood.

Alongside the tensions evident within the late medieval Church, that between the two male genders – masculinity and emasculinity – appears increasingly important. It provides a vital element in the changes which allow the Reformation to be considered a *trahison des clercs*. The Protestant Reformation forcefully linked masculinity and change in its deliberate rejection of emasculinity (and its female equivalent) by the affirmation of a masculine priesthood, made evident in marriage. These new Protestant pastors adopted an increasingly masculine, and increasingly patriarchal, role within the new religion. As members of a profession rather than a caste, as legitimately fathers and heads of families, they were, unmistakeably, men. (The Catholic priesthood also changed, but as it retained emasculinity, those changes do not affect the analysis here.)

Over the centuries the wheel had come full circle. The attempt to create a new gender had foundered on the enormity of the task. Perhaps that was because priesthood was usually a career rather than a vocation; perhaps it does affirm the polarization of two sexes

---

37. S. McSheffrey, *Gender and Heresy: Women and Men in Lollard Communities, 1420–1530* (Philadelphia, 1995), pp.57, 82–3.

38. S. Ozment, *When Fathers Ruled: Family Life in Reformation Europe* (Cambridge, Mass., and London, 1983), p.2.

and two genders. In 1523 the reformer Justus Jonas proclaimed that, 'If you are a man, it is no more in your power to live without a woman than it is to change your sex . . . it is the way God has created and made us.'[39] Yet post-Reformation Roman Catholicism maintained the search for emasculinity; there the battle between the two male genders is still fought, and produces tabloid exultation at each victory for masculinity. Meanwhile, in Protestantism, the angels were brought down to earth.

39. Cited in Ozment, *The Age of Reform*, p.391.

CHAPTER ELEVEN

Clergy, Masculinity and Transgression in Late Medieval England

P.H. CULLUM

Where did the secular clergy of the later Middle Ages fit into the gender order of their time? In the previous chapter Robert Swanson discussed medieval theoretical, and especially theological, conceptions of the gender identity of the clergy; in this chapter I shall explore some of the practical implications of the acquisition of clerical gender identity through the examination of a series of detailed case studies from late medieval England. In particular, I shall discuss the means by which gender identity was inculcated, ways in which clerical gender identity contrasted and conflicted with lay societal ideas of appropriate masculine behaviour, and the responses (of both laity and clergy) to transgressions of expected clerical behaviour.

Of particular interest to my study of the secular clergy is the fact that, far more than monks, they were expected to mix with lay people and were thus both more prone to the temptations of the lay world and also more exposed to lay ideologies about gender identity. The secular clergy also constituted a more ambivalent group than monks. The lower ranks of the secular clergy did not, in fact, have to renounce sex, and it was possible for a young man to take minor orders, but not to proceed to the priesthood. He could return to lay life, often while remaining involved in aspects of church administration.

The acquisition of clerical gender identity

Canon lawyers practising in the church courts might, by the fifteenth century, easily be married clerks. The late age at which entry to the major orders, and hence to the vows of celibacy took place, (eighteen to become sub-deacon, nineteen for deacon, twenty-four to be a priest) also meant that, at least from a modern perspective, their gender identity must have been largely formed before they accepted (or not) these aspects of their role. Studies of the acquisition of gender identity in the modern period suggest that children have a fixed gender identity by the age of eight, which is further developed by the process of education, in the pre- and early teens. Until the practice of child oblation largely died out in the thirteenth century, monks may well have acquired a monastic identity at much the same age as they were developing a gender identity and may have experienced little or no conflict between these two. By comparison, in the late medieval period most men probably became monks at around eighteen, in the final stage of monastic profession. David Knowles argued that Benedictines were supposed to be nineteen at profession but that there was much evidence in the fifteenth century for clothing at fifteen, and thus profession a year later at sixteen. Barbara Harvey argues that at Westminster in the early fifteenth century monks were likely to be over eighteen at profession, though from 1470 some could have been as young as fourteen at profession, having usually already spent a year as a novice.[1]

While late medieval monks may have had more problems in accepting their new identity than their predecessors, they were still younger than those who entered the secular priesthood. Indeed, in the years after the Black Death it would appear that it was quite common to delay entry to the major orders, as progression through the orders often came in successive ordination ceremonies. As priesthood could not (except with a dispensation) be granted before the age of twenty-four, it seems likely that a commitment to celibacy came only a year or so before this. It could be argued that this represented a measured and thoughtful choice, in the full knowledge of what was involved, however, the delay might also represent the putting off of a commitment to the last moment.[2] The choice of a clerical career and celibacy at around twenty-three or four or even later would have been made more stark by the fact that this was probably the age at which the intending priest's lay contemporaries would have been beginning to get married. In the later Middle Ages, far from an identity grown into through adolescence, priestly celibacy was often a choice made at a fork in the road,

1. Barbara Harvey, *Living and Dying in England, 1100–1540: The Monastic Experience* (Oxford, 1993), pp.118–21.
2. R.N. Swanson, *Church and Society in Late Medieval England* (Oxford, 1989), pp.42–3.

where a young man whose upbringing and education might have led either to a secular or an ecclesiastical career finally had to make a choice between the two. The secular clergy should thus be expected to have had a more fragile gender identity, because acquired later and with more alternatives available, and to transgress their gender roles more frequently than monks. Their conduct was therefore commented upon both by those who sought to give them advice, and by lay people. Transgressive clergy are, then, a particularly useful group to examine for contemporary assumptions about the nature of clerical gender. In this chapter I shall examine both lay and clerical discourse about such transgressive clergy.

In the context of the acquisition of gender identity it would be helpful to know more about the upbringing and education of intending priests. In the absence of a modern seminary training, how did young men acquire (if they did) a clerical gender identity? In the thirteenth century the post of holy water clerk had often been a kind of scholarship for a boy aiming at a clerical career, but had by the fifteenth century often been incorporated into the job of the parish clerk. The parish clerk himself was usually in minor orders and might be employed as a deacon, effectively receiving training like a modern curate. But by the fifteenth century this post had frequently become a dead end or an end in itself, no longer a first step for intending priests but a lifelong career for men who because they were only in minor orders could and did marry. Indeed, the separation of the clerkship from the priesthood is evidenced by the establishment in London of a fraternity of parish clerks which later became a livery company.[3] In the face of these blocks to a route to the priesthood which also involved both a practical parochial training and the inculcation of a clerical identity through residence in the incumbent's household, how was that identity acquired?

How common it was for boys or young men to enter a clerical household for training and at what age, and in what capacity, is far from clear. The boy who spent a period from March 1459 to June 1460 boarding in the all-male household of the two elderly chaplains of Munden's Chantry, Bridport (Dorset), may have been in the early stages of a clerical career.[4] This would have provided

---

3. Peter Heath, *English Parish Clergy on the Eve of the Reformation* (London, 1969), pp.19–20; Swanson, *Church and Society*, p.43.
4. K.L. Wood-Legh, *A Small Household of the Fifteenth Century, being the Account Book of Munden's Chantry, Bridport* (Manchester, 1956), pp.58–69. He was clearly not a servant as these were not recorded as receiving commons. He may have been receiving an education but that might itself be the beginning of a clerical career.

the social separation and distinct pattern of living which could have inculcated a particular gender identity. A study of clerical house-holds is difficult, given the survival of few domestic accounts, and is mainly possible only for the wealthier clergy, such as the residentiary canons of the secular cathedrals, who appear in the fifteenth cen-tury to have been more interested in bringing up the sons of the local gentry and urban elites who would then go on to secular careers.[5]

Some secular cathedrals did make arrangements to allow boys and young men to lead a common life, separate from the lay world, and be educated either at the chancellor's grammar school or in a choir school. By the fifteenth century most secular cathedrals had a house where choristers could live together, and most also provided the vicars-choral with either a common hall or close by the same period. A number also provided employment for choristers whose voices had broken and were too young to take the orders which would allow them to progress to become vicars-choral, but only Lincoln provided them with a common hall. Elsewhere they may have boarded with other members of the cathedral clergy.[6] Here one can find an environment which might inculcate a clerical gen-der identity, but the number of clergy affected would have been small. Even here it was no hermetically sealed life. By the fifteenth century the master of the York Minster grammar school was often a married clerk.[7] Despite a lifestyle designed to inculcate a clerical identity, the temptations of the flesh were sufficiently strong for vicars-choral of most cathedrals to be disciplined frequently, usually for fornication.

And what happened to those young men who found their way into the Church without living in such a household? The main sources for the names of medieval clergy are the ordination lists recorded in bishops' registers, but they give us no clue as to how or where the young men presenting themselves for ordination had trained or studied. Thus our first knowledge of most young clergy is probably at a point when their clerical identity was already well on the way to being formed. Of the formative influences on those young men who remained living with their own families while serv-ing as choristers, and perhaps parish clerks, and who may never

5. David Lepine, *A Brotherhood of Canons Serving God: English Secular Cathedrals in the Later Middle Ages* (Woodbridge, 1995), pp.127–9.

6. Kathleen Edwards, *English Secular Cathedrals in the Middle Ages* (2nd edn, Man-chester, 1967), pp.303–15.

7. R.B. Dobson, 'The Later Middle Ages, 1215–1500', in G.E. Aylmer and Reginald Cant, eds, *A History of York Minster* (Oxford, 1977), p.71.

have progressed beyond the ranks of the minor orders or the unbeneficed clergy, we have as yet only the slightest knowledge. Some of the dilemmas which faced (in particular) young clergy are explored below through a range of different sources.

Clerical status, gender identity and the laity

Given that clerical discipline required that they be celibate, and also forbade the carrying of arms because of the ban on members of the Church drawing blood, secular clergy, like monks, were, in principle if not always in practice, excluded from two of the activities which most obviously characterized the ideal of masculinity (certainly for the aristocracy and probably for those lower down the social scale), that is, fighting and reproducing. This might lead to the assumption that the clergy then fell into the feminine category. Women were not expected to fight, at least not in the formal sense, and celibacy and virginity were coming to be increasingly seen as feminine virtues by the later Middle Ages. The emphasis on the chastity of St Anne, St Elizabeth of Hungary, and the virgin saints is not parallelled in the lives of the male saints, except perhaps in the frequently told temptations of St Anthony, and even then attempted seduction by female devils was only one of the problems he faced.

Priests especially, clergy generally, performed their profession through speech. They sang, they spoke the mass, they heard confession. But speech was characterized as feminine, especially excessive speech. This contrasts with the written word, which was masculine and authoritative, and especially with the Latin written word which was authoritatively clerical and even divine ('in the beginning was the word and the word was with God'). Did this use of the spoken word make the clergy feminine? In terms of lay male perception it was one of the things which made the clergy attractive to women.

In Chaucer's 'Miller's Tale' 'hende Nicholas', a young scholar, is described both as being 'lyk a mayden meke for to see' and also as as having a 'myrie throte'.[8] Nicholas wins the love of the carpenter's wife by his fair speech. His rival Absolon, a parish clerk, also seeks to win Alison's love by serenading her, and by playing Herod. These vocal gymnastics both prove less attractive than Nicholas' voice because Absolon has a 'loud quynyble' (a 'high treble' suggests *The Riverside Chaucer*, but perhaps a loud whinny), which might

---

8. All references are to *The Riverside Chaucer*, ed. Larry D. Benson (3rd edn, Oxford, 1988), pp.68–77.

suggest he was less of a man than 'maidenly' Nicholas. Speech alone therefore is not enough to characterize the clergy as feminine, after all both these young men are shown as masculinely heterosexual, but their masculinity is in some sense qualified by their verbal activity. Indeed Absolon's desire to play Herod, which in those texts of the Mystery Plays which have survived, is a ranting part, despite the unsuitability of his voice, suggests some anxiety about his masculinity. And Herod, like Absolon, fails to achieve his goal. Both these young men could claim to be members of the secular clergy,[9] both are also clearly represented as lecherous, and each, though in different ways, also says something of the gender ambivalence of the clergy. Absolon cannot give a convincingly masculine performance, and Nicholas, though he can 'act the part' enough to get the woman, nevertheless looks like a girl.

This ambivalence is emphasized when Absolon on the holy day goes:

Sensynge the wyves of the parisshe faste;
And many a lovely look on hem he caste   (ll. 3341–2)

('Censing [i.e. wafting with incense] the wives of the parish eagerly/
And many a loving look on them he threw')

but for Alison:

Hath in his herte swich a love-longynge
That of no wyf took he noon offrynge;
For curteisie, he seyde, he wolde noon.   (ll. 3349–51)

('He has in his heart such a love-longing/That he would take no offering [i.e. money payment to the church on the festival] from any of the wives/For courtesy, he said, he would not [or did not want any].')[10]

The double entendre of this passage both suggests the sexual availability of the female parishioners and Absolon's unwillingness or inability to take advantage of it other than in respect of the one woman who does not want him. Between them Nicholas and Absolon illustrate the dilemma of young clergy, and perhaps explain the delinquent behaviour of certain of the clergy: to keep their vows and risk their masculinity; or to confirm their masculinity at the expense of their vows. These young men were thus in a double bind, likely to lose status whatever choice they made.

9. Heath, *Parish Clergy*, pp.19–20.
10. Both 'censing' and 'offering' carry sexual implications.

But priesthood was something to which only men could aspire; women were by their nature excluded from it. In this sense the priesthood was specifically male. Moreover, however much it may have been resented by laymen, any priest could perform in ways which were permitted to no layman. At confession and Communion a layman of whatever status must kneel before his priest to receive the sacraments which only a priest could deliver. The authority which priests exercised was therefore quintessentially masculine.

All this suggests a degree of ambivalence, even confusion, especially if we are wedded to a two-gender model. Were medieval secular clergy masculine, feminine or a third gender? In one respect medieval clergy did have to be real men. The Old Testament requirement that only perfect male animals (with both testicles) be offered to God, was taken to apply also to those ordained to the priesthood.[11] In practice, however, papal dispensation could be acquired in cases of physical handicap. These dispensations were rarely sought, in comparison with fairly common dispensations for illegitimacy, though whether this indicates that men who were not physically perfect did not seek the priesthood, whether physical imperfection was more embarrassing than illegitimacy and thus not admitted to, or whether it was not regarded as important is unclear.[12] The famous case of Abelard in the early twelfth century certainly indicates that public knowledge of castration was both hideously embarrassing, and no bar to entry into the monastic life and to the priesthood, though someone as well known as Abelard might have received preferential treatment. It may have become an issue in continuance as a priest by the fifteenth century, as a Worcester priest in 1448 sought a dispensation for self-castration, having been driven to this extremity by the tension between his wish to keep his vows and his sexual desires.[13]

Other secular clergy did not all find the possession of fully functioning sexual organs and an oath of celibacy to be wholly compatible either, but their response was more likely to involve breach of their vows. Fornication and fighting were the two misdemeanours for which clergy were most frequently disciplined by the archdeacons' courts, or by their own house. These too were the activities,

---

11. Leviticus 20:16–20; 22:24–5.
12. Heath, *Parish Clergy*, pp.16–18. The English cases are almost all for blemishes in the eyes, which were both very obvious, and presumably not embarrassing, *(C)alendar of (P)apal (L)etters*, vols. V–XIV, passim.
13. Heath, *Parish Clergy*, p.105; *CPL* X, p.401.

particularly the former, alongside hunting, trading, drinking and over-dressing, which John Myrc, an Austin canon, and author of the *Manuale Sacerdotis* (c.1400), a handbook for priests, most warned against:

Preste, þy self thow moste be chast,
And say þy serues wyþowten hast . . .
Of honde & mowþe þou moste be trewe,
And grete oþes thow moste enchewe,
In worde and dede þou moste be mylde, . . .
Dronkelec and glotonye,
Pruyde and slouþe and enue,
Alle þow moste putten a-way . . .
That þe nedeth, ete and drynke,
But sle þy lust for any thynge.
Tauernes also thow moste for-sake,
Wrastelynge, & schotynge, & such maner game,
Thow myȝte not vse wythowte blame.
Hawkynge, huntynge, and dawnsynge, . . .
Cutted clothes and pyked schone,
Thy god fame þey wol for-done.
Marketes and feyres I the for-bede . . .
In honeste clothes thow moste gon,
Baselard ny bawdryke were þow non.'   (ll. 23–48)[14]

('Priest, you must be chaste, /And say your service without haste . . . /Of hand and mouth you must be true [i.e. not lie], /And great oaths you must avoid, /In word and deed you must be mild, . . . /Drunkenness and gluttony, /Pride and sloth and envy, /You must put them all away . . . /Eat and drink as much as you need, /But slay lust above all things. /You must forsake taverns, /Wrestling and shooting (perhaps archery, but probably shooting at the cock, often associated with betting) and similar games/You may not be involved in without being censured./Hawking, hunting, and dancing . . . /Fashionable dagged clothes and pointed shoes, /Will destroy your good reputation. /I forbid you to go to markets and fairs . . . You must wear respectable clothes, /Do not wear a dagger or baldric' [a shoulder strap, used to support a sword or a hunting horn])

Thomas Laqueur has argued that in the medieval period there was no gender order, there was merely a notion of masculinity, and of not masculinity; in other words medieval society had a single-gender system. This might suggest that the medieval clergy were not-masculine, but not necessarily feminine. However, Laqueur is

---

14. *Instructions for Parish Priests by John Myrc*, ed., E. Peacock, EETS 31 (1868, revised 1902), p.2.

not a medievalist and most medievalists would reject his view as being simply a convenient means of providing a start line in the early modern period for the gender system, rather than a realistic understanding of medieval ideas of gender.[15] By contrast, studies of masculinity in the nineteenth and twentieth centuries have increasingly emphasized not just a distinction between masculine and feminine, but a more complex picture, not of a single homogenous 'masculinity' but of varieties of masculinity.[16] It is argued that these varieties relate particularly to class, to sexuality and to ethnicity, and that they are subject to change over time. If orders are substituted for classes, or perhaps cross-cut with them, this model applied to the Middle Ages would allow the medieval clergy to fulfil their obligations and yet remain real men, just a different kind of real man from their lay neighbours. If the clergy possessed a 'different form of masculinity', what form did that masculinity take, and how was it acquired?

I have argued that fighting and fornication were the two major markers of lay masculinity, but what does this tell us? It might, of course, simply mean that these are innate male characteristics. But this is too simple. Priests were expected to avoid these behaviours, and to control any impulses to them. However, I have suggested that a clerical gender identity was acquired late, and in many cases perhaps imperfectly. Thus for many clergy, being debarred from these activities might indeed mark them out as less than 'real men', or even as feminized. Hence clerical transgression of these rules might indicate anxiety about gender identity, and the need on the part of some clergy to prove that they were 'truly' masculine.

Transgressive clergy and the courts

In order to discuss clerical transgression I would like briefly to examine some evidence drawn from the Capitular Act Book of York Minster.[17] The Dean and Chapter of the Minster had jurisdiction

15. Thomas Laqueur, *Making Sex: Body and Gender from the Greeks to Freud* (Cambridge, Mass., and London, 1990), p.8. Note the way that he leaps 'across a millennial chasm' (p.63) from the authorities of the Classical and late Antique world to the world of the Renaissance and Reformation, between chapters two and three.

16. L. Davidoff and C. Hall, *Family Fortunes: Men and Women of the English Middle Class* (London, 1987); J.A. Mangan and J. Walvin, *Manliness and Morality: Middle-class Masculinity in Britain and America, 1800–1940* (Manchester, 1987); M. Roper and J. Tosh, eds, *Manful Assertions: Masculinities in Britain since 1800* (London, 1991); Lynne Segal, *Slow Motion: Changing Masculinities, Changing Men* (London, 1990).

17. BIHR D/C AB. 1. Act Book of the Dean and Chapter's Court, 1387–1494.

over all those living within the Liberty of St Peter in the city, as well as clergy serving the churches appropriated to the Minster throughout the diocese. Among a broad range of other material there are frequent presentments of both clergy and laypeople for a variety of misdemeanours. The vast majority of clerical cases dealt with sexual misconduct, although some cases of violence were also recorded. Whether this indicates that violence was an infrequent ocurrence or that the court was less concerned to discipline it is far from clear. It may suggest that for both transgressors and those imposing discipline, sexual activity was a more serious issue, a more clearly transgressive act. Accordingly, I would like to look at two contrasting cases: one of fornication, one implying the possibility of violence. These are both relatively rare cases where rather more than the bare outline of charge and penalty are recorded.

In 1397 *Dominus* Thomas de Watton, a vicar-choral of the Minster, was accused of fornicating with three women: Alice de Malton; Agnes, daughter of Thomas del Coke (with both of whom he had been convicted before); and Agnes Grynder, who was said to be pregnant as a result.[18] In itself this would tell us only about a minor cleric, unable to control his sexual appetites, very much the stuff of contemporary anti-clerical discourse. However, the charge went on to detail the scurrilous and obscene stories he had been telling in various local taverns. The two recorded stories were both tall tales about his sexual prowess. In one he claimed to have known carnally a certain woman (unnamed) fifteen times in a day and the following night. In the other he said that he had deflowered seven virgins in the town of Ripon (Yorkshire). The presumably drunken boasting (given the location in taverns) perhaps gives us an insight into what drove his persistent offending. The insistence on his sexual endurance and his irresistibility suggest a man deeply insecure about his masculinity.

The second case is less straightforward of interpretation. In 1421 Richard Kirkeby and William Wyvell, one a deacon, the other a chaplain, both also vicars-choral of the Minster, were charged with walking through the streets of York at eleven at night on the Eve of St John the Baptist, carrying poleaxes and wearing 'pallettes' or helmets on their heads and chaplets around their necks, against honesty and priestly dignity.[19] They admitted to having gone to see the St John's Eve fires but denied the poleaxes and helmets, saying they had been dressed as priests with chaplets on their heads. The

18. BIHR D/C AB 1 fos.2, 4.   19. *Ibid.*, f.61v.

court appears to have regarded it as a minor matter, for it merely admonished them.

The midsummer festival was widely celebrated with fires, wealthier citizens providing food and drink at their doors, and in York there were minstrels and a play.[20] In many towns the celebrations went on well into the night. It is therefore not surprising to find two priests out and about late in the evening to see the fun. But why were they carrying (or not) axes and wearing helmets and chaplets? As priests they should not have been carrying weapons, though marching watches bearing arms, while not attested at York, were common forms of marking the festival. Nor was their decoration, although appropriate to the time of year (the celebrations frequently involved the dressing of buildings with greenery and the wearing of garlands), suitable to their clerical estate. However, young clerics wearing garlands on their heads would have been dressed much like other young laymen, and this appears to have been how they were trying to present themselves to the capitular court. They seem to have been willing to present themselves in this way in order to draw attention away from the more serious issue of the bearing of arms.

While the clergy were generally banned from the carrying and use of weapons because of the canon law ban on priests shedding blood, this was reversed for a period during the Hundred Years' War. From about the middle of the fourteenth century to c.1418, on occasions of threat of invasion, the clergy were required to muster to perform as a defensive militia, in armour and carrying weapons. Few of them ever needed to use their weapons in anger, but this direct contravention of canon law does not appear to have generated ecclesiastical discussion, let alone controversy. This requirement was laid upon the clergy by the Crown but does not seem to have elicited any objection from the bishops, some of whom, like the archbishops of York and bishops of Durham, had long had a role in organizing resistance to Scottish invasions.[21] Indeed the only ones to have objected, like Langland and some of the Lollards, seem to have been marginal voices. This licensed transgression of clerical gender identity seems to have elicited none of the anxiety to be found in some of the early medieval sources discussed by

20. Ronald Hutton, *The Rise and Fall of Merry England* (Oxford, 1994), pp.37–40.

21. However, two grants of clerical taxation in the 1380s, significantly in the Northern Province, were only made on the condition that the clergy not have to array themselves: Bruce McNab, 'Obligations of the Church in English Society: military arrays of the clergy, 1369–1418', in W.C. Jordan, B. McNab, T.F. Ruiz, eds, *Order and Innovation in the Middle Ages: Essays in Honour of Joseph R. Strayer* (Princeton, N.J., 1976), pp.299–300.

Janet Nelson in this volume about the legitimacy, even for the nobility, of violence. Alison McHardy argues that this arming of the clergy, even for a limited period and in specific circumstances led to a blurring of the distinctions between the clergy and laity.[22]

We may have here indirect evidence that there was some kind of marching watch in York, albeit of an unofficial kind, and that these two young clerics were taking part in it. There had been general arrays of the clergy in 1415 and 1418, and Archbishop Bowet would be carried into battle against the Scots in 1422. In the context of the times it is quite possible that the two vicars-choral legitimately owned these arms.[23] Nevertheless, there must have been some concern about their activities or they would not have appeared before the court. Whether the concern was that they were appearing armed other than at an array of the clergy, or whether they were suspected of an intention to commit some act of violence under the cover of the midsummer festival, is unclear. Corroboration for the view that the vicars-choral were involved in, or afraid of, violence is given by the case of John Middleton, another vicar-choral, who in the same month was presented for spending the night in the house of his godmother and thereby causing suspicion. His defence was that he had taken refuge there from an unspecified group who wanted to attack him.[24]

The illicit violence of the clergy, involved in brawls and sometimes worse, evoked much more concern than the legitimated potential violence of the clerical arrays, but probably less than other clerical misdemeanours, such as breach of celibacy. The issue here seems to have been the matter of licence; violence could be permissible – indeed, required under some circumstances – whereas active sexuality was always a problem, both for ecclesiastical authorities and the lay society amongst which the clergy lived. This suggests that, by the later Middle Ages, clerical celibacy was, for both clergy and laity, more distinctly a marker of clerical gender identity than abstention from the use of weapons. Indeed, the classification of the clergy as 'spiritual gentlemen' may in part have sprung from an increased acceptance of their right to bear arms, and further broken down an earlier distinctly clerical identity based on powerlessness as well as celibacy. In the fifteenth century, priests, especially

22. A. McHardy, 'The clergy and the Hundred Years' War', in W.J. Shiels, ed., *The Church and War*, Studies in Church History 20 (1983), pp.171–79.

23. In 1418 a group of Worcester clergy were armed '*cum loricis et palettes ac curteis lanceis vel pollaxis*'; McNab, 'Military arrays', p.304.

24. Frederick Harrison, *Life in a Medieval College* (London, 1952), p.71.

those in the beneficed and higher reaches of the Church, were increasingly seen as assimilated to the status of the gentry. In 1486 *The Book of St Albans* enumerated nine ranks of gentry, of whom the last were the spiritual gentry.[25] This may reflect in part the increased dominance of gentry and aristocracy in the upper levels of the Church, and probably affected the lower reaches of the Church much less, but it still indicates a partial dissolution of clerical identity.

Transgressive clergy and anti-clerical literature

It is not just in the courts that we find evidence of clerical misdemeanour, but also in the discourse of literary production, both of the laity and of the clergy. Indeed, in much of this writing, particularly of the late fourteenth and early fifteenth centuries, there is an assumption of clerical sexual activity, more rarely of violence. The reasons why clergy should be concerned about this are fairly clear, but what about the laity? Was this simply a concern with clerical discipline, or did the active sexuality and violence of some clergy transgress gender hierarchies? Did laymen feel that they were more masculine than clergy or that clergy were less than masculine, and thus resent the behaviour of transgressive clergy as blurring a gender hierarchy?

I will explore these issues through a discussion of an inquisition postmortem and two lyrics, all of which share similar assumptions about clerical gender. The inquisition postmortem is a document created by a group of secular men, the jurors, called on by the coroner to explain the death of a chaplain. Although an historical document, it is also a fiction, drawing on the discourse to be found in the literary material.

The inquest was into the death of Hugh de Weston, a chaplain, killed on Christmas Day 1287 in Acton Scott (Shropshire) by John de Quercubus.[26] In the evening a group of men were singing outside the tavern, when Hugh the chaplain, 'immensely drunk' according to the lay jurors, came up and began quarrelling with them. John was one of the singers, apparently carolling to, or perhaps

---

25. D.N. Lepine, 'The origins and careers of the canons of Exeter Cathedral, 1300–1455', in Christopher Harper-Bill, ed., *Religious Belief and Ecclesiastical Careers in Late Medieval England*, (Woodbridge, 1991), p.97.

26. *Calendar of Inquisitions Miscellaneous*, 1, no. 2306, also printed in H. Rothwell, ed., *English Historical Documents, III, (1189–1327)* (London, 1975), no. 198, p.828.

serenading, 'certain women who were standing by in a field'. Hugh allegedly hated John because of his good singing and because Hugh was also interested in the women, so he took a sword and attacked John, hitting him on the head and wounding his left hand. John begged for God's peace on his knees and then ran away, but when the chaplain cornered him, stabbed him in the chest with a knife, killing him. The absolute accuracy of the account, given by a group of laymen anxious to exonerate a fellow layman of blame, may be open to doubt, though doubtless alcohol, vying for the favours of women, and weapons were all involved.

What the jury did was to use popular anti-clerical topoi to construct an account of what had happened which laid all the blame at the feet of the dead man. The chaplain is constructed as drunk, lecherous – 'affecting the women nearby' – and also violent. (Interestingly, he is also apparently enraged by the singing, which trespasses on his own area of expertise.)[27] He is the aggressor throughout, wielding a sword to his opponent's knife (i.e. an illegitimate weapon against a legitimate one). By contrast, his killer is 'standing by', implicitly an innocent bystander, whose reaction to being struck with a sword is to kneel and speak peace, and then to run away, only drawing his knife in self-defence when cornered, wounded and in justifiable fear of his life. John Myrc's advice to priests to slay lust, forsake taverns and wear no daggers, while written more than a century later, was clearly part of a common tradition about what the clergy too often failed to do. The jurors of Acton Scott were able to use that tradition to portray Hugh as a bad priest and thus entirely responsible for his own death. They thereby disguised but also acknowledged a lay victory over the clergy; a layman had excluded, in the most permanent way possible from the lay sphere of activity (paying court to the young women of their community), the upstart clerk who had tried to muscle in on their rights.

The poems are from *Medieval English Lyrics*, edited by R.T. Davies: no. 73, 'Jankyn, the clerical seducer' and no. 108, 'A night with a holy water clerk'. Both are argued by Davies to be by clergy, though both are anonymous.[28] Both are written from the perspective of the

27. Cf. the lyrics discussed below: no.73, line 20 'Jankyn craketh a merye note', no.108, line 17 'Jack preyede in my faire face'.
28. One is from British Library MS Sloane 2593, the other from Gonville and Caius Camb MS 383. R.T. Davies, ed., *Medieval English Lyrics* (London, 1966 edition), pp.162–3, 204–6, discussed pp.336–7, 347–8. There is a double entendre on 'holy water' in the second of these lyrics. It was the job of the clerk to sprinkle the congregation with holy water during the main Sunday Mass.

young woman seduced by a young secular clerk and left with child. In the first of these the subject of the lyric, Alison, describes how she enjoys hearing Jankyn doing his job, beginning the office, reading the Epistle, with the refrain 'Kyrie, so kyrie, /Jankyn singeth merye, /With Aleison' and only reveals at the end 'Alas I go with childe'.[29] The speaker of the second poem describes how 'Ladd I the dance a Midsomer Day' and attracted the attention of Jack, and how dancing led to kissing, to wooing and to a night together.

How are we to read these lyrics? Are they simply didactic, as P.J.P. Goldberg has argued, warning young women against seducers and particularly clerical ones who cannot marry, whatever they may say?[30] Jack, the holy water clerk, was probably still in minor orders, perhaps only with a first tonsure, but Jankyn who reads the Epistle and carries the Pax brede to the congregation was probably a sub-deacon or deacon, in major orders, though he could have been performing the office of a deacon as a parish clerk and thus still in minor orders. In the case of the holy water clerk, at least, his status was distinctly ambiguous; he could still marry and become a parish clerk, and the frequency of married parish clerks by the date of the poem (c.1450) has already been noted. His seduction of the young woman was through the promise of a pair of gloves, a traditional betrothal gift.[31]

The trouble with the minor clergy was not that they could not marry, but that they could. A promise of marriage was all too easily believed by inexperienced young women, because there were married clergy around. For young clerks too, particularly those without good prospects of promotion in the uncertain world of the clerical job market, the temptation to settle for a steady, if meagre, living and the compensations of marriage may have been considerable. For the parents of the young women at whom these cautionary tales were aimed – those who were interested in a good marriage for their daughters – a parish clerk was no great catch. For though these minor clergy could marry, by doing so almost all of them ended any hope of promotion in the Church. In a very few cases where the clerk had acquired an appropriate university education,

---

29. There is a pun on the prayer Kyrie Eleison – 'Lord have mercy', and the name Alison. The Kyrie is found at the beginning of the Mass.

30. P.J.P. Goldberg, 'Leaving mother at home: young women after the Plague', unpublished paper given at the Berkshire Conference on the History of Women, Vassar College (1993), pp.7–8.

31. 'A peire white gloves, I ha to thine were (wear)'.... 'Com hom after thy gloves that I thee bihette (promised)', 'A Night with a Holy Water Clerk', ll. 24, 27.

a good living could be made in the ecclesiastical courts, for which promotion to the priesthood was unnecessary. But the majority of the above cases, fictional or real, did not involve such men; most were unlikely to rise above the lower ranks of the beneficed clergy at best. An apprentice, once out of his articles, might with the help of a good wife make something of himself, and possibly might make himself a master. A married parish clerk would always have a master to answer to. Marriage for the minor clergy was not, there-fore, a good idea: from their own perspective, from the perspective of their superiors in the Church, or from those of the young women with whom they became involved and their families. In this sense a clerk, even a married one, was less of a man than a layman with his own workshop or landholding. (This of course begs the question of the masculinity of those laymen who spent their lives as wage labourers; the gender identity of urban apprentices is discussed above in chapter 4.)

Because marriage was such a bad idea, in relation to a further career, many clergy must have hoped to avoid it. However, the ambiguity of the situation made it ripe for exploitation by those who wished to do so. In some sense these lyrics may be celebra-tory of clerical misdemeanours. I argued earlier that discussions of modern masculinity have usually pointed to a range of masculin-ities existing together. However, these masculinities are not usually treated as being equal, a selection of lifestyles from which young men can freely choose. Some forms of masculinity carry more weight than others, and not all are equally open. R.W. Connell distin-guishes between dominant or hegemonic masculinity (which varies in form according to time and place), and subordinate, complicit and marginal forms of masculinity, which also vary but in relation to the dominant form of masculinity.[32] Subordinate and particu-larly marginal masculinities may be defined by hegemonic mascu-linity as bearing those qualities or characteristics which hegemonic masculinity finds inadequate or even unacceptable, i.e. a projection of the 'other' onto a minority group, hence modern associations of male homosexuality with effeminacy. Such marginal groups may choose to valorize the negative characteristics projected onto them. The emphasis of the ban on certain kinds of behaviour may para-doxically, have acted as a licence to behave in precisely those ways. Literary and cultural stereotypes of the unchaste clerk made it easier for clerks tempted to fornication to yield to temptation. Hugh de

32. R.W. Connell, *Masculinities* (Cambridge, 1995), pp.76–81.

Weston of Acton Scott may have been represented as fulfilling the bad clerical stereotype, but he was outside the tavern, he was carrying a weapon, and he may well have been interested in the nearby women.

The extent to which clerical masculinity was a marginal masculinity is problematic, and there are good reasons, such as the dominance of the Church in most areas of life, for arguing that it was not. But if we are discussing not a single clerical masculinity, but one of a variety, as the earlier distinction between monastic and secular clerical masculinity might indicate, then it could be argued that most of the cases discussed did belong to a particular marginal, or at least subordinate, clerical masculinity. In all the cases, both literary and historical, the men share a common characteristic beyond that of belonging to the clergy. As well as being not fully masculine, they were also not fully socially adult. Indeed, their lack of masculinity may have been predicated upon this lack of full social adulthood. For a layman, becoming the head of an independent household, which was usually bound up with marriage, was the marker of full adulthood. He was now the master in his own home. None of the clerics discussed were heads of establishments (I hesitate to use the term 'head of household' because that is not clear from the evidence). The vicars-choral of York Minster lived communally under a head; Hugh de Weston was a chaplain, probably under the authority of a parish priest, even if not living in his house, as were all the literary characters. Under these circumstances other markers of social adulthood, such as sexual activity, may have assumed disproportionate importance to these men.

To the authorities of Church and town, however, the disruptive and ungoverned sexuality, the drunkenness and minor violence of these mostly young men were precisely the markers of youthful masculinity. But most of these 'Lost Boys' would never grow up.[33] Their sexuality would never be channelled within marriage. The expansion of employment for lesser clergy as household, guild and chantry chaplains, as stipendiary and mass priests, meant that most of them could look forward at best to a life of reasonable security as an employee of family or guild, but more likely one of insecurity, working by the day, the week or the year. All employees, often in someone else's household, frequently under lay authority, they were

---

33. Richard Tyttesbury sought papal absolution in 1398 for his youthful failings as an Oxford student, when he had brawled, revealed confessions and celebrated mass in unsuitable places, but he had made good as a canon of Exeter Cathedral. Cited in Lepine, *A Brotherhood of Canons*, p.156.

rarely able to establish their own households. Only a few could hope for security and perhaps independence as a beneficed chantry priest. Most of them would spend their lives in some sort of social late adolescence.

Robert Swanson argues in this volume that emasculinity became a less tenable identity in the later Middle Ages, and I would tend to agree that the distinctiveness of a clerical masculinity was blurred by a number of factors. At one level the increase in lay literacy and the possibility of making a career as an administrator without the necessity of taking orders undermined one of the clergy's main claims to superior knowledge and also limited the need for educated men to enter the clergy. Hence, perhaps, the frequency of delay in entering orders for better-educated men – if a benefice did not appear then they could still make a career as laymen. In other respects, the laicization of certain roles within the Church, such as that of parish clerk, both limited the opportunities for young men to acquire a clerical gender identity within a clerical household at an early age, and also blurred the distinctions between the lay and the clerical estate.

Conclusion

By way of conclusion I would like to offer an analogy between the relationship of clerical and lay masculinity in the later Middle Ages and black and white masculinity in the modern period. This draws particularly on the experience of America but also applies to Britain. In a culture where black men have been treated by white men as less than fully masculine and, historically, as less than human, more recently, through lesser access to economic and political independence, both sides have tended to see black men as more sexual than white men. For white men this has been a by-product of their view of black men as less than human, a projection of a troubling 'animal' sexuality onto 'the other'; for black men, internalizing dominant white values, it has nonetheless been a compensation for inability or difficulty in maintaining themselves and their families economically. 'I may not be able to provide for a family, but sexually I am more of a man than he is.'[34] For some clergy in the later Middle Ages, uncertain of their own clerical gender identity, acquired so late and so fragilely, it was better to break their

34. This metaphor was inspired by reading Segal, *Slow Motion*, pp.169–204.

vows and prove themselves sexually as 'real men', risking the punishment that came from rejection of their 'official' gender identity, than to accept emasculinity with its ambivalent advantages and all too obvious problems. To paraphrase Lynne Segal, to avoid being 'not-man-enough' it might be necessary to be 'too-masculine-by-half'.[35]

35. *Ibid.*, p.185.

PART THREE

Masculinity and the Written Word: Text and Context

Women and Hunting-birds are Easy to Tame: Aristocratic Masculinity and the Early German Love-Lyric

M. CHINCA

What can images of men in medieval literature contribute to our understanding of historical masculinity? In a recent book Simon Gaunt points out that although literature may not reflect past reality, it nevertheless is part of the historical record:

> The principal interest of literary texts from the historical viewpoint [is not] their mimetic qualities, but their status as fragments of collective memory or . . . collective fantasy. The question 'was the world really like that?' which medievalists, both historians and literary critics, have frequently asked of the texts they work on is largely redundant, and all too often non-literary evidence suggests that medieval literature does not accurately reflect contemporary social structures or practices. But rather than discard literature as having no historical value, we could perhaps ask more pertinent historicizing questions of texts. Why did writers choose to represent the world in this way? What was the symbolic value of these representations and fantasies to contemporary readers?[1]

Applied to our question, this means that literary images of men can tell us something about the collective memories and fantasies of medieval people concerning masculinity: their beliefs about what a man was or ought to be and, occasionally, their uncertainties about the meaning of manhood. This is as much a part of the history of masculinity as hard facts about what men in the past characteristically did; it is part of the record of human subjects' attempts at making sense of the bodies they inhabit.[2]

---

1. Simon Gaunt, *Gender and Genre in Medieval French Literature* (Cambridge, 1995), pp.7–8.
2. For recent work on this topic, see the essays in Sarah Kay and Miri Rubin, eds, *Framing Medieval Bodies* (Manchester, 1994).

If it is an axiom that masculinity is defined in relation to its opposite, femininity, then the lyrics of the poet Der von Kürenberg offer interesting evidence of how German nobles in the second half of the twelfth century made sense of masculinity. All of the fifteen strophes that make up the surviving corpus are love-lyrics; their theme is the relationship between the sexes and they are, moreover, spoken by both men's and women's voices. The voices in the 'women's strophes' ('Frauenstrophen'), as they are called, are patently not the authentic voices of women: they are the product of male poetic imagination and consequently are really documents of a particular kind of masculinity. The use of female personae is a distinctive feature of Kürenberg and other poets who, together with him, are the earliest recorded exponents of the court love-lyric in Germany. Collectively, these poets (the others are Dietmar von Aist, Meinloh von Sevelingen, the Burggraf von Regensburg and the Burggraf von Rietenburg) are known as the 'Danubians', because they appear to come from the part of the German-speaking world traversed by the River Danube, i.e. present-day Austria and Bavaria. Der von Kürenberg has always held a special place in literary history as the first recorded minnesinger (the term by which medieval German love-poets are usually called), though it is not easy to establish whether he was the first of the Danubians, all of whom are dated approximately to the period 1150–80. Possibly Kürenberg was active in the 1160s; at any rate ministerials with the family name de Cúrnberg or Churnperch are attested in the service of the the lords of Wilheringen, near Linz (1161), and the counts of Schalah in upper Bavaria (1166).[3]

I begin with a textual analysis of both the male and the female voices in Kürenberg's lyrics; then, in order to establish the meaning these gendered images might have assumed for their aristocratic public, I consider the possible contexts in which these utterances were performed.

Male and female voices in the lyrics of Der von Kürenberg

The aristocratic status of the male and female voices is evident from the terms by which they refer to each other. The male lover is

---

3. Günther Schweikle, 'Der von Kürenberg', in *Die deutsche Literatur des Mittelalters: Verfasserlexikon*, V (2nd edn, Berlin, 1985), cols 454–61. Olive Sayce, *The Medieval German Lyric 1150–1300: The Development of its Themes and Forms in their European Context* (Oxford, 1982), ch. 3, gives a convenient survey in English of the Danubian lyric.

a knight (strophe IV), sometimes additionally qualified as courtly (III), noble (VI), handsome (XV); the female lover is a noble-woman (V, XII, XIII). The class allegiance and class consciousness of the lyric personae are also revealed in their allusions to the male aristocratic pursuits of warfare (the knight in strophe XII asks for his charger and his armour) and falconry (strophes VIII, IX and XV), and in the admonition that it would be improper for a lady to love beneath her class, 'except if you love a man of low birth; that I do not allow you' (XI).[4]

The speech of these voices, which are clearly marked for social status, is determined by literary convention. The situation basic to almost all of Kürenberg's lyrics is the lovers' separation; con-sequently, most of the songs consist of speech acts appropriate for parted lovers: they send messages to the absent other, express sorrow and hope, narrate past successes in order to boast about their desirability. The assumption of separation is a genre constraint; the different speech acts imaginable in this situation constitute the generic repertoire. All this is reflected in the names traditionally given by literary historians to the various song-types in Kürenberg's œuvre, 'Botenlied' (a song in which the lovers communicate via a messenger, e.g. strophe I), 'Frauenklage' (a woman's plaint; the lady laments the loss or unobtainability of the man she desires, e.g. strophes III, VII, X), 'Wechsel' (an exchange between two lovers, who do not address each other directly, but speak in turn about a common theme, e.g. strophes I and II, IV and V).[5]

Genre is not the only determinant of the lovers' speech; it is also determined by their gender. A high proportion of the lovers' utter-ances is grounded in reminiscence and the narration of past events; female and male voices do not, however, have the same relation-ship to the past. First, an example of a woman reminiscing:

> X   Ez gât mir vonme herzen,   daz ich geweine.
>   ich und mîn geselle   müezen uns scheiden.
>   daz machent lügenære,   got, der gebe in leit.
>   der uns zwei versuonde,   vil wol des wære ich gemeit.

---

4. The most accessible editions of all of Kürenberg's surviving songs, with parallel translation into modern German and commentary, are Günther Schweikle, *Die mittelhochdeutsche Minnelyrik*, vol. 1, *Die frühe Minnelyrik* (Darmstadt, 1977), and Ingrid Kasten, *Deutsche Lyrik des frühen und hohen Mittelalters* (Frankfurt, 1995); Gayle Agler-Beck, *Der von Kürenberg: Edition, Notes and Commentary* (Amsterdam, 1978) is another useful edition, with commentary and interpretation in English. All references and quotations in this chapter are from Schweikle's edition.

5. For a general survey of song-types in medieval German lyric see Günther Schweikle, *Minnesang* (Stuttgart, 1989), pp.119–53.

(It comes from my heart that I cry. My lover and I must part; that is
the fault of liars, may God send them grief. If anyone were to recon-
cile the two of us, I would indeed be glad.)

The speech act that constitutes the present song, the woman's tear-
ful plaint, has its cause in anterior events: liars said something to
provoke a falling out with her lover. The strophe is representative of other women's verses in Kürenberg's œuvre; the speaker is
affected by the past, in the double sense of being the victim of events
and being moved to express sorrow and desire (seen also in strophes III, VI, VII, VIII, IX). Contrast this with an example of male
reminiscence:

> XV   Wîb unde vederspil,   die werdent lîhte zam.
>   swer si ze rehte lucket,   sô suochent si den man.
>   als warb ein schœne ritter   umbe eine frouwen guot.
>   als ich dar an gedenke,   sô stêt wol hôhe mîn muot.

(Women and hunting-birds are easy to tame. If one knows the right
way to entice them, they seek out their man. Thus a handsome
knight wooed a good lady. When I recall this, it brings me great
cheer.)

The difference is not simply that the past here gives grounds for
exultation rather than desire and sorrow. The speaker, who insinu-
ates that he is the handsome knight, recollects a past in which he is
master, not victim, of the will of others. Moreover, although he
recollects a singular occurrence (successful 'enticing' of the lady),
this success is presented as *iterable*; the sententious statement with
which the strophe begins establishes that the narrated incident is
merely one example of the knight's skill in 'taming', a skill he will
carry on applying. Thus whereas women are contained within a
past they cannot change, men use the past to illustrate their ability
to determine events then, now, and in the future.[6] This difference
between the female and male voices is also produced in another
way. The 'genre constraint' referred to above of the lovers' separation is breached in some of the strophes with male voices. In two of
them, we hear men telling women directly how they are to behave:

> XI   Wîb vil schœne,   nû var du sam mir.
>   lieb unde leide,   daz teile ich sant dir.
>   die wîle unz ich daz leben hân,   sô bist du mir vil liep,
>   wan minnestu einen bœsen,   des engan ich dir niet.

6. Rolf Grimminger, *Poetik des frühen Minnesangs* (Munich, 1969), pp.73–4, talks
about 'elegaic time' in the women's laments, which move between past joy and
present sorrow.

(Most beautiful woman, come now with me. With you I will share joy and sorrow. I will love you dearly for as long as I live, except if you love a man of low birth; that I do not allow you.)

XIII Der tunkel sterne,   sam der birget sich,
      als tuo du frouwe schône,   sô du sehest mich,
      sô lâ du dîniu ougen gên   an einen andern man.
      son weiz doch lützel ieman,   wiez under uns zwein ist getân.

(As the dark star hides itself, likewise you should behave, beautiful lady, when you see me, let your eyes gaze upon another man. Then nobody will know how things stand between us.)

These are statements in which the past does not figure at all; instead the men issue instructions in the present which will set the shape of their relationships for the future.

From this brief typology of men's and women's voices it should be clear that we are dealing with constructions of masculinity and femininity; moreover, because they are made and performed by a male poet they reveal how men construct their self-image in opposition to women. Reduced to categorical oppositions, we may say that men are defined as active and mobile, their field of operation covering past, present and future, whereas women are defined as passive and fixed into their past. The validity of these gender categories is also demonstrated negatively, in a strophe where the female voice usurps the male role (and which, incidentally, contains the poet's only reference to himself):

IV   Ich stuont mir nehtint spâte   an einer zinne.
     dô hôrt ich einen ritter   vil wol singen
     in Kürenberges wîse   al ûz der menigîn.
     er muoz mir diu lant rûmen,   alder ich geniete mich sîn.

(Late last night I stood on the battlement. Then I heard a knight singing excellently, in the manner of Kürenberg, above the crowd. He must leave my territory, or I will make him mine.)

The corpus contains two male responses to the demands of this imperious lady, who speaks like a feudal ruler (she has territorial possessions; *rûmen diu lant* is a legal term, meaning 'to be banished').[7] In both cases, the lady is rebuffed:

7. Rüdiger Krohn, 'Begehren und Aufbegehren im Wechsel: Zum Verfahren von Parodie und Protest bei einigen Liedern des Kürenbergers', in R. Krohn, ed., *Liebe als Literatur: Aufsätze zur erotischen Dichtung in Deutschland* (Munich, 1983), pp.117–42, in particular pp.124–8.

XII   Nû bring mir her vil balde   mîn ros, mîn îsengewant,
      wan ich muoz einer frouwen   rûmen diu lant.
      diu wil mich des betwingen,   daz ich ir holt sî.
      si muoz der mîner minne   iemer darbende sîn.

(Now bring me my steed and my armour without delay, for I must
leave a lady's territory. She wants to force me to be her devoted man.
She will have to do without my love forever.)

The knight acts within the parameters set by the lady, but in a way
that preserves his independence and mobility. He refuses to be
compelled to serve her in love (*holt sîn* means both 'to love' and 'to
serve (e.g. as a vassal)') and emphasizes that the lady will not get
what she really wants. This last point is repeated in a burlesque
manner in the other response, the strophe that follows immediately in the manuscripts and which has often been considered
unauthentic:[8]

V   Jô stuont ich nehtint spâte   vor dînem bette.
      dô getorste ich dich, frouwe,   niwet wecken.
      'des gehazze iemer   got den dînen lîp!
      jô enwas ich niht ein eber   wilde', sô sprach daz wîp.

(Truly I stood late last night before your bed. I did not dare to wake
you, lady. 'May God forever hate you on that account! I wasn't a wild
boar, you know,' said the woman.)

Here, in another strophe with face-to-face communication, the
knight appears to have subordinated himself to his mistress, but his
subordination works once again to deprive her (and him) of what
she really desires.

The performance context

So far, I have established only that the texts contain a set of propositions about masculinity (and femininity). I have not yet said
anything about the *significance* of these propositions for those who
performed and listened to the lyrics. This significance is not only in
the words; it is created above all through performance in a social
context. Depending on who performed, in what manner, and for
what public, the textual propositions might be either affirmed or
questioned. These are questions of literary *pragmatics* (a term borrowed from linguistics, where it means the study of how language is
used in social interaction); in order to answer them we have to rely

8. *Ibid.*, pp.127–8.

on hypothetical models. In the case of these early lyrics, we do not have any hard information about performance practice and the social dimension of poetic utterance. The two manuscripts in which Kürenberg's lyrics are preserved postdate their composition by around 150 years; the large Heidelberg manuscript was compiled around 1300, and the recently discovered Budapest fragment has been dated to the period 1280–1300.[9] Both of them present the songs as texts for reading, without the accompanying music. We do not know, therefore, how the strophes recorded on parchment were sung; nor do we know whether and how these largely mono-strophic songs were combined in longer performance sequences. Sometimes the scribes have written down in sequence strophes that apparently belong together (I and II, IV and V, VIII and IX), but they sometimes have separated others (XII is related to IV; perhaps the scribe of the Heidelberg manuscript has placed it later because of a tendency to group the women's and the men's strophes in the corpus together). We are not sure whether other strophes were originally related to one another in longer cycles and if so, which ones. Many combinations are possible in theory, so that most experts assume that the strophes could have been sung in variable sequences. The choice of sequence would have depended on the singer and the situation; the meaning of the strophes would have been determined by this, and other performance variables, such as choice of melody and style of singing.[10] All of this extratextual context has been lost in the transition from orality to writing, and is only partly and speculatively recoverable from the written record of the manuscripts.

We rely, then, on hypothetical models in order to get some purchase on these questions of literary pragmatics. Two models have been proposed. According to the first one, Kürenberg's lyrics would have affirmed and reinforced the image of patriarchal and sexist masculinity they contain. According to the second model, the lyrics would have allowed room for reflexion on masculinity.

9. Gisela Kornrumpf, 'Heidelberger Liederhandschrift C', in *Die deutsche Literatur des Mittelalters: Verfasserlexikon*, III (2nd edn, Berlin, 1981), cols 584–97; A. Vizkelety and K.-A. Wirth, 'Funde zum Minnesang: Blätter aus einer bebilderten Liederhandschrift', *Beiträge zur Geschichte der deutschen Sprache und Literatur* 107 (1985), pp.366–75; A. Vizkelety, 'Die Budapester Liederhandschrift', *Beiträge zur Geschichte der deutschen Sprache und Literatur* 110 (1988), pp.387–407.

10. The improvisatory nature of performance has not always been taken suffi-ciently into account by those who have tried to order Kürenberg's strophes in fixed cycles. For a survey of these attempts (and another proposal) see Christel Schmidt, *Die Lieder der Kürenberg-Sammlung: Einzelstrophen oder zyklische Einheiten?* (Göppingen, 1980).

The first model interprets the lyric as an example of the collect-ive behaviour of noblemen. In an essay published in 1989 Wolfgang Haubrichs suggested that the early German love-lyric, including Kürenberg's, may have been an exclusively male activity, performed by men before an audience composed entirely of men. That would make the lyric similar to other noblemen's sports and pastimes – horsemanship, swordsmanship, archery, jousting, hunting – the com-mon denominator of which is that they are all forms of ritual male behaviour whose functions are to display aristocratic masculinity and to confer distinction upon the practitioners. The lyric can be said to perform these functions in a number of ways: it allows male singers to boast about sexual conquests (Kürenberg's strophe about women and hunting-birds is a prime example of this); it enables them to insinuate their desirability (the function of the women's strophes which lament the loss or unobtainability of the lover); finally, the lyric allows the male poet to enhance his status com-pared with other men by showing off his accomplishment as a singer (Kürenberg alludes to his singing as what makes him stand out from the crowd). Both by their content and by the manner of their execution, the lyrics give proof of aristocratic masculinity, defined as prowess and distinction.[11]

Haubrichs thus proposes a homology between textual content and contextual function. The lyrics are a performance of the patri-archal masculinity they represent. They are male *behaviour*, not only in the sense that they are sung and listened to by men, but in the further sense that their performance – along with other ritualized sports and pastimes – *is* masculinity. All of this behaviour expresses an aristocratic male *habitus*, a term that Haubrichs uses several times and which he defines in an earlier essay as the unconscious prin-ciples that define the behaviour common to all members of a group.[12] It is important to read the 1989 essay together with these earlier remarks in order to realize the full implications of what Haubrichs is proposing for lyrics like Kürenberg's. He follows Bourdieu, his acknowledged source for the notion of *habitus*, in arguing that soci-eties with no specialized education system rely on other institutions,

---

11. Wolfgang Haubrichs, 'Männerrollen und Frauenrollen im frühen deutschen Minnesang', *Zeitschrift für Literaturwissenschaft und Linguistik* 74 (1989), pp.39–57, here pp.54–7; Krohn, 'Begehren und Aufbegehren', pp.126–7, also suggests an all-male audience.

12. Wolfgang Haubrichs, '*Reiner muot* und *kiusche site*: Argumentationsmuster und situative Differenzen in der staufischen Kreuzzugslyrik zwischen 1188/89 und 1227/28', in R. Krohn, B. Thum and P. Wapnewski, eds, *Stauferzeit: Geschichte, Literatur, Kunst* (Stuttgart, 1978), pp.295–324, here p.302.

such as myth, art and ritual, in order to inculcate *habitus*.[13] Performing lyrics is one of the rituals in which the *habitus* of aristocratic
masculinity is reproduced, in both senses of the verb: the *habitus* is
expressed, and it is inculcated in its public.[14]

According to Bourdieu, the principles of the *habitus* are transmitted practically, or through symbolic forms, like myth or ritual,
that do not admit of questioning; for that reason the principles 'are
placed beyond the grasp of consciousness, and hence cannot be
touched by voluntary, deliberate transformation'.[15] Haubrichs follows Bourdieu in describing early minnesang, including Kürenberg,
as 'an art drawn from experience, which does not become reflect-
ive because it has no need of argument'.[16] The lyric is one more
thing, in addition to fighting, hunting, riding and so on, that
noblemen self-evidently do; its performance therefore attracts no
debate. This seems to me to involve a confusion between the lyric
personae, who do often speak without reflecting, and the perform-
ers and public, who may have reflected on the roles they performed
and listened to.[17] If the lyric is unreflective, this is not because it is
intrinsically so, but because it is *used* unreflectingly. Such a use is
conceivable for an all-male public indulging in homosocial bonding through collective rehearsal of their gender stereotypes, but we
cannot be sure that this was the only kind of public or performance
context for the lyric. All of the named poets of early minnesang
were men, but we do not know that their audience was always
composed entirely of men. Kürenberg does not address any of his
lyrics explicitly to other men, unlike the troubadour William of
Aquitaine, with whom he has so often been compared and who
appeals in several songs to his male *companho*.[18] In fact, Haubrichs
has to base his argument partly on surmise (the content of the
songs is unsuitable for performance in mixed company) and partly
on information contained in contemporary literary sources.[19] For

---

13. *Ibid.*; compare Pierre Bourdieu, *Outline of a Theory of Practice* (Cambridge, 1977), p.167.

14. Haubrichs, 'Männerrollen', pp.54, 57.

15. Bourdieu, *Outline*, p.94.

16. Haubrichs, 'Männerrollen', p.54 (my translation of 'eine Kunst aus Erfahrung, die nicht reflexiv wird, weil sie der Argumentation nicht bedarf').

17. Grimminger, *Poetik*, pp.70–3, 82–5, 88–90, argues that the lyrics were intended to provoke reflexion in their audience; for further discussion of this question see Mark Chinca, 'Knowledge and practice in the early German love-lyric', *Forum for Modern Language Studies* 33 (1997), pp.204–16.

18. *The Poetry of William VII, Count of Poitiers, IX Duke of Aquitaine*, ed. and trans. Gerald A. Bond (New York & London, 1982), songs I, II, III.

19. Haubrichs, 'Männerrollen', pp.53, 54–5.

instance, the *Kaiserchronik* (*c.*1140/50) gives a list of recreations at a courtly festival which describes how the knights 'talked about fine horses and good dogs, they talked about hunting-birds and many other pastimes, they talked about beautiful ladies';[20] Heinrich von Melk's verse homily on the theme of *memento mori* (*c.*1160/80) complains that 'wherever knights gather they start swapping stories about how many women so-and-so has fornicated with; they are incapable of covering their disgrace and boast only about women'.[21] These passages evoke an all-male social setting in which lyrics might also have been sung, but perhaps that was not the only context for early minnesang.

In fact Haubrichs does not take account of literary evidence, sometimes in the very same sources, that points to the inclusion of women in the audience for the lyric. In one of Kürenberg's own songs, the strophe uttered by the imperious lady (IV), the poet is heard (or maybe overheard) by a woman. Heinrich von Melk presses home his lesson about the vanity of life in this world by confronting an imaginary lady with the corpse of her princely lover and asking her what remains now of the qualities that made him so attractive to women when he was living. Among these qualities is his tongue, 'with which he could sing love-songs [*trovt liet*] pleasingly'; the effectiveness of this detail for the lady presupposes that she habitually heard and was pleased by his singing.[22] Finally, the *Kaiserchronik* contains a little anecdote about an incident that supposedly took place in the reign of Tarquin the Proud. It is worth examining this passage in some detail, because it too hints at the possible existence of another pragmatic context for lyric, alongside the exclusively masculine one proposed by Haubrichs. The Romans are laying siege to Viterbo; during an armistice a lady from the city engages one of the Romans, Totila, in conversation. She addresses him: 'Totila, you noble man, come closer to the ladies; you are so bold and a thoroughly fine hero so far as your physical strength is concerned. In God's name, pray answer my question. Which of these two things would you prefer as a man of honour: that a beautiful lady should make love to you all night through, or that you should go armed tomorrow morning to fight with a man you consider your equal in

20. *Kaiserchronik*, ed. E. Schröder (Hannover, 1895), ll. 4424–7.
21. Heinrich von Melk, *Von des todes gehugde*, ed. Thomas Bein *et al.* (Stuttgart, 1994), ll. 354–8.
22. *Ibid.*, ll. 612–13. Haubrichs, 'Männerrollen', pp.40–1, does quote this passage as evidence that love-lyrics formed part of an aristocratic culture in which both men and women participated, but by the end of the same essay, when he discusses the pragmatic context of singing, he seems to have forgotten this point.

boldness? If the choice were yours, which would you rather do?'[23]
What is interesting in this anecdote is that masculinity is not boast-
fully asserted in an all-male environment, but is the object of discussion by both sexes. A lady requires a nobleman to reflect on
masculine honour and prowess. Totila's answer is interesting too
because he declares his incompetence as judge, and admits that the
lady may know better than he does. He replies to her challenge, 'I
do not know if I can give a good answer to your question. I will tell
you in truth: no valiant man should ever lose courage when he is
required to prove his honour with his sword, nor should he boast
of his chivalry, in case things go badly for him afterwards. With
love, however, it stands thus: nothing alive can resist it. If a man
really feels the love of good women, he will become well if he is
sick, and be rejuvenated if he is old. Ladies make a very courtly and
bold man of him; nothing can harm him. You ask me too much;
I am a simple man who does not know how to answer your question well.'[24]

The Totila anecdote is not actually about lyrics, but it indicates
another context in which songs like Kürenberg's might have been
performed. Joachim Bumke has given this context the name of
'Minnegeselligkeit'. The German word is more easily paraphrased
than translated; what Bumke means is discussions of love conducted
as a convivial pastime by men and women at court. This is the
second of my two pragmatic models. Courtly love-talk revolved
around the discussion of theoretical questions like the one put to
Totila by the lady of Viterbo (the same question is in fact discussed,
explicitly or implicitly, in a number of texts). According to Bumke,
this culture of debate and discussion was particularly developed in
twelfth-century France, where we have the evidence of debating
poems and treatises such as Andreas Capellanus' *De amore*; examples from Germany are fewer, but here too there was a culture
of 'Minnegeselligkeit' which incidents like the Totila anecdote
either reflected or were intended to foster.[25]

Although Bumke does not include Kürenberg in his discussion
of 'Minnegeselligkeit', it seems to me that his lyrics could have
been part of such a culture. The implications of this pragmatic
model are twofold: masculinity is debated in (and maybe around)

---

23. *Kaiserchronik*, ll. 4581–96.   24. *Ibid.*, ll. 4599–618.
25. Joachim Bumke, *Höfische Kultur: Literatur und Gesellschaft im hohen Mittelalter*
(Munich, 1986), pp.569–82. Bumke's term 'Minnegeselligkeit' is translated as 'the
conviviality of love' in the English version of his book, *Courtly Culture: Literature and
Society in the High Middle Ages*, trans. Thomas Dunlap (Berkeley, 1991), pp.404–13.

the lyrics, rather than displayed and asserted; the singers and the public are not enacting their unconscious *habitus*, but are aware of their involvement in a literary game. The literariness of Kürenberg's lyrics is evident in strophes IV, V and XII, the ones that portray the imperious lady and men's reactions to her. We are dealing here with a parody of the literary convention of courtly love service or *fin' amors*, a convention that was established in the troubadour lyric of Southern France and was beginning to enter the Danubian lyric by the 1160s.[26] The singer of *this* kind of love-lyric assumes the role of an abject lover, who serves his lady with his singing in the hope of gaining her favour. The imperious lady of strophe IV is the *domina* of troubadour convention who hears the poet's song; but whereas the lady's power is normally demonstrated in her aloofness and indifference (indeed, we seldom hear her voice in the poetry of *fin' amors*), in this parody her superiority is expressed in an open demand for sex which is made to appear ridiculous when it turns out to have been addressed to a male lover who functions according to a quite different set of genre conventions (strophe XII). The two strophes in sequence work like a game of literary consequences: modern *domina* meets old-fashioned knight; she says, he says. The parody possibly extends to the male role; the knight may refuse the lady, but by choosing exile he reveals that he cannot tame her.[27] In strophe V, the one that editors have often considered unauthentic, there is parody of both male and female roles in *fin' amors*. The servile lover is brought to his lady's bedside; both her power (exaggerated as the ferocity of a wild boar) and his timidness are mocked.

Literary roles are the object of a game in which they are held up at a distance and confronted with each other. The parody is pervasive: women who try to exercise power, men who play the subordinate, perhaps even men whose proud masculinity expresses itself in running away, are made to appear ridiculous. It is possible to read the most famous of all of Kürenberg's songs as a questioning of this same masculinity. The 'Falkenlied' is usually assumed to be spoken by a woman, who regrets the loss of her lover, symbolized by the falcon; it would then be like other songs in which the woman still laments the past events she was powerless to influence.

26. Krohn, 'Begehren und Aufbegehren', pp.124–7; Ingrid Kasten, *Frauendienst bei Trobadors und Minnesängern im 12. Jahrhundert: Zur Entwicklung und Adaption eines literarischen Konzepts* (Heidelberg, 1986), pp.212–18. A detailed account of the Danubian poets' borrowings from the troubadours is given by Sayce, *The Medieval German Lyric*, pp.83–101.

27. Krohn concedes in principle that *fin' amors* and traditional roles are alike parodied (p.123), but his actual interpretation of the songs focuses on parody of the troubadour model alone.

VIII   Ich zôch mir einen valken   mêre danne ein jâr.
       dô ich in gezamete   als ich in wolte hân
       und ich im sîn gevidere   mit golde wol bewant,
       er huob sich ûf vil hôhe   und floug in anderiu lant.

(I trained a falcon for over a year. When I had tamed him to my liking and had adorned his plumage with gold, he soared up high and flew away to other lands.)

IX   Sît sach ich den valken   schône fliegen.
      er fuorte an sînem fuoze   sîdîne riemen,
      und was im sîn gevidere   alrôt guldîn.
      got sende si zesamene,   die geliebe wellen gerne sîn.

(Since that time I saw the falcon flying beautifully. On his foot he wore silken jesses and his plumage was all red gold. May God unite those who yearn to be lovers.)

There are good arguments for assuming a female persona. The sentiments fit the generic codes of masculinity and femininity outlined at the beginning of this essay; the falcon appears in other medieval German literature as a metaphor for the male lover (in the *Nibelungenlied*, for instance, Kriemhild has a dream in which she trains a falcon which is torn to pieces by two eagles; the falcon symbolizes her future husband, Siegfried).[28] Yet there are also cogent arguments for assuming that the words in this song are spoken by a man. Kürenberg's own strophe XV compares women to hunting-birds; in a lyric by Kürenberg's contemporary, Dietmar von Aist, a female persona likens herself to a falcon;[29] the falcons used for hunting were in fact often females (they are bigger and stronger than the male). Even the use of the masculine pronoun does not stand in the way of associating the falcon with a woman; its function is purely grammatical (the noun *der valke* is masculine) and treatises of falconry frequently do refer to a female bird as *der valke*, which they distinguish from the male *terz* or *terzel*.[30] If the 'Falkenlied' is

28. *Das Nibelungenlied*, ed., H. de Boor (20th edn, Wiesbaden, 1972), strophes 13–19.

29. 'Ez stuont ein frouwe alleine', Schweikle, *Die mittelhochdeutsche Minnelyrik*, p.146, song VI.

30. This is only the barest summary of the arguments; for a much fuller review, with references to the extensive secondary literature, see Agler-Beck, *Der von Kürenberg*, pp.114–31, and Irene Erfen-Hänsch, 'Von Falken und Frauen: Bemerkungen zur frühen deutschen Liebeslyrik', in Ulrich Müller, ed., *Minne ist ein swærez spil: Neue Untersuchungen zum Minnesang und zur Geschichte der Liebe im Mittelalter* (Göppingen, 1986), pp.143–68, especially pp.149–56. The classic discussion of the falcon song remains Peter Wapnewski, 'Des Kürenbergers Falkenlied', *Euphorion* 53 (1959), pp.1–19, reprinted in Peter Wapnewski, *Waz ist minne? Studien zur Mittelhochdeutschen Lyrik* (Munich, 1975), pp.23–46.

spoken by a man, then this is a very different picture of masculinity from the one we have become accustomed to in Kürenberg's lyrics. A male voice would be admitting to failure, and would be articulating the 'typically' female sentiments of loss and desire.

It is not a matter of deciding that the 'Falkenlied' must be spoken by either a woman or a man. The point is that these strophes are ambivalent, so that a singer could have performed them as either a woman's song or a man's. If he chose the first possibility, then the song could have complemented the male role articulated in strophe XV; the sum of these strophes performed together would be, as Grimminger has put it, that 'women and falcons can be tamed by the man, but not men and falcons by the woman'.[31] But if the 'Falkenlied' was sung in a male voice, and accompanied by strophe XV, the two songs comment on each other in one of two possible ways. Either the singer of the 'Falkenlied' has failed because, unlike his boasting counterpart, he is incompetent in the art of *rehte lucken*, the right way of enticing women; or the man who boasts about his facility in taming will not be boasting in a year's time.[32]

Just as one cannot say that the lover in the 'Falkenlied' is categorically male or female, so, too, it cannot be said that strophe XV was intended as its companion-piece.[33] These are simply potential realizations in a performance practice that was improvisatory. The important point is that a singer could have chosen to present roles in a way that fosters questions about the content and meaning of masculinity, rather as Totila is provoked by the lady of Viterbo.

Conclusions

I have discussed two models of literary pragmatics that might be appropriate to Kürenberg's lyrics. Each carries particular assumptions about the performance context and each makes the lyrics into a particular kind of document of aristocratic masculinity in the second half of the twelfth century. One model interprets the lyrics as part of the collective behaviour of noblemen; it assumes an

---

31. *Poetik*, p.115 (my translation of 'Frauen und Falken können vom Mann gezähmt werden, Männer und Falken von der Frau nicht').

32. Erfen-Hänsch, 'Von Falken und Frauen', pp.152, 156, who points out that an aristocratic audience familiar with the art of training falcons could not take seriously the claim that hunting-birds are easily tamed.

33. For another possible combination see Krohn, 'Begehren und Aufbegehren', pp.130–3.

exclusively male public and assigns to the songs the function of reproducing and reinforcing patriarchal and sexist masculinity. The other model situates the lyrics within an incipient culture of 'Minnegeselligkeit'; it assumes that the songs were enjoyed by both noblemen and noblewomen as a literary game in which masculinity could become an object of debate and discussion. Either of these models might correspond to historical reality, or (because it is possible that the lyrics were performed in more than one context) both of them, or even (because we must admit we do not know anything for certain) neither of them. Whatever the case, one thing may be asserted confidently about the masculinity represented in Kürenberg's lyrics: its meaning is established by use. The anthropologist Michael Carrithers argues that the collective representations by which a culture inculcates and judges social behaviour do not overdetermine but, as he pointedly puts it, *under*determine actual behaviour. He writes, 'Themes and images are powerless in themselves, but are empowered by people using them to interpret their relations to each other in specific situations.'[34] In our case, this means that those who empowered literary images of masculinity, the poets and their public, might sometimes have gone with the grain of those images in pragmatic contexts that encouraged them to do so (e.g. in situations of homosocial bonding), but in other contexts (when for instance men are negotiating their relations to women rather than to one another) they might not have. It is this underdetermining quality of literary images of masculinity that needs to be emphasized in any pragmatic model or models we may care to hypothesize.

34. Michael Carrithers, *Why Humans Have Cultures: Explaining Anthropology and Social Diversity* (Oxford, 1992), p.65.

CHAPTER THIRTEEN

The Medieval Male Couple and the Language of Homosociality

M.J. AILES

Men were largely defined in the Middle Ages, as well as in many, if not most, other periods, by their relationships with other men – father and son, lord and vassal, uncle and nephew, companions in arms. This chapter explores the typology of the medieval male couple as it is expressed in medieval literature; focusing in particular on French epic may suggest a method for the interpretation of how male friendship was expressed in the Middle Ages.[1] This study looks at the evidence of the language used in that literature and in some historical documents, to express close, even passionate, male friendship, in the twelfth and early thirteenth centuries. Although the language is often passionate it is not, I shall argue, homo-erotic, and I will demonstrate that a number of recent studies of medieval homosexuality proceed from a series of fundamental misunderstandings of the conventions of medieval literary texts. I will show that the language forms part of the public affirmation of masculine identity, an identity realized in the context of a man's relationship with other men. Such relationships, which we may call homosocial, underpin the activities of the characters in the French *chansons de geste* and also have a significant place in some romances.[2] Although the *chansons de geste* as a genre contain very little introspection,

---

1. There has been much debate about the sexual practices of a number of medieval men. See, for example, P. Chaplais, *Piers Gaveston: Edward II's Adoptive Brother* (Oxford, 1992); John Gillingham, *Richard Coeur de Lion: Kingship, Chivalry and War in the Twelfth Century* (London, 1994), p.120 and pp.133–36; J. Boswell, *Christianity, Social Tolerance and Homosexuality: Gay People in Western Europe from the beginning of the Christian era to the Fourteenth Century* (Chicago, 1980) considers Richard to have been homosexual (pp.231–32) but questions whether William Rufus was (pp.229–31); D.S. Mailey, *Homosexuality and the Western Christian Tradition* (London, 1955; reprint, 1975), p.123 wrote that 'there is no doubt . . . that William Rufus was an invert'.

2. On the concept of 'homosocial' see Eve Kosofsky Sedgwick, *Between Men: English Literature and Male Homosocial Desire* (New York, 1985).

since they are texts which were both read and performed it is possible to begin to explore both the literary conventions employed and the extent to which the texts reflect something of the social reality of the largely aristocratic environment in which they were devised, written down and performed (discussed above, chapter 12).

The background of the medieval male couple

It is important to consider briefly the background of the medieval 'male couple'. The two main sources for the expression of this bond were the Classical tradition and the Bible. In the Classical tradition we find commonly the expression of homosexual feelings. Indeed, homosexuality may have been tolerated well into the Christian era.[3] According to John Boswell, 'in many ancient societies . . . friends of the same sex borrowed from the standard vocabulary of homosexual love to express their feelings in erotic terms'.[4] Alongside this homosexual tradition there developed the ideal of *amicitia perfecta*. Cicero's *Laelius de amicitia* (composed 44 BC) was widely read during the Middle Ages. However, it is important to remember that only limited numbers of Classical texts were available in the Middle Ages, and that these were interpreted through the filter of contemporary Christian ideals. Thus, Bernard of Clairvaux in the twelfth century would not have read Cicero or Seneca as they were originally intended, or indeed as we would today (see below, chapter 14).[5]

The Bible was the other main literary source for the expression of love between men, or more simply, for the expression of love. Again the filter through which we read the biblical texts affects our attitude to what we find there.[6] In the New Testament there is an apparent tenderness between John 'the Beloved Disciple' and Christ,

3. Boswell, *Christianity*, pp.169–206; James A. Brundage, *Law, Sex and Christian Society in Medieval Europe* (Chicago, 1987), pp.212–4 gives a more complex picture; he is in general agreement that condemnation and repression of homosexuality increased during the later Middle Ages, see pp.472–74. There has, of course, since the time of St Paul, always been a vein of asceticism in Christianity which favoured total abstinence, see *ibid.*, pp.80ff.

4. Boswell, *Christianity*, p.135.

5. Reginald Hyatte, *The Arts of Friendship: The Idealization of Friendship in Medieval and Renaissance Literature* (Leiden, 1994), p.26; on the availablity of texts see pp.38–39; for a very concise summary of the influence of antiquity on Christian friendship see Gerald A. Bond, *The Loving Subject, Desire, Eloquence and Power in Romanesque France* (Philadelphia, 1995), p.49.

6. Jean Leclercq, *Monks and Love in Twelfth-Century France: Psycho-Historical Essays* (Oxford, 1979).

which is foreign to our culture, but the main biblical example of friendship, in the Middle Ages as today, was that between David and Jonathan. If we look at the description of the love between David and Jonathan, we see great tenderness:[7] 'Jonathan, Saul's son, delighted much in David' (1 Sam 19:2); 'He loved him as he loved his own soul' (1 Sam 20:17). This is most fully expressed in David's lament for Jonathan:

> I am distressed for thee, my brother Jonathan: very pleasant hast thou been unto me; thy love to me was wonderful [as the love of a mother for her son], passing the love of woman.   (2 Sam 1:23, 26)

This is an expression of love which is not eroticized. The love is intense, 'passing the love of woman', passionate even, but there is no concentration here on the physical attributes of the beloved as there would be in sexual love.

The Middle Ages inherited from these two main sources two very different ways of presenting passionate male friendship; from the Classical tradition came the homoerotic expression and from both Classical and biblical traditions came a non-eroticized expression of male love.

The male couple in the chanson de geste

ROLAND AND CHARLEMAGNE, ROLAND AND OLIVER

In the male couple of the *chanson de geste* we may also find tender, uneroticized, expression of love. This love may be particular but not necessarily totally exclusive as is, generally, sexual love.[8] The best known male couple of the epic is Roland and Oliver in the *Chanson de Roland*, written down c.1100, yet in that text the most intense expression of love comes from the lips of the emperor Charlemagne, Roland's uncle and feudal lord.

As David's love for Jonathan is expressed most tenderly in the *planctus*, the lamentation for the beloved, so is the love of Charlemagne for Roland given its most extensive development after Roland's death:[9]

7. Boswell, *Christianity*, pp.252 and 299 discusses this relationship; Hyatte, *Friendship*, pp.32, 60, 84–86; Chaplais, *Piers Gaveston*, pp.13–14. I have given the Authorized Version of the Bible as the nearest English equivalent to the Vulgate, although it is not a direct translation of it.

8. Hyatte, *Friendship*, pp.33–86.

9. F. Whitehead, ed., *La Chanson de Roland* (Oxford, 1970, repd with new introduction by T.D. Hemming, Bristol, 1993). For the translation used in this paper see Glyn Burgess, trans., *The Song of Roland* (Harmondsworth, 1990).

l. 2887   'Beloved Roland, may God have mercy on you!
No man has ever seen such a knight
For starting great battles and bringing them to an end.
Now my fame has begun its decline.'

l. 2898   'Beloved Roland, may God place your soul amidst the flowers
Of paradise, amongst the glorious ones.
How unfortunate was your coming to Spain, lord!
Never will a day dawn without my feeling sorrow for you.
How my strength and my ardour will decrease!
I shall never have anyone to sustain my honour;
I do not think I have a single friend on earth;
I may have kinsmen, but there is none so valiant.'

R. Lafont has seen in this expression of intense love a combination of the legend that Roland is the fruit of an incestuous relationship between Charlemagne and his sister, a legend for which there is no other evidence as early as the extant *Chanson de Roland*, and a reminiscence of an older Germanic tradition of homosexuality.[10] Even if one accepts that the uncle–nephew relationship in Old French literature does derive from an older homosexual model, there is nothing sexual in the extant text. It is important to understand here the nature of the epic text. Unlike romances, epics did not normally make a character's emotions and thoughts clear through internal analysis. The emotions are seen through actions and expressed in the words of the characters. What we have in this extended *planctus* is the 'externalization' of Charlemagne's feelings for Roland. The extent of his loss is portrayed not only by his words, but also in physical action:[11]

l. 2876   He sees his nephew lying on the green grass;
It is no wonder that Charles is distressed.
He dismounts and made his way swiftly to where he lay;
He takes him in both hands
And, such is his anguish, faints upon him.

l. 2906   He tears out handfuls of his hair

10. Robert Lafont, 'Oncles et neveus', in J. Aubailly *et al.*, eds, *Et c'est la fin pour quoy sommes ensemble: Hommage à Jean Dufournet*, 3 vols (Paris, 1993), pp.839–54. The later *Karlamagnussaga* sees Charlemagne confess this to St Giles; a reference to St Giles in the *Chanson de Roland*, which gives Roland a unique position as Charlemagne's nephew, may indicate that the legend was already known at the time of the *Chanson de Roland*; see J. Duggan, 'The generation of the episode of Baligant' *Romance Philology* 30 (1976), pp.59–81, n.109.

11. W.G. van Emden, *La Chanson de Roland* (London, 1995), p.83, writes that 'physical signs of grief, hyperbolic here, as elsewhere, punctuate the words'.

Not only does Charlemagne faint, but 100,000 French warriors both cry and faint with him, for pity: 'A hundred thousand Franks fall to the ground in a faint' (l. 2932). None of this in any way undermines or demeans their masculinity – nor, although the emotion is expressed physically, is it erotic. Physical manifestations of his sorrow are also present when Charlemagne tells Aude, Roland's fiancée, about Roland's death: 'He weeps and tugs at his white beard' (l. 3712).

In Charlemagne's *planctus*, his lament over the death of Roland, he addresses the dead hero as 'Ami', ambiguously both friend and lover in French, and speaks of his great loss. The physical expression of this loss is simply the conventional externalization of feeling of the *chanson de geste* and the words which are used are not in themselves erotic. There is, for example, in four *laisses* (verses) of lament only one reference to Roland's physical attributes and that is a brief one: 'Beloved Roland, valiant man, noble [or handsome] youth' (l. 2916).

The main emphasis of the lament is Roland's prowess and the loss of esteem which Charlemagne will suffer through the loss of his 'quens cataignes'. Certainly there is tenderness when Charlemagne takes the body of his nephew in his arms (l. 2879) but the passion is not an erotic one. Roland in turn has shown great tenderness at the time of the death of the archbishop Turpin:

l. 2251 He mourns him out loud, in the fashion of his land:
       'O noble man, knight of high birth,
       This day I entrust you to the Glorious One in heaven.
       Never will any man serve him more willingly;
       Since the apostles there was never such a prophet
       For maintaining the faith and winning men over.
       May your soul know no suffering
       And find the gate of paradise wide open'.

In a later version of the Roland story, the *Rhymed Roland* (dated c.1180), this is elaborated through an explicit comparison with Roland's love for Oliver:[12]

l. 2544 When Roland saw the archbishop dying
       He had such sorrow, greater than he had ever known,
       Except over the death of Oliver, whom he loved so much.

                                    (MS P)

12. Raoul Mortier, ed., *Les Textes de la Chanson de Roland*, 9 vols (Paris, 1940–44); the relevant MSS are edited in the following vols: V4 in vol. 2; C in vol. 4; V7 (not edited but reproduced as photographs of the MS) in vol. 5; P in vol. 6; T in vol. 7.

Two manuscripts of the *Rhymed Roland* (C and V7) follow this with a prayer for Oliver and the archbishop. These elaborations both stress the extent of Roland's love for Turpin, while at the same time showing it to be less than the love he had for Oliver – thus the love between Roland and Oliver does not deny the possibility of other loves but rather transcends them. Just before his death Oliver speaks of their approaching separation: 'In great sorrow we shall part this day' (l. 1977), words which are echoed by the narrator as Oliver dies: 'See how they part with such great love!' (l. 2009). Even before Oliver's death Roland begins to lament:

> l. 1984 'No man will ever be your equal. [tun cors cuntrevaillet]
> O, fair land of France, how bereft you will be today
> Of good vassals, destroyed and ruined!'

To understand the significance of the apparently physical 'tun cors' it is important to observe here that Old French often uses 'tun cors' or 'mun cors' to refer to 'yourself' and 'myself', and in any case the value of Oliver is here presented in the context of the men lost to France – i.e. as a fighter. Roland's *planctus* at the death of Oliver certainly shows strong passion:

> l. 2027 'Lord companion, how sad that you were so bold;
> We have been together for days and years.
> You have caused me no harm and I have not wronged you.
> Now that you are dead, it grieves me to remain alive.'

Again, as Roland laments, the physical manifestations of sorrow are there as part of the narrative technique of the *chanson de geste*. However, if we see tenderness in this relationship, it also contains violence – at least of words. When they quarrel it is with virulence. Indeed Simon Gaunt has recently written of the 'real threat' to the individual coming from the 'person who is most like himself'.[13]

The word for love 'amor' or 'amer' in the *Roland* needs a study to itself. It is used of relationships between men, but covers a wide range of relationships from the political alliance (l. 121, the messengers from Marsile greet Charlemagne 'par amur et par bien'), through the feudal (Ganelon served Charlemagne 'par amur e par feid' l. 3801, cf. l. 3770), to the personal (Roland lamenting Oliver l. 2009). The role of Aude, Oliver's sister and Roland's fiancée, is to

---

13. S. Gaunt, *Gender and Genre in Medieval French Literature* (Cambridge, 1995), p.35; on the later redaction of the *Roland* contained in the Paris MS see up to p.46.

cement the love between the men – a common use of women in medieval epic.[14]

The verb 'aimer' is also used of the relationship between Roland and Oliver in *Girart de Vienne* (c.1180). They are on opposite sides, Roland with his uncle, Charlemagne, Oliver with his uncle, Girart de Vienne. They have been fighting in single combat when they are stopped by an angel of God and subsequently pledge *compagnonage*.[15]

> They went to rest under a tree; there they pledged and affirmed companionage for the rest of their lives. Roland spoke . . . 'My lord Oliver, let it never be hidden from you. I pledge you my loyalty, that I love you more than any man born of woman, except for Charlemagne, that strong crowned king. Since God wishes that we should be reconciled, I shall never own a castle, or a city, burgh or town, tower or fortified place which we shall not share, if that pleases you. I shall take Aude, if you give her to me, and, if I can, before four days have passed, you will have peace with Charlemagne and be reconciled with him. If he [Charlemagne] will not do my will and give you friendship I will join you in the city and he will have war for the rest of his life.'   (ll. 5931–5948)

Roland's words contain a strange inconsistency vis-à-vis Charlemagne. His feudal duty and love for Charlemagne is at first set apart and beyond this pledge to Oliver (l. 5937–38) yet he threatens to go over to the same side as Oliver if Charlemagne will not accept him. It may be that this is to show that such a rejection is so inconceivable to Roland that he feels he can safely threaten, without any risk of actually having to chose between Charlemagne and Oliver. Oliver's response is first to thank God and then to reply in similar vein to Roland:

> 'My lord Roland I will not hide from you any longer that I love you more than any man born of woman. I give you my sister most willingly, by this agreement, as it was said by you, that we should have peace with Charlemagne. Now unlace this jewelled helmet so that we may kiss and embrace.'   (ll. 5954–60)

They proceed to take off their helmets and kiss one another. The whole scene is very stylized and is parallelled in other broadly

---

14. S. Kay, *The Chansons de Geste in the Age of Romance* (Oxford, 1995), p.148; Aude's other function in the text is to valorize Roland, dying when she hears of his death, refusing the socially more advantageous marriage with Charlemagne's son; see van Emden, *La Chanson de Roland*, p.91.

15. Wolfgang van Emden, ed., *Girart de Vienne by Bertrand de Bar-sur-Aube* (Paris, Picard, 1997); the translation is my own.

contemporary texts such as the romance *Tirant le Blanc*.[16] The physical expression of their commitment of one another, seen through the kiss, is part of the normal technique of the genre.[17] The gift of the woman as an element of that bond is again common in *chansons de geste* and it has been suggested that this motif represents the subordination of heterosexual to homosocial ties.[18] The actual expression of the pledge is made in very practical terms, very similar to the wording of the few documents extant detailing the relationship between 'real' companions in arms – the main concern seems to be the sharing of booty and the giving of Aude to Roland.

The documentary evidence for the swearing of companions in arms is scanty and mostly late. Maurice Keen translates one of the few documents recording such agreements, a document between the dukes of Clarence and Orleans in 1412:[19]

> I, Thomas, the King's son, Duke of Clarence, swear and promise on the faith of my body, and by all the oaths which a preudom can make, that I will be good and true kinsman, brother and companion-in-arms to my very dear and very beloved cousin, Charles Duke of Orleans, and that I will serve him, aid him, counsel him, and protect his honour and well-being in all my ways and to the best of my powers, saving and excepting my allegiance reserved to my sovereign lord the King. And this oath I promise to keep loyally and to fulfil to the utmost of my ability, and never, whatever may happen will I go against it. And in witness hereof I have written this letter, and signed it with my hand and sealed it with my seal this twelfth day of November the year 1412.

Like Roland swearing to Oliver, the loyalty owed by the companion is seen as subject to that owed to the overlord. Keen also highlights the very practical nature of some elements of these agreements. The expression of the wording is feudal: 'serve'; 'aid'; 'counsel' – yet, as Keen points out, one major difference between this and the feudal relationship is that this is a relationship of equals; the relationship between Charlemagne and Roland is indeed feudal, that of lord and vassal, but Roland and Oliver are of equal status, neither subject to the other.

16. Maurice Keen, 'Brotherhood in arms', *History* 47 (1962), pp.1–17, p.9.

17. On the kiss of friendship as part of the feudal rite see M. Bloch, *Feudal Society*, 2 vols, English trans. (2nd edn, London, 1962), I, p.162 and p.180.

18. Kay, *Chansons*, p.148.

19. The original is found in *Pièces inédites sur le règne de Charles VI, Mémoires pour servir à l'histoire de France* (Paris, 1863), p.359; Keen, 'Brotherhood in arms', translates this example on p.6.

AMI AND AMILE

In the *chansons de geste*, even more closely identified by their relationship with one another, are the epic heroes Ami and Amile. The legend of these two men was a popular one in the Middle Ages and survives in a number of genres, including an Old French epic, an Anglo-Norman verse narrative and a Middle English romance. I refer here to the French epic, but the theme of friendship is given at least as much emphasis in the two insular versions.[20] Recent studies carried out by Jane Gilbert stress their identity with one another.[21] If other characters try constantly, and in vain, to tell them apart, the two heroes constantly seek closer identification.[22] They use few words when they meet each other for the first time since their baptism as infants, but their feelings are expressed physically:

> They embraced each other with such strength; they kissed so fervently and held each other so tenderly, so that it nearly killed them; they broke their stirrups and fell to the ground.   (ll. 179–82)

The hugging and kissing is not necessarily erotic, but is rather typical of the hyperbolic expression of the *chanson de geste*. In these lines, however, lies the only possible hint of irony in a text which seems to accept the importance of this friendship above all other relationships – line 182 uses a formula of the type normally used in battle scenes. Its application here as the friends meet for the first time may seem inappropriate, even parodic.[23] This is a text which exalts friendship above all else, even to the extent that Amile is willing to behead his own sons so that through their blood Ami may be cured of his leprosy. Belissant, Amile's wife, pledges not to come between her husband and his companion. The men customarily greet each other with a hug and a kiss – yet the bed-sharing in this text is always between a man and a woman. There is no

20. William Calin, *The French Tradition and the Literature of Medieval England* (Toronto, 1994), pp.483–90, contains an analysis of the Middle English text, *Ami et Amile*, ed., P.F. Dembowski (Paris, 1969); the translation is my own.

21. Jane Gilbert, 'Comparing Like with Like', PhD thesis (Cambridge, 1993), forthcoming as *The Double in Medieval French and English Narrative*. Gilbert sees the relationship between the two men as 'an eroticised and gender-differentiated one', p.25, n.29, placing it further towards the sexual end of the homosocial–homosexual continuum than I consider to be the case; see also Gaunt, *Gender and Genre*, p.46; Kay, *Chansons*, pp.152–5, discusses *Ami and Amile* in a section entitled 'The monstrous double'. See also *idem*, 'Seduction and suppression in *Ami et Amile*', *French Studies* 44 (1990), pp.129–42.

22. Gilbert, 'Comparing Like with Like', pp.8–55.

23. The parodic use of formulae is one of the main subjects explored by Anne Elizabeth Cobby, *Ambivalent Conventions, Formula and Parody in Old French* (Amsterdam, 1995).

ambiguity about the nature of their relationship. Both men have wives and sleep with them. When Amile shares a bed with Ami's wife Lubias, Ami makes him promise not to have sexual relations with her – he would not have exacted such a promise if he had not expected his companion to feel tempted to do so.

RAOUL AND BERNIER

The typical language of the male bond in the epic is feudal or familial. The friends will address one another as 'frere' or speak of serving one another. The 'feudal' model of the male couple is at its most developed in the twelfth-century epic *Raoul de Cambrai* in the relationship between the unruly Raoul and his socially inferior friend, Bernier. In this text the expressions of affection are much more one-sided:[24]

> Handsome Count Raoul was amazingly fond of young Bernier, [. . . ?] Ybert of Ribemont's son. Nowhere could you have found a handsomer boy, more skilled at handling shield or staff, [l. 280] or at speaking wisely in a royal court; despite all that, he was known as a bastard. Handsome Raoul loved him and promptly made him his squire, [though?] he was an odd choice of companion. (ll. 275–84)

Raoul arms Bernier, giving him the best of everything: 'The next day Raoul that praiseworthy count, knighted Bernier with the best arms he could obtain' (ll. 402–4).

Later, when Raoul is fighting Bernier's family, Bernier's mother asks Bernier why he is fighting against his own kin. Bernier expresses himself in terms of feudal duty:

> 'By St Thomas!' Bernier replied, 'I would rather not do it for all the wealth of Baghdad. Raoul my overlord is more villainous than Judas: [yet] he is my overlord, he gives me horses and clothing and arms and oriental silks. I wouldn't fail him, not [even] for the fief of Damascus, until such time as all can declare: "Bernier, you are in the right!".' (ll. 1204–10)

It is only later, during a violent quarrel between the two men, on account of Raoul ordering the burning of the nunnery of which Bernier's mother is Abbess, that Bernier uses the verb 'aimer': 'What appalling friendship this is! I have loved you, served you and supported you . . .' (ll. 1525–6). Even here 'aimer' goes with 'servir'. And here, after the burning of the nunnery and striking a blow

24. Sarah Kay, ed. and trans., *Raoul de Cambrai* (Oxford, 1992).

against Bernier, it is Raoul who begs for reconciliation 'par grant amor'. Bernier does not respond to Raoul's pleadings and there ensues a terrible and bloody war, culminating in the death of Raoul at the hand of Bernier. Raoul's death does draw tears from Bernier, but his *planctus* concentrates on what he owes to Raoul:

> His tears began to fall under his helmet as he cried out loud 'Oh my lord Raoul, son of noble-hearted lady, you armed me a knight, I'll not deny, but you have made me pay dearly for it since . . .'.
>
> (ll. 2954–7)

The strongest expressions of emotion in this text are, as in the *Chanson de Roland*, between an uncle and his nephew, as Guerri mourns the death of his nephew Raoul, and expresses his great anger towards the man who killed him:

> Look here is Guerri on a tall bay charger. He finds his nephew, and was overcome with dismay – he mourns him as follows: 'Nephew,' he said, 'I feel great grief for you. I shall never love whoever it was who killed you, nor make peace or any settlement or truce with them . . .' . . . Guerri falls in a faint on the noble baron's breast. 'Nephew,' he said, 'this is a terrible business . . . By our Lord . . . those who have wrested you from me will never have any peace . . .'.
>
> (ll. 2986–3017)

The epic technique of repeating the material over three *laisses*, the epic verse-form, is the same technique as that used for the affective scene of Roland's death in the *Chanson de Roland* and puts great emphasis on Guerri's distress.

Gaunt sees the Bernier–Raoul relationship as the extension of the friend as the 'alter ego' who presents, nonetheless the real threat to the hero.[25] Certainly, if the male couple of the *chanson de geste* is realized most fully in the near-identity of Ami and Amile, the limits of that friendship are seen in Raoul and Bernier. However, though Gaunt stresses the similarities between Raoul and Bernier in terms of their characterization he also points out their differences. The poet makes their inequality clear from the first introduction of Bernier, commenting, 'though he was an odd choice of companion' (l. 284, above).[26] We are continually reminded that however worthy Bernier may be, and although he is of aristocratic stock, he is a bastard. Bernier is identified both through his lineage and through his relationship with Raoul. His relationship with his

25. Gaunt, *Gender and Genre*, p.61; see also Kay, *Chansons*, pp.152–5.
26. Gaunt, *Gender and Genre*, pp.56–61.

mother, while a mainspring of both the emotional force and the action of the narrative, is not an identifying feature.

GUI AND BOVE

In the Occitan epic, *Daurel et Beton*, we again have the death of one companion at the hand of the other – this time through treachery. This is another text which uses the language of feudalism, indeed the establishment of the relationship between the two companions, Gui and Bove, prefigures that between Bove and Charlemagne. Under the terms of their agreement as companions Gui will provide Bove with military service – in return he receives joint lordship over Bove's assets during his life and on his death will, if he dies childless, inherit everything, including Bove's wife. The temptation to ensure that Bove will die before he engenders any heirs was obviously too much for his companion, who treacherously kills him. From the beginning, however, this is an unequal relationship; Gui is Bove's 'man'; his relative inequality is further stressed by his poverty.[27]

It seems that the friendships which are valorized in the epic are largely those of equals, even near-co-identities – such as Roland and Oliver, Ami and Amile – or at least between men of equal worth rather than the unequal relationships based on a feudal hierarchical structure. This does not mean that these equal relationships do not have their own dramas and problems; there are difficulties between Roland and Oliver and Ami and Amile do not have a problem-free relationship. It does mean that these relationships are ultimately successful, despite death or interference from outside pressures such as heterosexual relationships.

The male couple in romances

We might expect the *chanson de geste* to valorize friendship above the heterosexual relationship – it is after all generally considered

27. J. de Caluwé, 'Les liens féodaux dans Daurel et Beton', in Jean Marie d'Heur and Nicoletta Cherubini, eds, *Etudes de philologie romane et d'histoire littéraire, offertes à Jules Horrent* (Liège, 1980), pp.105–14, stresses from the beginning the inequality of the two men. He discusses the development in the French tradition of the Germanic concept of *compagnonage*; he sees a two-stranded development in French as the concept is divided into a hierarchical, feudal relationship and one between two men serving one lord with *compagnonage* referring only to the latter; he also examines the strength of feeling shown by Beuve as 'une amitié plus forte que l'amour' p.106; see also Kay, *Chansons*, pp.155–69; Arthur S. Kimmel, ed., *Daurel et Beton* (Chapel Hill, N.C., 1971). This text is also analysed by Gaunt, *Gender and Genre*, pp.66–9.

to be a masculine genre.[28] It describes a world largely inhabited by men, and may have found its most ready audience in all-male environments; we know, for example that the *Chanson de Roland* was performed before the Battle of Hastings. But what of romance? Here, apparently, the heterosexual couple is at the heart of the narrative. Some romances do, however, valorize the male couple. In Thomas's version of the Tristan story, Tristan's friendship with Kaherdin, his wife's brother, proves less tempestuous, more stable, than his relationship with either his mistress, Yseut, or his wife, Yseut of the White Hands. There is no doubt that Tristan feels strong desire towards Yseut, and Kaherdin shows a great desire for Brangain, Yseut's maid, but Kaherdin expresses himself towards Tristan with great tenderness:[29]

> Caerdin sees Tristran weeping, he hears him lament and despair and it makes him very sad, so that he replies with tender affection. 'Dear companion', he says, 'do not weep, and I will do all you wish. Believe me my friend, to make you well I shall go very close to death . . . By the loyalty which I owe you, it will not be my fault or for want of anything that I can do or for any distress or hardship if I fail to exert all my strength to carry out your wish . . .'
>
> (ll. 2437–52, trans., p.343)

The rhetoric is typical of the romance genre, but the physical manifestations of sorrow come equally from the epic tradition. As they part, both Tristan and Kaherdin weep and kiss one another.

Analysing another romance, the prose *Lancelot*, Reginald Hyatte sees in the 'chivalric friendship' of the knights an idealization of 'fine amor' – courtly love, a love at once spiritual and physical.[30] Yet the tradition of male friendship is surely far older than that of courtly love and has its own conventional expression. The words of Roland to Oliver, the hugs and kisses of Ami and Amile, the tears of Kaherdin and Tristan belong to the tradition of David and Jonathan; it is a love which is intense, passionate and may be expressed in physical ways, but which is not erotic. It probably makes more sense to see courtly love – the idealization of heterosexual

28. Kay questions the received idea that romance gives a more significant role to women than does epic in 'Contesting romance influences', *Comparative Literature Studies* 32 (1995), pp.320–4; see also *idem, Chansons*, pp.26–48.

29. Thomas, *Le Roman de Tristan*, ed., Felix Lecoy (Paris, 1991), trans. A.T. Hatto, with Gottfried von Strassburg's *Tristan* (Harmondsworth, 1960), pp.301–52.

30. Hyatte, *Friendship*, pp.91–102 analyses the relationship between Kaherdin and Tristan; I would disagree with Hyatte's conclusion that Thomas 'subordinates the activity and fate of chivalric friendship to the pursuit of fine amor', p.102; Hyatte's analysis of the prose *Lancelot* is on pp.102–21.

love – as drawing upon the tradition of male friendship. Courtly love, like the expression of affection between men, typically uses the language of feudalism and of the family. A lover may address his beloved as 'suer', 'sister', or, in the Provencal lyric as 'dompna', 'lord' – but the male homosocial context for this language precedes its use in a sexual context.

On the rare occasions when homosexuality is alluded to in the vernacular literature it is made as a serious charge against a character. Thus in the twelfth-century *Roman d'Enéas* Lavinia's mother accuses Enéas of homosexuality in a vain attempt to turn her daughter from him:[31]

> 'What have you said, foolish madwoman? Do you know to whom you have given yourself? This wretch is of the sort who have hardly any interest in women. He prefers the opposite trade: he will not eat hens but he loves very much the flesh of the cock. He would prefer to embrace a boy rather than you or any other woman. He does not know how to play with women and would not parley at the wicket-gate; but he loves very much the breech of a young man. Have you not heard how he mistreated Dido? Never did a woman have any good from him, nor do I think you will have, from a traitor and a sodomite (*un sodomite*) . . . If he finds any sweet boy, it will seem fair and good to him that you let him pursue his love. And if he can attract the boy by means of you, he will not find it too outrageous to make an exchange, so that the boy will have his pleasure from you, while in turn sufficing for him. He will gladly let the boy mount you, if he in turn can ride him.'   (ll. 8565–8594)

This is an extremely explicit accusation, but it is clearly unfounded and born out of malice. Lavinia does not believe her mother, but rather realizes that Enéas may reciprocate her feelings (ll. 9702–4, trans., p.226). Later we are given a detailed analysis of Enéas' feelings as he suffers for love (ll. 8900–9109, also ll. 9915 ff.). The outcome of the story, the happy marriage of Enéas and Lavinia, also belies the accusation. It is interesting that it is in any case based on his desertion of Dido and not on his lament for his friend Pallas (ll. 6147–6213, trans. pp.176–770). This lament is very much in the tradition of the epic *planctus*, although it does contain a brief reference to Pallas' physical appearance:

> 'Yesterday morning you were so handsome that there was not a more seemly youth under the heavens. In a short time I see you changed,

---

31. J.J. Saverda de Grave, ed., *Roman d'Enéas*, 2 vols, Classiques français du moyen âge (Paris, 1925, 1929); trans. John A. Yunck as *Eneas: A Twelfth-Century French Romance* (New York and London, 1974).

paled and all discoloured: your whiteness is all darkened, your color all turned to perse. Handsome creature, seemly youth, as the sun withers the rose, so has death quickly undone you, and withered all and changed all . . .'   (ll. 6187–96)

This is but a short passage in a very long lament and has its roots in the literary tradition. There is some reference in the *Roland* to the discoloration of the dead hero (l. 2895 – 'Cors ad gaillard, perdue ad sa culur' – 'his body is robust but drained of all its colour'). The lament in the *Enéas* is moreover an elaboration of the lament in Virgil (Aeneid Book XI). The lyrical comparison with a flower is found in Virgil though not in Aeneas' lament, but in the poet's own comments.

If the accusation against Eneas is clearly false, that against Lanval in Marie de France's *lai* 'Lanval' is even more demonstrably so, and is again clearly the fruit of malice. In a 'Potiphar's wife' scenario, the queen, repulsed by Lanval, who has a fairy-mistress, accuses him wildly: 'I have been told often enough that you have no desire for women. You have well-trained young men and enjoy yourself with them' (ll. 279–82).[32]

Other heroes are deemed incomplete when they are not known to be involved in a heterosexual affair.[33] Again these are generally false doubts anyway. Male friendships in French literature in the Middle Ages are just that, however passionate the feelings involved. The violence of any accusations of homosexuality could well be a consequence of the importance of homosocial bonds in the definition of masculine status; there could be no room for ambiguity. While homosociality was prescribed, homosexuality was proscribed.[34]

Homoerotic Latin literature

It cannot be denied that homoerotic poetry existed during the Middle Ages – just that it is not to be found in these vernacular genres, which exalt a non-eroticized passionate male friendship. It is in the Latin literature of the Middle Ages that the influence of the homoerotic literature of the Classical period is seen most clearly.

32. *Marie de France, Lais*, ed. A. Ewart, Blackwells French Texts (Oxford, 1969); reprinted with a new introduction by Glyn S. Burgess (Bristol, 1995); Glyn Burgess and Keith Busby, trans., *The Lais of Marie de France* (Harmondsworth, 1986).

33. See e.g. Marie de France, 'Guigemar', *Lais*, ll. 57–58.

34. John Tosh, 'What should historians do with masculinity? Reflections on nineteenth-century Britain', *HWJ* 38 (1994), pp.186–7.

Although the openly erotic poems are mostly from the early Middle Ages, and writings against homosexuality increase from the twelfth century,[35] some twelfth-century lyrics are at least evocative of homosexual love. Jeffrey Richards ascribes the 'flourishing genre of erotic love poetry addressed by males to other males' to 'the revival of interest in and study of Classical texts'.[36] These texts must be viewed then primarily as literary constructs, regardless of whether they have any roots in the 'reality' of the poet's experience or not. The following poem by Hilary the Englishman is quite typical of his poetry:[37]

> 'To an English Boy'
> Handsome boy, flower's beauty,
> Shining gem, I want you to know
> That your face's beauty
> For me was the torch of love.
>
> As soon as I saw you, desire
> Struck me, but I despair,
> For my Dido restrains me:
> I dread her wrath.
>
> O how happy I would be
> If, through a new replacement
> As is the custom,
> I could slough off this love affair.
>
> I will succeed, I believe,
> For I give myself to you as fair game;
> I'll be the loot, you the robber –
> To such a robber I surrender.
>
> Even the ruler of the gods
> Was once a ravisher of boys.
> If he were here now, he would sweep away
> So handsome a youth to his heavenly bed.
>
> Then at last in the celestial palace
> Ready for either duty –
> Now in bed, now with the cup –
> Two in one you would please Jove.

35. For example, in the writings of Alan de Lille and Bernard of Clairvaux. See above n.4. See also Thomas Stehling, ed., *Medieval Latin Poems of Male Love and Friendship, Garland Library of Medieval Literature*, Series A, 20 vols (New York and London, 1984), VII, pp.xxii–xxiii.

36. J. Richards, *Sex, Dissidence and Damnation: Minority Groups in the Middle Ages* (London, 1991), p.137.

37. Stehling, ed., *Medieval Latin Poems*, pp.74–5.

Here we have overtly homosexual poetry. Hilary wrote others in similar vein, addressing 'puer pulcher' (pretty boy), 'puer unice' (the unparalleled boy; 'unice' also has the meaning of 'unmarried man'), 'puer speciose' (handsome boy), 'decor unice' (unparalleled beauty). In the words of Thomas Stehling, 'writing [love poems to men] would . . . be first understood as writing on a conventional topic of poetry'.[38]

Bishop Baudri of Bourgeuil was another writer of sensual poetry, but this is more ambiguous than the poetry of Hilary. Baudri de Bourgeuil wrote several poems about Alexander, the young man whose death is lamented in this poem:[39]

> Though my care has given inscriptions to many sepulchres,
> It gives none more tearful than this one.
> For here lies Alexander, flower of youth,
> Cause of grief generally for the world, but especially for his friends.
> The beauty of other youths yielded to his
> More than nard yields to the rose or heather to the violet.
> You have seen the neck of this dead boy at last
> Droop like the broken lily on its stalk.
> The clerics of Tours lament for him; anyone
> Who has compassion for tender age weeps.

Here is the concentration on the physical beauty of the beloved, so noticeably lacking in the vernacular laments and affirmations of friendship. Baudri's poetry is complex and ambiguous, sensual, yet often urging the dedicatee to chastity, or praising him/her for chastity – for Baudri wrote such letter poems to individuals of both sexes. It is also presented as a *iocus amoris* – a love game.[40] Of course, as a bishop Baudri may have felt obliged to include a conventional admonition to chastity and as Gerald Bond states in his recent study 'the force of Baudri's letter-poems . . . lies precisely in their hazardous play with the taboo, their display of the dialectic between the public language of restraint and the private thought of release embedded in a generic framework whose inherent duplicity reinforces the reader's inability to resolve the ambiguities'.[41] It is this generic framework which must be remembered, for if the expression of male love in the *chanson de geste* is governed by the

38. *Ibid.*, p.xx.
39. *Ibid.*, pp.44–45; other poems by Baudri de Bourgeuil are given on pp.38–55. Stehling briefly discusses Baudri's poems as 'illustrative of the complexity of emotions a man might feel for a boy', pp.xxi–xxii; see also *Baudri de Bourgeuil, Oeuvres Poétiques*, ed., Phyllis Abrahams (Paris, 1926; reprinted Geneva, 1974), pp.89–90.
40. Bond, *The Loving Subject*, pp.54–7.   41. *Ibid.*, p.36.

conventions of the genre, so too is the expression in Latin lyric, but here the inherited tradition is more erotic. Elsewhere the language, although tender or passionate, does not have the same concentration on the physical. In a letter-poem addressed to Raoul, a monk, Baudri writes of him as his alter ego and of 'being of one soul':[42]

> A honeyed letter of my friend Raoul came to me with a perfume of great friendship; what sort of replies shall I send to my friend Raoul which the favour of our marvellous friendship will reinforce? I shall talk to myself, the reply having greeted Raoul, who lives within me as a great part of me, my alter ego, or myself, if two spirits can be one and if two bodies can become one and the same body.

The last two lines of this are particularly important: '(my) other self or (my own self), if (our) two spirits can be one and if (our) two bodies can become the same body' ('Alter ego, vel ego si sint duo spiritu unus, /ique duo fiant corpora corpus idem'). This last line could be taken as sexual or could simply be a figurative extension of the concept of 'alter ego'; the use of the subjunctive form implies that they do not reflect a reality, but rather something that cannot be – two spirits cannot become one. The penultimate line has resonances of David's lament for Jonathan.[43] The twelfth-century philosopher and theologian Abelard wrote a poetic version of David's lament which also contains the idea of being 'one in spirit':[44]

> l. 45   Jonathan, more than a brother to me.
>   One in spirit with me,
>   What sins, what crimes
>   Have sundered our hearts?

Peter Dronke gives a brief analysis of this poem in the context of the other five *planctus* written by Abelard. Dronke interprets ll. 47–48 as expressing a 'shared agony of guilt . . . which is never explained within the *planctus* . . .'.[45] These lines do not, however, necessarily refer to sexual sin, or indeed to sins committed by David and Jonathan; they could refer to the sins of another, e.g. Saul, which cause their separation, or even suggest ironically their innocence. Unlike Baudri, Abelard is not writing erotic poetry, not even sensual poetry. Here the Latin text seems closer to the vernacular tradition of passionate friendship, receiving its most tender expression in the lament. The feelings expressed in Abelard's poem are close to those expressed by Roland as he lamented Oliver's death:

42. Abrahams, ed., *Oeuvres Poétiques*, p.55.   43. Bond, *The Loving Subject*, p.49.
44. Stehling, ed., *Medieval Latin Poems*, pp.62–7, gives the whole poem.
45. Peter Dronke, *Poetic Individuality in the Middle Ages* (Oxford, 1970), p.116.

l. 75   I should have died happily,
         For love can do nothing
         Greater than this,
         And to outlive you
         Is to die at every moment:
         Half a soul is not
         Enough for life.

Boswell comments on this poem: 'whether or not he intended to portray the relationship as sexual he certainly used erotic vocabulary to invest it with pathos'.[46] This illustrates well the problem in dealing with this material, in that eroticism is clearly dependent on the reader. The conscious intertext here may be the biblical 'Greater love hath no man than this that he lay down his life for his friend' (John 15:13). The intensity of expression is what we find in the vernacular literature.

The expression in most of these texts is governed by convention and inherited tradition–conventions of the genre. This has certain implications when we read chronicle or epistolary evidence for historical figures. The chronicler Roger of Howden wrote of the love between Richard the Lion-Heart and Philip of France:[47]

> Richard, duke of Aquitaine, son of the king of England, remained with Philip the king of France, who honoured him for so long that they ate every day at the same table and from the same dish, and at night their beds did not separate them. And the King of France loved him as his own soul; and they loved each other so much that the king of England was absolutely astonished at the passionate love between them and marvelled at it.

This passage has contributed considerably to what John Gillingham has called 'the modern myth' of Richard I's sexual practices.[48] Gillingham's comments on the passage from Roger of Howden are worth quoting in full: 'To a modern reader the meaning of these words may seem obvious. But it is a mistake to assume that ritual gestures such as kisses or sleeping in the same bed retain a uniform meaning in all ages . . . What Richard and Philip were doing was not making love but making a political gesture.' Gillingham goes on to mention William the Marshal sharing a bed with Henry II, as

46. Boswell, *Christianity*, p.238.

47. Roger of Howden, *Gesta Henrici Secundi*, ed., William Stubbs (London, 1867), translated in Boswell, *Christianity*, p.231; see also H.T. Riley, *The Annals of Roger de Hovenden*, 2 vols (London, 1853), II, pp.63–4.

48. Gillingham, *Richard Coeur de Lion*, p.120.

another example of the use of the bed-sharing motif in a political context.[49]

Bed-sharing apart – and beds in the Middle Ages were valuable commodities, the property of the privileged and often mentioned specifically in wills – the description of Philip and Richard's love for one another is no more erotic than that of many literary characters. There is, moreover, some evidence of direct influence of epic on the way chronicle narratives are related so we should not be surprised to find a chronicler describing the love between two men in conventional, stylized terms reminiscent of Roland and Oliver, Ami and Amile or Raoul and Bernier. Indeed, in the lack of physical detail it is more like the epic companions than the more homoerotic language found in some of the Latin lyrics. On the other hand, if Ambroise's description of Richard's love for Berengaria, in his *Estoire de la guerre sainte*, is at best the view of the common soldier it is more probably just as conventional as the expression of his affection for Philip, and tells us nothing of his real feelings: 'And the king had loved her greatly, since the time when he was first count of Poitou' (ll. 1150–1).[50]

Other evidence for Richard I's supposed homosexuality has, of course, been put forward, most notably the story of the hermit's reproof to Richard to 'remember the destruction of Sodom and abstain from illicit acts'. Both Boswell and Gillingham trace the development of the concept of the 'sins of Sodom' as being identified specifically and exclusively with homosexuality and place this as a later development.[51] Vern Bullough writes of the ambiguity of the terms 'sodomy' and 'sinning against nature'.[52] Richards suggests that sodomy had a meaning similar to that used today, but wider, embracing all non-procreative sexual acts.[53] The interpretation of this passage as a warning against homosexuality tells us, as Gillingham puts it, a great deal about the culture of our own generation, its unfamiliarity with the Old Testament and its wider interest in sex.[54] Boswell writes of Richard I that 'it is difficult to

49. *Ibid.*, p.135; see P. Meyer, ed., *Histoire de Guillaume le Maréchal*, 3 vols (Paris, 1891–1901), II, p.324, ll. 898–94.

50. *Ambroise, Histoire de la Guerre sainte*, ed. Gaston Paris, (Paris, 1897), ll. 1150–52; a translation of *Ambroise* by M.J. Ailes is in progress, with historical notes by Malcolm Barber; see Gillingham, *Richard Coeur de Lion*, p.130, n.46, on diplomatic considerations for the marriage.

51. Boswell, *Christianity*, pp.92–4 and Gillingham, *Richard Coeur de Lion*, p.134.

52. Vern L. Bullough, 'The sin against nature and homosexuality', in V.L. Bullough and J. Brundage, eds, *Sexual Practices and the Medieval Church* (Buffalo, 1982) pp.55–71.

53. Richards, *Sex, Dissidence and Damnation*, p.135.

54. Gillingham, *Richard Coeur de Lion*, p.134.

question the unanimity and equanimity with which chroniclers allude to the sexual orientation of Richard I'.[55] However, this is a concept which seems to owe more to misunderstanding of conventional expression than to more concrete evidence. It is possible that Richard I did have homosexual or bisexual inclinations – but the evidence, in particular the oft-quoted passage from Roger of Howden, does not prove it.

If we look at another historical figure accepted as being homosexual by Boswell, Aelred, Abbot of Rievaulx and friend of David II of Scotland, we find similarly ambiguous evidence. In Aelred's case we have both theoretical writing and evidence of his own, intense, feelings of friendship. He wrote extensively on the subject in both his *Speculum Caritatis* (the *Mirror of Charity*)[56] and in *De Spirituali Amicitia* (*Spiritual Friendship*). Although expressing reservations about Cicero, he was heavily influenced by him. In *Spiritual Friendship* Aelred writes of a 'friend cleaving to his friend in the spirit of Christ, becomes one heart and soul with him and thus, rising by the steps of love to the friendship of Christ is made one spirit with him in one kiss'.[57] Squire, in his biography of Aelred describes this as 'transporting Cicero's notion of union in friendship into the scriptural love language of the Song of Songs'.[58] This is also the language in which David mourns Jonathan in the Old Testament, or that used to express the lamentation by Abelard, or that of Roland's lament for Oliver and Charlemagne's lament for Roland. To read into, for example, Aelred's *Act of Contrition* (extracts given below) any specific reference to homosexuality would be to misunderstand the use he is making of his biblical sources, and the conventional nature of such acts of contrition:[59]

> For when in bitterness of soul
> I view my former life,
> it scares and frightens me that I should be called shepherd,
> for I am surely crazy if I do not know myself
> unworthy of the name.
> Your holy mercy is upon me,

55. Boswell, *Christianity*, p.231.

56. Extracts of both texts are translated in P. Matarasso, ed., *The Cistercian World: Monastic Writings of the Twelfth Century* (Harmondsworth, 1993). Both texts are translated in *The Works of Aelred of Rievaulx*, Cistercian Publications, Massachusetts, Cistercian Father series; the *Speculum Caritatis* is no. 17 and *De Spirituali Amicitia*, no. 5.

57. See also Hyatte, *Friendship*, pp.62–9.

58. Aelred Squire, *Aelred of Rievaulx: A Study* (London, 1969), p.106.

59. *The Works of Aelred of Rievaulx*, vol. 1, no. 2, p.106; on conventional expressions of contrition at this period see J.C. Payen, *Le Motif du repentir dans la littérature française médiévale* (Geneva, 1967).

to snatch my wretched soul out of the nether hell.
You show mercy as you will;
your pity succours him whom you are pleased to pity;
and such is your forgiveness of my sin,
that you do not avenge yourself by damning me,
nor do you even overwhelm me with reproaches;
And even when you accuse me you love me no less.
. . . before you is my heart's confession of the countless sins
from which your mercy has been pleased to free my hapless soul.

(ll. 1–13, 18–19)

Aelred, as a good monk, takes his sins seriously, and, as part of his series of pastoral prayers he includes a prayer for his own needs:[60]

I ask you, by the power of your most sweet name,
and by your holy manhood's mystery,
to put away my sins and heal the languors of my soul
mindful only of your goodness, not
of my ingratitude.
Further, against the vices and the evil passions
which still assault my soul,
(whether they come from past bad habit, or
from my immeasurable daily negligence,
whether their source is in the weakness
of my corrupt and vitiated nature,
or in the secret tempting of malignant spirits)
against their vices, Lord, may your sweet grace
afford me strength and courage;
that I may not consent thereto, nor let them reign
in this my mortal body
nor yield my members to be instruments of wickedness.
. . . May he quench with the dew of his blessing
the heat of my desires,
and with this power put to death
my carnal impulses and fleshly lusts.   (ll. 24–40, 51–54)

Boswell states that 'there can be little question that Aelred was gay and that his erotic attraction to men was a dominant force in his life'.[61] Aelred was certainly not chaste during the earlier part of his life. The nature of his sexual experience is not, however, explicit.[62]

---

60. *The Works of Aelred of Rievaulx*, vol. 1.   61. Boswell, *Christianity*, p.222.
62. Squire, *Aelred of Rievaulx*, referring to the prologue of *De Amicitia*, writes of 'Aelred's own account of how he lost his heart first to one boy and then to another during his schooldays', p.12; however, these are the affections of a boy, not a man. Aelred wrote in *De Institutione Reclusarem*, trans. as the 'Rule of the Life of a Recluse', in *The Works of Aelred of Rievaulx*, vol. 1 of his own loss of chastity, pp.93–4, but not of the nature of his experiences.

It must be borne in mind that in the Middle Ages, especially for a monk, all sexual temptations would be seen as 'evil passions'. In *De Institutione Inclusarum*, written to his sister, he seems to be referring to himself when he writes:[63]

> I know a monk who at the beginning of his monastic life was afraid of threats to his chastity from the promptings of nature, from the force of bad habit and from the suggestions of the wily tempter and so declared war on himself, was filled with savage hatred for his own flesh and sought nothing more than what would afflict it. Accordingly he weakened his body by fasting, and by depriving it of its lawful due suppressed its simplest movements. But when he was forced by weakness to allow himself more, the flesh came to life again and upset the tranquillity which he thought he had acquired. . . . the spirit of fornication still harassed him . . . his heart was beset with forbidden affections . . .

For a twelfth-century monk, any expression of sexuality was a 'forbidden affection' – not just homosexuality. In the same work, within a context of encouragement to control all sexuality he refers to homosexual desire as 'that abominable sin . . . [which] meets with more relentless condemnation than any other crime'.[64] There is nothing in his confessional writings to indicate that he himself found his passions directed solely towards men. One of his closest relationships was with David II of Scotland and a eulogy of David is found in his *Genealogia Regum Anglorum*.[65] In this eulogy he expresses himself in strong terms of affection, referring twice to David as his 'sweetest lord and friend' and remembers the 'embraces and kisses in which you dismissed me' as Aelred himself 'sprinkle[s] and shower[s] . . . tears for you and pour out my affection and my whole spirit'.[66] Again, if we accept the shedding of tears, embraces and kisses as the acceptable expression of affection between men, as between women, this is tender, but not erotic. It may not be possible to say that Aelred felt no sexual desire towards David of Scotland – but is equally impossible to say that he did. As expressed by P. Matarasso 'friendship for Aelred has its beginning and end in God'.[67] Reading the dialogue of *Spiritual Friendship* this is clear

---

63. Aelred, *De institutione inclusarem*, p.66.   64. *Ibid.*, pp.66–67.

65. V. Wall, 'Repaying a debt of friendship: Aelred of Rievaulx and his *Genealogia Rerum Anglorum*', in Anne E. Curry, ed., *Thirty Years of Medieval Studies at the University of Reading, 1965–95: A Celebration* (Reading, 1996), pp.89–94, examines the friendship; on his lament for David see Squire, *Aelred of Rievaulx*, pp.82ff.

66. Wall, 'Repaying a debt', p.93.

67. Matarasso, ed., *Cistercian Writings*, p.169; see the extract from 'On spiritual friendship', p.179: 'This foundation [of spiritual love] is the love of God.'

– and we should never underestimate the centrality of God in the life of a man like Aelred.

Conclusion

While different conventions rule in different forms of writing, in historical, as well as 'literary' texts, the expression of emotion is largely a formal, rhetorical matter. It behoves us then to be careful in our interpretations of such expressions and we should be careful to observe the genre constraints of medieval texts. Homoerotic literature can be as much a matter of observing generic norms, as is the expression of homosociality. In the vernacular literature, in particular the *chanson de geste*, homosociality is expressed physically, in 'body language' as well as in words of great intensity. Chronicles and other written sources also use literary conventions; indeed such physical and verbal conventions are culturally determined as well as defined by literary genre and may also reflect 'real' actions. I can do no better here than to echo the words of Dom Jean Leclercq: 'In such matters we must be careful not to project on to a less erotically preoccupied society the artificially stimulated and commercially exploited eroticism of our own sex-ridden age'.[68]

68. Leclercq, *Monks and Love*, p.100.

CHAPTER FOURTEEN

Love, Separation and Male Friendship: Words and Actions in Saint Anselm's Letters to his Friends

J.P. HASELDINE

The twelfth century was the century of love. The letters of Abelard and Héloïse, the romances of Chrétien de Troyes, Aelred of Rievaulx's treatises on spiritual love and friendship remain the most visible highlights of what was a new, all-pervasive literature of love: romantic heroes were guided by the powerful affections it inspired, while human feelings and divine love took their place in the theology of sin and redemption. Saint Bernard's sermons on the Song of Songs stand at the centre of a tradition which elevated erotic verse to the level of sublime divine allegory. Love was not merely a literary fashion, it reflected a new vision of the world in which human experience was given a central role. God himself, in the reflections of thinkers like Saint Anselm, was converted from a stern and arbitrary judge into a loving father.[1]

In this climate the monastic vocation had never been so popular. Vigorous and austere reform programmes inspired an unprecedented expansion in the numbers of westerners renouncing the world and all its ties. Cloistered, forbidden by the Rule not only sexual union but even particular personal friendships,[2] monks of

---

1. On these themes see R.W. Southern, *Medieval Humanism and Other Studies* (Oxford, 1970); *idem, Scholastic Humanism and the Unification of Europe* (Oxford, 1995); and M.-D. Chenu, *Nature, Man and Society in the Twelfth Century,* trans. J. Taylor and L.K. Little (Chicago, 1968). Jesus was also seen, in some respects, as a loving mother: C. Walker Bynum, *Jesus as Mother: Studies in the Spirituality of the High Middle Ages* (Berkeley, 1982). The cultural phenomenon of the 'twelfth-century renaissance' began, of course, before the turn of the year 1100, and the work of Anselm (1033–1109) represents an important contribution.

2. *The Rule of St Benedict,* trans. J. McCann (London, 1970), especially chs 54, 63, 69 and 71.

many orders yet made a remarkable contribution to the cult of love, producing, in the numerous letters which they exchanged, some of the most open and touching expressions of longing and desire in our literature. Here monks, clerics and bishops told of their ardent passion for one another, how they longed to embrace and to kiss, how they grieved inconsolably in the absence of their friends, how they were bound by enduring chains of love. They speak of the union of their souls, of the fusion of their hearts in the intense heat of love, of intimate and unspoken knowledge of one another's thoughts and feelings. From declarations of the simple need for physical presence to heightened visions of the metaphysical union of souls, this, to modern ears at least, is the intimate, private language of the lover. As Saint Bernard said in a letter to Prior Thomas of Beverley, 'What need of words? A fervent spirit and eager heart cannot be expressed by the tongue alone. . . . Remember your promise and do not deny me any longer the satisfaction of your presence, I who love you so truly and will love you for ever.'[3]

In contrast to the situation described by Robert Swanson in chapter 10 of this volume, in which the gendered status of some ecclesiastics – the secular clergy – was renegotiated, the status of monks was unambiguous. There was no debate about whether or not monks *should* have sexual partnerships with women, or accord intimate, particular relationships of any type a place in their lives. The bonds forged and developed through the monastic letter collections examined in this chapter represent an idealized form of public behaviour which was not determined by the tensions of ambiguous status experienced by the secular clergy, nor developed with reference to reciprocal female behaviour. Rather, these expressions arose in a context in which the rules of celibate masculine behaviour were already firmly established. Further, these relationships commonly arose between men who had never met. Admission to bonds and circles of friendship was highly selective but the principles of selection were not primarily emotional, and often involved a high degree of formality. This alone must influence our reading of their affective content.

The ardent expressions of love and friendship in these letters can tell us about the ways in which the writers idealized and conducted their relationships with other men, and so about their

---

3. *The Letters of St Bernard of Clairvaux*, trans. B. Scott James (London, 1953), no. 109, pp.158–9.

notions of what constituted acceptable masculine behaviour.[4] The connection between the language used and the experience conveyed, however, is not a simple one. Both the literary genre and the intellectual tradition framing these expressions must be given due consideration. Letter writing and the production of letter collections held a place in the literature of the Middle Ages which might be compared to that of the novel today: it was the medium through which a broad spectrum of thought from the meditative and poignant to the polemical and philosophical was conveyed to a wide audience. Theologians, canon lawyers, political disputants and propagandists all took advantage of its attributes of brevity and flexibility. Letter writing was an art, and letter collections were refined and stylish compilations, carefully preserved for posterity.[5]

The cult of love and the cultivation of friendship

If the compilation and dissemination of letter collections is at least a recognizable, if not a currently fashionable, literary activity, the intellectual tradition of friendship which we encounter here takes us into truly unfamiliar territory. In modern western culture love and friendship are distinct if occasionally overlapping areas of emotional experience: they are usually different in intensity, certainly different in the expectations and activities associated with the emotion, and can lead to fundamentally different social and legal obligations. Love is particular and exclusive (although distinct loves may coexist, such as that for family and for partner), while friendship can be bestowed more widely and does not lead to relationships which are institutionally or legally defined. Furthermore, while concepts of betrayal are pertinent to friendship, shifts in alignment are regarded as normal, whereas shifts in love relationships are frequently condemned as faithless, or at least regarded as emotionally problematic.

4. The participation of women in circles of correspondence and in the cultivation of love and friendship is a topic which merits treatment of its own at length, but see K. Cherewatuk and U. Wiethaus, eds, *Dear Sister: Medieval Women and the Epistolary Genre* (Philadelphia, 1993). The majority of letters of love and friendship in this period were exchanged between men, more specifically between monks, bishops and occasionally clerics.

5. G. Constable, *Letters and Letter Collections*, Typologie des sources du moyen-âge occidental, fasc. 17 (Turnhoult, 1976); and G. Constable, ed., *The Letters of Peter the Venerable*, 2 vols (Cambridge, Mass., 1967), II, pp.1–44.

A letter of Anselm to a recently departed 'beloved friend', Gilbert Crispin, recalls their friendship in terms of actions and emotions which we would associate with a quite different order of relationship:

> I often perceived how great and how true this affection was when it displayed itself face to face, lip to lip, embrace to embrace. . . . For just as someone who has great possessions knows not what it is to be in need . . . so someone who finds pleasure in a friend knows not the languor of the soul without one. . . . I pray with you that when we see each other again we should once more revive, face to face, lip to lip, embrace to embrace, our unforgotten love.[6]

In medieval letters love and friendship are bound together so closely as to be dependent on one another. Friendship is frequently the occasion of love, and love the appropriate affection to express towards a friend. An important consequence of this is that love is commonly extended beyond the exclusive, private world of two intimates and carried across a wide network of friends. What we would recognize as a private language reserved for intimate correspondence or conversation between individuals, where wider disclosure may be regarded as an act of betrayal, was advertised freely to all who cared to read it.

This fusion of love and friendship is taken yet further beyond the bounds of intimacy. It was frequently invoked between quite distant acquaintances and even strangers. In fact the Middle Ages inherited from the ancient world a theory of friendship (*amicitia*) predicated on a conceptual relationship between the private, emotional sphere and public life which was fundamentally different from our own. Personal relationships were seen to have an integral and natural role in public life and social cohesion. These ideas were best known in the twelfth century through Cicero's treatise *de Amicitia*. Cicero himself was reflecting a long and continuous tradition of ancient thought in according human friendship a central role in the natural order: 'in nature and the entire universe whatever

---

6. All quotations from the letters of Saint Anselm are taken from *The Letters of Saint Anselm of Canterbury*, trans. W. Fröhlich, 3 vols (Kalamazoo, Mich., 1990–94), hereafter *Letters of Anselm*. References to the standard Latin edition, F.S. Schmitt, ed., *S. Anselmi Cantuariensis Archiepiscopi Opera Omnia* 6 vols (Edinburgh 1946–61, reprint Stuttgart 1968), hereafter *AOO*, follow in parentheses (the numeration of the letters is the same in both). This quotation: *Letters of Anselm* I, no. 130, p.305, (*AOO*, III, pp.272–3). The link between friendship and love is clear here; on the question of gestural language and kissing, see below p.252), and also R.W. Southern, *Saint Anselm. A Portrait in a Landscape* (Cambridge, 1990), pp.153–4.

things are at rest and whatever are in motion are united by friendship and scattered by discord'.[7]

At the heart of this concept was the belief that the origins of
such feelings as love and friendship were external to the individual
human psyche and so did not depend on personal affection or
even acquaintance. They were in fact the product of the operation
of natural virtue and not of the inner emotions and feelings of the
subject. True friendship (*vera amicitia*) was almost a force of nature,
creating disinterested bonds which united the virtuous to the benefit of the public good. Its key features were a clear distinction
between false and true friendship (the one motivated by utility or
profit, the other by virtue) and the belief that true friendship was
eternal, an aspect of the greater scheme of the universe. Medieval
thinkers set divine love in place of natural virtue as the motive
force behind friendship. Love then became both the origin of friendship and the normal and appropriate medium for its expression.[8]
Love for strangers, on account of the attractions exerted by virtue,
which was for Cicero always a theoretical possibility, was for many
Christian writers a powerful reality. Where Cicero had speculated
that, '. . . on account of their virtue and uprightness we love, in one
sense, even those whom we have never seen', Saint Bernard could
declare, in a letter to a monk: 'Although you are not known to us
personally, although you are far away in the flesh, yet you are a
friend and friendship makes you known to us now and here with us'.[9]

Friendship between individuals occupied a central role in political thought as an ethical force for the maintenance of order and
social cohesion.[10] But how can we approach the reality of the relationships whose existence breathed life into this theoretical concept?
The idea that friendship and love are social bonds which imply
levels of obligation and responsibility and which can be analysed

7. W.A. Falconer, ed., *Cicero; De Senectute, de Amicitia, de Divinatione*, Loeb Classical Library (London and Cambridge, Mass., 1923), see *de Amicitia* s. 7. 24, pp.134–5.
8. Note the statement by Aelred of Rievaulx: 'The fountain and source of friendship is love. There can be love without friendship, but friendship without love is
impossible', *Aelred of Rievaulx, Spiritual Friendship*, trans. M.E. Laker (Kalamazoo,
Mich., 1977), p.91.
9. *Cicero, De Amicitia* 8. 28, pp.138–9, (my translation adapts that in the Loeb
edition); Saint Bernard: J. Leclercq and H. Rochais eds, *Sancti Bernardi Opera*, 8 vols
(Rome, 1957–77), vii., 259, no. 103, my translation. On Cicero's theory of friendship
see P.A. Brunt, '*Amicitia* in the late Roman Republic', *Proceedings of the Cambridge
Philological Society* new ser. II, 191 (1965), pp.1–20.
10. See above, chapters 7 and 9; see also J.P. Haseldine, 'Friendship, equality and
universal harmony', in O. Leaman, ed., *Friendship East and West: Philosophical Perspectives* (Richmond, Surrey, 1996), pp.192–214.

and cultivated is not one unique to this cultural context. Formalized, even highly ritualized, social structures based on relationships which modern western culture tends to isolate as purely private are not uncommon.[11] Where a language of powerful emotions such as love and friendship, rather than honour or adoptive kinship, is chosen to forge and articulate these sorts of bonds it clearly does not indicate sexual or even exclusive ties. The choice, however, is a significant one and can tell us a great deal about the shared values of those who participate in the bonds. In the case of medieval friendship the concept of homosociality has been invoked to explore the values inherent in non-erotic expressions of male love in a variety of literary sources, often in explicit contrast to homosexuality or homoeroticism. This offers an analytical tool for understanding the motivations and assumptions which governed the mutual interactions of men (see above, chapter 13). Medieval letter collections, however, offer another avenue for the exploration of these activities – one directly related to their function.

In these documents we are dealing not with literary reflections on, or descriptions of, friendships written by observers but with the medium of the cultivation of friendship itself. Letters were the means by which friendship was requested, granted, affirmed and called upon. Participation in circles and networks of friendship was reinforced through explicit and repeated reference to the guiding ideals of love and friendship.[12] These letters, their exchange, their contents and the evidence they provide about the behaviour expected of and experienced by the friends are invaluable in recreating the relationship itself through the activities and conduct which defined, articulated and advanced it. Indeed, the image of masculinity implicit in this cult of male love and friendship can only usefully emerge from a close examination of both the words and the actions which actually comprised these exchanges.

Setting the language of friendship in its context in this way immediately presents a problem of interpretation. Writers commonly addressed expressions of love and friendship of equal warmth

11. See e.g. G. Herman, *Ritualised Friendship and the Greek City* (Cambridge, 1987); on the anthropology of friendship see E. Leyton, ed., *The Compact: Selected dimensions of friendship*, Newfoundland Social and Economic Papers no. 3 (St John's, Newfoundland, 1974), and for modern, sociological studies see R. Blieszner and R.G. Adams, eds, *Adult Friendship* (Newbury Park, Calif., 1992); and G.A. Allan, *A Sociology of Friendship and Kinship* (London, 1979).

12. See also I.N. Wood, 'Administration, law and culture in Merovingian Gaul', in R. McKitterick, ed., *The Uses of Literacy in Medieval Europe* (Cambridge, 1990), pp.63–81.

to a wide variety of recipients. These could include personal acquaintances, strangers and entire monastic communities. It is very difficult to distinguish from the language itself what the prior relationship is. 'Beloved friends' often turn out to be unacquainted. Without external evidence it is dangerous to hazard guesses as to the affective relationship which may or may not underlie a literary friendship.[13] A friendship could even begin with a formal approach to a complete stranger. Significantly, actual meeting was not essential either to the formation or the continuance of the friendship. In each quotation from Saint Bernard above the recipient of the letter was a stranger, and Bernard does not hide this fact.[14] Further, descriptions of friendship tend to stress its eternal nature. The ideal relationship is a static one. There is very little concern with, or analysis of, the growth of emotional attachment, shifting moods or progress towards intimacy. Entry is immediate and often formal; souls are united once and for all; personalities are not seen to grow together. Thus while the range of expressions encountered can include passionate declarations, introspective analyses of the state of the writer's soul and explorations of the mutual actions and gestures which constitute friendly behaviour between men, the genre and the milieu in which they are developed suggest a radically different use of this seemingly familiar language. Friendship is held to confer an equality on its participants which overrides inequalities of rank and social origin, but not – in the manner of romantic love – on grounds of subjective affection. It would seem, rather, to signify inclusion in a group, with the repetition of these themes among members of a select circle operating as a rehearsal and advertisement of collective identity.

The functions of friendship networks

This raises two questions: What was the function of this formal cultivation of friendship? And why, given its context, was its mode of expression so overtly affective? Recent interpretations of this

13. For case studies of particular letter collections see J.P. Haseldine, 'Understanding the language of *amicitia*. The friendship circle of Peter of Celle (c.1115–1183)', *JMH* 20 (1994), pp.237–60 and J. McLoughlin, '*Amicitia* in practice: John of Salisbury (c.1120–1180) and his circle', in D. Williams, ed., *England in the Twelfth Century*, Proceedings of the 1988 Harlaxton Symposium (Woodbridge, 1990), pp.165–81.

14. See above, notes 3 and 9; see also Anselm's letter 85, below and note 25, which is a response to a formal request for friendship.

literature have fallen into two broad categories: there are those which regard friendship as a reflection of the exploration of individual identity and spirituality, and those which see it primarily as a function of political network-formation. Interpretations in the first category have ranged from the overtly sexual (friendship as the expression of a gay subculture) to the psychological and spiritual (friendship as emotion sublimated in spiritual ascent to God). In between these, and providing some salutary criticisms of earlier work, is Brian McGuire's comprehensive study of friendship and community.[15] While addressing the question of personal relationships in the broader context of community and society, this study regards the problem fundamentally as one of the interaction between two discrete spheres, defining friendship in terms of intimate relationships, with an important spiritual dimension, and using the sources to uncover what 'medieval men and women sought [through friendship]: self-knowledge, the enjoyment of life, the commitment of community, and the experience of God'.[16]

Works in the second category address the role of friendship in motivating political activity and forging networks of mutual support and co-operation. Both the formality of friendship and its context are taken into account and interpretations offered for instances where affective bonds are clearly not involved. The potential power of friendship was shown in the case of Gregory VII by Ian Robinson, who described the revolutionary pope as creating: '. . . a friendship network which seems to have extended to all the major regions of Western Christendom . . . the purpose of which was the implementation of reform against local opposition'.[17]

If we are to understand the significance of the cultivation of friendship in the real contexts where we encounter it, and not to leave it isolated in the realms of abstract spiritual philosophy or a soul-searching literature of the emotions, then we must attempt to understand it as operating on both sides of what might seem to

---

15. B.P. McGuire, *Friendship and Community. The Monastic Experience 350–1250* (Kalamazoo, Mich., 1988). On friendship as gay subculture, J. Boswell, *Christianity, Social Tolerance and Homosexuality: Gay People in Western Europe from the Beginning of the Christian Era to the Fourteenth Century* (Chicago, 1980), and criticisms of this approach in Southern, *Saint Anselm*, pp.147–54 and McGuire, *Friendship and Community*, p.244. On friendship and spiritual ascent see J. Leclercq, *Monks and Love in Twelfth-Century France* (Oxford, 1979).

16. McGuire, *Friendship and Community*, p.l, and see p.xv.

17. I.S. Robinson, 'The friendship network of Gregory VII', *History* 63 (1978), p.2. See also McLoughlin, '*Amicitia* in practice', and J.P. Haseldine, 'Friendship and rivalry: The role of *amicitia* in twelfth-century monastic relations', *JEccH* 44 (1993), pp.390–414.

modern sensibilities to be a wide gulf. Allegiances and solidarities can be conveyed in a variety of terms and codes, including appeals to partisan loyalty, or unity in defence of points of principle (for example, ecclesiastical liberty, or Christian unity), without invoking the warmth and depth of feeling which are expressly conveyed here. At the same time, if the primary function of this language is held to be the exploration, revelation or advancement of private, affective relationships, then its extension into many other contexts, an activity pursued with conscious deliberation by many writers over centuries, would be no more than a bland and empty rhetoric. This is not to say that personal, affective friendships and loves did not exist, nor that degrees of love and friendship were not distinguished in daily life. Rather, certain relationships were chosen to be elevated to the level of formal, literary *amicitiae*, and not all of these were based on affective bonds or even personal acquaintance. What we would call friendship was only one (and not necessarily the most important) route into an *amicitia* relationship.[18]

By using friendship and love to articulate social bonds, allegiances and solidarities the correspondents were advertising their adherence to a defined body of ideas which they shared, and so to an ideology which united them. But if such participation in circles of friendship implied real obligations, as an increasing body of evidence suggests, did it also constitute a language of criticism, or of the definition of ideal male roles, which informed or guided the conduct of the men who partook in it? If, that is to say, this language does indeed constitute a collective rehearsal of group identity, as its context suggests, this does not in itself resolve the question of its chosen content and mode of expression. An understanding of this language will reflect something of what eleventh-and twelfth-century society deemed to be the attitudes and conduct appropriate to the public man.

Saint Anselm and friendship

Among the most important and penetrating investigations into the connection between private language and a broader public sphere is Southern's study of Saint Anselm, whose letters of friendship he characterized as 'public statements about the rewards of the life

18. See Haseldine, 'Understanding the language of *amicitia*', pp.258–60.

dedicated to God'.[19] Anselm (prior of Bec 1063–1078, abbot 1078–1093, and archbishop of Canterbury 1093–1109) has figured prominently in recent debates largely because, especially before Southern wrote, he was widely seen as presenting a model of purely private, affective friendship. Southern drew a distinction between Anselm's monastic letters of friendship (most, but not all, of which were written before his departure from Bec to become archbishop of Canterbury) and the later letters, largely concerned with church business. He did not, however, base this distinction on a separation of the private and public spheres of Anselm's life. Rather, friendship was a function of the pursuit of the monastic life, monastic life was central to Anselm's vision of the world, and consequently friendship was always a central part of his professed life, not an optional indulgence or private escape – it is simply that in the earlier letters we see Anselm reflecting on the *monastic* aspect of friendship with fewer distractions.[20]

Southern thus analyses Anselm's central and unique contribution to the literature of friendship at its intellectual peak, developed at times when Anselm was most free to devote his attention to it. However, his letters can tell us other things about the cultural context in which he wrote, for Anselm did not refrain from the pursuit of friendship in later life, even in letters which went beyond his inner circle and were concerned with matters of church business and politics. Taking Anselm's collection as a whole, two aspects which we have already identified as crucial to understanding the function of friendship – the contexts in which the language of friendship is employed and the real actions associated with its cultivation – can illuminate some of the broader assumptions about the cultivation of friendship which he shared with his contemporaries.

LOVE IN CONTEXT: SEPARATION AND SHARING

One of the strongest themes to emerge in Anselm's letters is that of separation from his friends. Many of his finest passages on friendship were inspired by such separations. This theme is frequently associated with others which, as we have seen, are central to the concept of friendship: the existence of love and friendship in absence, and the eternal nature of friendship. Anselm articulates his love and grief with other images common to *amicitia* literature.

19. Southern, *Saint Anselm* is the best modern work on Anselm; this quotation p.147.
20. c.f. *Ibid.*, pp.138–65.

Love is the union of souls; the friend is the other half of his soul; love burns with hot flames; friends are fused together; the image of the friend is impressed on his heart, or fixed in his memory. There is also a gestural imagery of tears, embraces and kissing, although, as we shall see, this is surprisingly rare in Anselm's letters, even those to his closest intimates.

A typical passage (here again in a letter to Gilbert Crispin, who had left Bec to join Archbishop Lanfranc's household in Canterbury), illustrates the way in which Anselm often ran these themes together to achieve a heightened, emotive expression:

> . . . my soul . . . will never be consoled for its separation except by recovering its other half, my sundered soul. The anguish of my heart whenever I think about it is my witness; the tears shrouding my eyes and pouring down my face and over my fingers as I write are my witness. . . . Truly a person does not have knowledge of good and evil if he has not experienced both. For, never having experienced your absence, I did not know how delectable it was for me to be with you, how bitter without you.[21]

This poignant expression of loss of innocence, of emotional self-discovery through love and separation, is followed immediately by this disarmingly brisk assessment of the situation: 'But, through this very separation of ours, you have the presence of another whom you certainly love not less but more'.[22]

Jealous irony is not a convincing interpretation of this passage, given the tone of the letter as a whole. In fact most of Anselm's letters to the monks of Bec have a remarkable lack of exclusivity. Indeed, when Anselm writes to his most frequent correspondents, and those whom we might expect (but can never be certain) also fell into the category of affective friends, he is often most explicit in his instructions that the feelings of friendship expressed to the recipient be passed on impartially to others often less well known to him, and received in equal measure by all, even at times the entire community.[23] Letter 205, for example, assures the monks of Bec, '. . . how much and how truly I have always loved you, and how much and how deeply I have longed for you'. The community has grown since Anselm's departure, but the new monks are not excluded from the love of, even from sharing something of the memory of, the ex-abbot they never knew:

21. *Letters of Anselm* I, no. 84, p.219, (*AOO*, III, p.209).
22. *Ibid.* Possibly a reference to Lanfranc, see *ibid.* p.220, n.3.
23. See Southern, *Saint Anselm*, pp.143–7.

If not all of you know this from experience [i.e. how much he loves them], for God has increased your numbers since I left you, learn it from those who do know . . . Therefore I beg and beseech all of you equally that the memory and love of me in the hearts of those who have it may not cool down and that it may be enkindled and sustained in the minds of those who do not know me.[24]

Furthermore, similarly ardent language is directed to complete strangers, as in letter 85, to one Walter of Saint Wandrille, who is specifically addressed 'not as a stranger, but as a close friend':

> If my heart were harder than stone and colder than ice, then it would still have to grow warm at the fire of your love and be softened by the oil of your sweet address. Your letter, so full of the wholesome advice by which your sweet love and beloved prudence deigned to make yourself known to my poverty is aglow with such ardour of charity, scented with such fragrance of kindness and merry with such sweetness that my mind will not rest until my eyes have seen his face, my ears have heard his voice and my soul has enjoyed the presence of him who, without knowing me, obscure as I am, freely took me on with such love.[25]

Nor are expressions of friendship absent from letters dealing with far less personal issues, such as disputes and ecclesiastical business. Indeed emphatic invocations of friendship were an important part of dispute resolution for Anselm as for his contemporaries, and formed an integral part of the wide spectrum of contexts where reference to friendship was considered appropriate and normal.[26] While there is a preponderance of a certain type of expression in Anselm's letters to the monks of Bec, friendship and love are certainly not restricted to this sphere.

If Anselm's feelings for his friends are neither exclusive nor jealous, but are rather capable of extension even beyond the reasonable demands of impartiality to embrace virtual or complete strangers, there is, accordingly, little concern with the development of the emotional, as opposed to the spiritual, content of the *amicitia*

---

24. *Letters of Anselm*, II, no. 205, p.144, (*AOO*, IV, pp.97–8).
25. *Ibid.*, I, no. 85, pp.220–21, (*AOO*, III, pp.209–10). See also e.g. *ibid.*, I, no. 133, pp.309–10, (*AOO*, III, pp.275–6).
26. See e.g. the sequence of letters concerned with a dispute over market rights in Kent (*ibid.*, III, nos 356–9, pp.95–100, *AOO*, V, pp.297–301), where his opponents are referred to as friends more emphatically than his own deputies and allies. The large and complex question of the role of friendship in dispute resolution and diplomacy in the eleventh and twelfth centuries awaits a comprehensive study. The topic is addressed in Haseldine, 'Friendship and rivalry' and McLoughlin, '*Amicitia* in practice'.

bond once this is contracted or acknowledged. The implications of Anselm's priorities in this regard are apparent where the desire to see friends conflicts with monastic discipline. Letter 79 to the monk Maurice of Bec is one example of many:

> Although the more I love you the more I want to have you with me, yet because I cannot have you I love you even more. . . . you . . . should patiently bear our separation as being ordered by Providence, as long as our lord and father, the venerable Archbishop Lanfranc commands it; lest by impatience you in any way diminish the very qualities for which I love you most. For although I love you greatly and desire you to cling to me by living in our community with me, yet I desire even more that you cleave inseparably to a good way of life.[27]

Monastic obedience is not only superior to love, it is part of the very nature of the love upon which their friendship rests. To give up any part of it for the sake of love would diminish the very love for which the action was contemplated, and so be a self-defeating act. Thus we come full circle: separation, the inspiration of Anselm's expression of grief and love, is here almost essential to the continuance of that love on a solid foundation. Far from the demands of monastic life being a bar to the development of friendship, it alone, with all its restrictions on intimate communication, gives life to what Anselm values as *true* friendship. With this thought we may turn to the question of the real actions associated with friendship.

LOVE IN ACTION: OBEDIENCE AND DISTANCE

As the medium through which friendship was forged, conveyed and invoked, letters provide more than simply images of the ideal friend. Interpreted with caution, they can reveal the workings and conventions of that relationship. In 1093 Anselm, in a pragmatic mood for which he is rarely given credit, gave the abbot and monks of Bec a lesson in the cultivation of friends:

> Remember . . . how I always used to gain friends for the church of Bec: following this example, hasten to gain friends for yourselves from all sides by exercising the good deed of hospitality, dispensing generosity to all men, and when you do not have the opportunity of doing good works, by according at least the gift of a kind word. Never consider that you have enough friends, but whether rich or poor, let them all be bound to you by brotherly love. This will be to

27. *Letters of Anselm*, I, no. 79, p.210, (*AOO*, III, p.202).

the advantage of your church and promote the welfare of those you love.[28]

We must take this reflection of the experienced reality of Anselm's friendship into account along with his apparently more intimate passages. Letters were often only one part of an exchange which might also include verbal messages entrusted to a bearer, and gifts. The letter itself might be considered a gift; it might contain spiritual advice, or a promise of either practical or spiritual aid (that is, prayers), or information relevant to a current dispute. Letters can also furnish evidence of the gestures exchanged when friends met. Not every aspect of these complex communications is recoverable, but our understanding of Anselm's expectations of his male friends is advanced by an examination of those actions which evidently merited reflection in his letter collection. These can be divided into four themes: exchanges (of letters, gifts, prayers etc.); spiritual admonition, exhortation and advice; gestures (kissing, embracing etc.); and obligations and responsibilities (including interventions in disputes, requests for help or references to specific obligations attendant upon friends).

The concept of gift-exchange, or the non-commercial transfer of commodities to forge or express relationships, is one familiar to historians, and an activity in which we might expect formally constituted friends to engage.[29] The single commodity whose exchange is repeatedly stressed, requested and confirmed in Anselm's letters of friendship, however, is prayer. To pray for one another was clearly a principal duty of friends. The exchange of letters is also an activity discussed as well as participated in, and linked to the maintenance of friendship. The exchange of books is sometimes associated with friendship, and exchanges of actual gifts are alluded to, but appear at times to be problematic. Anselm frequently remarks on the gift as superfluous to the offer of true friendship. A desire to avoid any association with simony may be reflected here, and there was probably more gift exchange than the letters reveal. Nevertheless, we may say with confidence that the relationship presented in the letters attached value principally to the mutual exchange of prayers and of letters.[30]

28. *Ibid.*, II, no. 165, pp.58–9, (*AOO*, IV, p.39). See also *ibid.*, II, no. 185, especially the last paragraph, p.106, (*AOO*, IV, pp.69–71), but note the warning against the wrong sort of friendship in *ibid.*, I, no. 81, at p.215, (*AOO*, III, pp.205–6).

29. See e.g. G. Duby, *The Early Growth of the European Economy* (London, 1974), pp.48–57.

30. A brief survey of the collection reveals, as a rough initial estimate, over 60 references to mutual prayers and around 40 each to the exchange of letters and books, compared to fewer than 20 references to other gifts.

It is hard to overestimate the centrality of spiritual admonition, exhortation and advice in Anselm's letters. It is clearly fundamental to the cultivation of friendship, and more than one-fifth of the letter collection is devoted to it. Often it is part of the process of forming bonds of friendship, as the example above, from the letter to Walter of Saint Wandrille, indicates.[31] Occasionally, advice is specifically directed, as in attempts to persuade laymen or secular clerics to become monks; often an exhortation is requested; but in the majority of cases this manner of writing appears simply to be the natural medium for the communication of friendship. Indeed, in terms of sheer numbers of words written, this reaffirmation of the spirituality at the heart of monastic life far outweighs actual discussion of the bond of friendship itself.

References to physical gesture, as opposed to metaphorical gestures – to embracing, as opposed to the embrace of souls, for example – are surprisingly rare in Anselm's letters. Where they are mentioned it is often as things to be hoped for in the future, or alongside exhortations to put monastic obedience before the desire to travel to see the friend, rather than simple descriptions of real past actions. The account given in letter 36 to Albert, a potential recruit, sheds light on the connection between the emotion expressed and the actual nature of the personal contact involved:

> From the time I was able to get to know you well, in fact, my heart has never ceased longing for and loving you. And you ought not to doubt this if you recall the journey we made together from Bec to Rouen. For then we harmonised so amicably in conversation that our mutual love, which had already been conceived in the mind and through which we had come to know one another in the beginning, displayed itself more fully . . .[32]

A mutual love conceived in the mind predated this encounter, a letter from Albert had reactivated the friendship, and the full display of friendship referred to was Albert's expression of his desire to become a monk, which it is now Anselm's goal to bring about. The only action associated with this longing and loving is harmonious conversation. There is indeed little reference throughout the collection to the necessity or centrality of ardent gestures or of meeting to enact such gestures. Such passages are outnumbered by

---

31. Letter 85, ref. n.25 above.
32. *Letters of Anselm*, I, no. 36, pp.131–2, (*AOO*, III, pp.143–4); but see letter 130, quoted above, ref. n.6, for one of the rare examples of a reference to emotional gestures (purportedly) enacted in reality.

those which stress obedience and the need to give up the desire to travel and meet which might, as we have seen above, undermine the very basis of the love itself, monastic discipline.[33]

The details and extent of the practical responsibilities and obligations attendant upon friends constitute an area of study in their own right. It is essential, however, to stress here that they represent an integral part of the expected behaviour of the friend. It may be that Anselm invokes *amicitia* less frequently than others in cases of urgent need, but, as the examples cited above demonstrate, there is no implication that he considered it a discrete category of activity.[34] He accorded it a ready place in his more worldly dealings, and respected the obligations and responsibilities which it conveyed. In this passage from a letter to Bishop Samson of Worcester, concerning Anselm's dispute with York over the profession of obedience to Canterbury, Anselm invokes their friendship as the first of two compelling sources of obligation:

> I therefore ask you as a friend and one who has made his profession to our church that, against this injury . . . [you] be a help to me in checking such an intolerable presumption.[35]

Conclusions

The unrestrained language which the potent fusion of friendship and love permitted in the letters of the eleventh and twelfth centuries drew its force not from romantic abandon but from its deliberate and controlled application in practice. Grounded in a distinct intellectual and philosophical tradition, it derived ethical value from its interaction with other moral and social considerations. It did not, in the manner of romantic love, transcend all else through a moral force independent of other ties and obligations. For Anselm, loving male friendship was an integral part of the monastic vocation. It was not restricted or muted by the demands of that life – by the renunciation of particular private friendships, or of sexual relations – but was rather enhanced and enlarged by it. As a spiritual reality it could not exist on any other terms. Anselm's letters not only offer an insight into his own remarkable and original mind,

---

33. Most significant references to gesture in the letters are metaphorical rather than descriptive of real past actions, or refer to the future; see e.g. letter 241, *ibid.*, II, p.220, 'I long to embrace your friendship' (*AOO*, IV, p.149).
34. See letter 165, quoted above, ref. n.30, and letters 356–9, cited above n.28.
35. *Letters of Anselm*, III, no. 464, p.257, (*AOO*, V, p.413).

but also reflect the living tradition of friendship which he shared with many medieval writers, a tradition built around the public exchange of declarations of love and dominated, above all, by the act of spiritual admonition. Friendship, however, did not offer the easy comfort of retreat into a private emotional domain. It was a difficult and challenging part of the life of the eleventh- and twelfth-century Church.

The Gregorian reform had presented Europe with a revolutionary vision of Christian unity centred on Rome. While this was never a simple collision between 'state' and 'Church', and while the ideal of absolute papal supremacy encountered resistance in many churches, it did open up for ecclesiastics the prospect of a common interest and identity beyond the range of traditional, regional political ties.[36] Friendship was instrumental in expressing these wider allegiances.[37] It combined the ancient theory of human friendships as central to political order with a theology of love which was at the forefront of a new intellectual movement. As such it reflected the shared educational and literary background of monks, bishops and clerics and stressed their common membership of the Church. The language of friendship was a powerful medium through which they could convey their mutual obligations, allegiances and common concerns – a convention akin, perhaps, to gift-exchange or even vassalage or patronage, but one ideally suited to churchmen.[38]

It would be all too easy, however, to reduce this vibrant literature to the empty rhetoric of political network-formation and to overlook the significance of the deliberate and public cultivation of so potent a language, with such consistency, over decades, by men dedicated to lives of austerity and renunciation. Other codes would surely have functioned equally well for the simple declaration of common interest or allegiance, and presented fewer of the sorts of ethical conflicts with which we have seen Anselm struggling. Given the circumstances of their composition, it is well to take seriously the choice of imagery and the ardour of the language employed, and to ask what model of reciprocal male behaviour is being constructed. The study of friendship is of central importance for illuminating emergent identities among important groups in medieval

---

36. For an introduction to the vast literature on the Gregorian reform see G. Tellenbach, *The Church in Western Europe from the Tenth to the Early Twelfth Century* (Cambridge, 1993).

37. As demonstrated in Robinson, 'The friendship network of Gregory VII'.

38. But note also that friendship conveyed a degree of equality, while patronage, by definition, is based on inequality.

society, but this does not divest the language of its emotive content. The most interesting feature of these letters is, rather, how such a passionate and tender language was seen not only to accord with, but to convey better than any other, the public relations of powerful and influential men. There can be no doubt that the writers of these letters, even when less exalted than Saint Anselm, were figures of the establishment, often of considerable authority. Their concerns, as we have seen, were often with questions of obedience or the rightful exercise of power. In these documents they were not concerned with emotional development, with what the modern world would term 'personal growth', but with projecting their role as figures of piety and authority. What is remarkable is that this carefully contrived image of the male, projected deliberately in a literary genre aimed as much at posterity as at contemporaries, is couched in a language which in subsequent ages came to seem entirely inappropriate to powerful male figures.

Love, permeating the learning and literature of the time, and friendship, long established intellectually and philosophically as a force for social order, provided churchmen with a distinctive language of their own. It was a language which reflected their common intellectual background and expressed their new sense of identity at a time when reform was challenging old allegiances and customs and offering a revolutionary view of Christian unity. Those who cultivated friendship constituted a privileged circle of educated clerics. The image of the man as friend and lover cherished in the letter collections of the central Middle Ages is the picture of a member of a new international elite. It is not a vulnerable or an introspective image, but it is an unashamedly passionate one.

Bibliographical Essay

D.M. HADLEY

This bibliographical essay suggests further reading related to the subjects and sources of evidence discussed in this volume. For each chapter I have cited studies which will enable the reader to explore further the subjects discussed in that chapter, offering a cross-section of literature related to the issues addressed by individual chapters. These works set the subject in its broader context; they need not have any particular interest in gender, and accordingly they reveal the ways in which the relevant issues have been treated in more traditional studies. Masculinity has received scant treatment from medievalists, thus, in addition to citing the few available studies of masculinity, I have also included work on other aspects of gender, in particular those studies which present interesting and challenging view of gender issues through their concentration on female status and identity. For the purpose of comparison I have cited studies which deal with the issues discussed in individual chapters in other regions or periods of medieval Europe, and studies of masculinity from other periods of history. Finally, where possible I have indicated the availability of translations into English of the main texts examined in individual chapters; for those texts in the original the reader is directed to the footnotes of the chapter concerned.

Chapter One: Introduction: Medieval Masculinities

The best general introduction to the development of gender studies within the historical discipline is Joan Scott, 'Gender: a useful category of historical analysis', *AHR* 91 (1986), pp.1053–75. Extended discussion is to be found in Scott's *Gender and the Politics of History* (New York and London, 1988). For an overview of studies of gender by medievalists since the 1960s see Janet Nelson, 'Family, gender and sexuality in the Middle Ages', in Michael Bentley, ed.,

Companion to Historiography (London, 1997), pp.153–76. A collection of papers about gender and medieval history appeared in *Speculum* 68 (1993), including: Nancy Partner, 'Studying medieval women: sex, gender, feminism', pp.305–8; Judith Bennett, 'Medievalism and feminism', pp.309–31; Carol Clover, 'Regardless of sex: men, women and power in early northern Europe', pp.363–87; Kathleen Biddick, 'Genders, bodies, borders: technologies of the visible', pp.389–418; Nancy Partner, 'No sex, no gender', pp.419–43; and Allen Frantzen, 'When women aren't enough', pp.445–71.

The following journals contain papers on aspects of gender in historical periods, although the medieval content is not great: *Gender and History* (1989–); *Women's History Review* (1992–); *Journal of Homosexuality* (1973–); *Signs* (1976–); *The Journal of Family History* (1976–); *History Workshop Journal* (1976–); and *Journal of the History of Sexuality* (1990–).

Useful introductions to the study of masculinity include John Tosh, 'What should historians do with masculinity? Reflections on nineteenth-century Britain', *HWJ* 38 (1994), pp.179–202; Michael Roper and John Tosh, eds, *Manful Assertions: Masculinities in Britain since 1800* (London, 1991); Frank Mort, 'Crisis points: masculinities in history and social theory', *Gender and History* 6 (1994), pp.124–30; L. Segal, *Slow Motion: Changing Masculinities, Changing Men* (London, 1990); R.W. Connell, *Masculinities* (Cambridge, 1995). An introduction to the so-called 'men's studies' is provided by Harry Brod, ed., *The Making of Masculinities: The New Men's Studies* (Boston, 1987); D. Gilmour, *Manhood in the Making: Cultural Constructs of Masculinity* (New Haven, Conn., 1990). For an anthropological perspective, see Andrea Cornwall and Nancy Lindisfarne, eds, *Dislocating Masculinity. Comparative Ethnographies* (London, 1994). On masculinities in the Middle Ages the most important recent work is Clare Lees, ed., *Medieval Masculinities. Regarding Men in the Middle Ages* (Minneapolis and London, 1994); and J.J. Cohen and B. Wheeler, eds, *Becoming Male in the Middle Ages* (New York, 1997).

There are numerous studies of women in the Middle Ages, but few of them may be appropriately described as studies of gender, since they do little more than 'add women' to medieval history. For a general bibliographical introduction and discussion of the best work on the early Middle Ages (pre-1100) see Nelson, 'Family, gender and sexuality in the Middle Ages'. Studies of note on this period include J.M.H. Smith, 'Gender and ideology in the earlier Middle Ages', in R.N. Swanson, ed., *Gender and the Christian Religion*, Studies in Church History 34 (1998), pp.51–73; S.F. Wemple, *Women in*

Frankish Society: Marriage and the Cloister, 500–900 (Philadelphia, 1981); G. Halsall, *Settlement and Social Organization. The Merovingian Region of Metz* (Cambridge, 1995), which also discusses archaeological evidence for the period; H. Leyser, *Medieval Women, A Social History of Women* (London, 1995), which also includes much on the later Middle Ages.

Gender issues have received more attention from late medievalists. Notable studies of late medieval women in England include Jeremy Goldberg, *Women, Work and Life-Cycle in a Medieval Economy: Women in York and Yorkshire c.1300–1520* (Oxford, 1992); a collection of papers edited by Goldberg: *Woman is a Worthy Wight: Women in English Society c.1200–1500* (Stroud, 1992), recently republished in paperback under the title *Women in Medieval English Society* (Stroud, 1997); Sue Sheridan Walker, ed., *Wife and Widow in Medieval England* (Michigan, 1993). For a more theoretically explicit discussion of the position of women in later medieval English society see Steve Rigby, 'Gender as social closure: women' in his *English Society in the Later Middle Ages* (London, 1995). For a wider European perspective, on both the early and later medieval periods, the collected works of David Herlihy provide a starting point: *Women, Family and Society in Medieval Europe* (Providence, Rhode Is. and Oxford, 1995). A variety of studies are to be found in M. Erler and M. Kowaleski, eds, *Women and Power in the Middle Ages* (Chicago, 1988); Susan Mosher Stuard, ed., *Women in Medieval Society* (Philadelphia, 1976); and J. Kirshner and S.F. Wemple, eds, *Women of the Medieval World* (Oxford, 1995). On women, and some men, in Byzantine society see Liz James, ed., *Women, Men and Eunuchs: Gender in Byzantium* (London and New York, 1997). Caroline Walker Bynum's study of female religiosity *Holy Feast and Holy Fast: the Religious Significance of Food to Medieval Women* (Berkeley and Los Angeles, 1987) has been extremely influential; for a critique see, K. Biddick, 'Genders, bodies, borders: technologies of the visible', *Speculum* 68 (1993), pp.389–418.

The impact of feminism on medieval studies is discussed in Judith Bennett, 'Medievalism and feminism', *Speculum* 68 (1993), pp.309–31; and Allen Frantzen, 'When women aren't enough', *ibid.*, pp.445–71. The biannual bibliographies of the *Medieval Feminist Newsletter* provide a valuable bibliographical guide. B. Gottlieb discusses the danger of anachronism in the application of the term 'feminist' to prominent medieval women in 'Feminism in the fifteenth century', J. Kirshner and S.F. Wemple, eds, *Women of the Medieval World* (Oxford, 1985), pp.337–64.

Medievalists have been greatly influenced by studies of gender, sexuality, the body and social identity in relation to other periods. This is reflected in this volume, and the following (in addition to those already cited) have clearly influenced many of the contributors: J. Boswell, *Christianity, Social Tolerance and Homosexuality: Gay People in Western Europe from the Beginning of the Christian Era to the Fourteenth Century* (Chicago, 1980). P. Bourdieu, *Outline of a Theory of Practice* (Cambridge, 1977); Judith Butler, *Gender Trouble: Feminism and the Subversion of Identity* (New York, 1990); M. Douglas, *Purity and Danger: an Analysis of the Concepts of Pollution and Taboo* (London, 1966); *idem, Natural Symbols: Explorations in Cosmology* (Harmondsworth, 1970); M. Foucault, *The History of Sexuality*, 3 vols, trans. R. Hurley (Harmondsworth, 1981–92); G. Herdt, ed., *Third Sex, Third Gender: Beyond Sexual Dimorphism in Culture and History* (New York, 1994); Eve Kosofsky Sedgwick, *Between Men: English Literature and Male Homosocial Desire* (New York, 1985).

Chapter Two: 'Death Makes the Man'? Burial Rite and the Construction of Masculinities in the Early Middle Ages

The best introduction to gender and archaeology is Joan Gero and Meg Conkey, eds, *Engendering Archaeology: Women and Prehistory* (Oxford, 1991). The chapters by Conkey and Gero ('Tensions, pluralities and engendering archaeology: an introduction to women and prehistory', pp.3–30) and Alison Wylie ('Gender theory and the archaeological record why is there no theory of gender?', pp.31–54) provide wide-ranging surveys of the development of gender theory in archaeology, and the rest of the volume applies this to various prehistoric contexts. A recent volume which looks at both gender and children in the archaeological record (including a number of papers on the medieval period) is Jenny Moore and Eleanor Scott, eds, *Invisible People and Processes. Writing Gender and Childhood into European Archaeology* (London, 1996). A useful review of gender and medieval archaeology is Roberta Gilchrist, 'Ambivalent bodies: gender and medieval archaeology', in *ibid.*, pp.42–58. See also the introduction to her book, *Gender and Material Culture: the Archaeology of Religious Women* (London, 1994). An interesting study of burial rite and society is I. Morris, *Death-Ritual and Social Structure in Classical Antiquity* (Cambridge, 1992).

The following provide the best introductions to gender and medieval cemeteries: R. Bertelsen, *Were They All Men? An Examination of Sex Roles in Prehistoric Society* (Stavanger, 1985), which, despite its title, is largely about the Viking period (c.AD800–1050); K. Brush, 'Gender and mortuary analysis in pagan Anglo-Saxon archaeology', *Archaeological Review from Cambridge* vii (1) (1988), pp.76–89; G. Halsall, *Settlement and Social Organization. The Merovingian Region of Metz* (Cambridge, 1995); *idem*, 'Female status and power in early Merovingian central Austrasia: the burial evidence', *EME* 5 (1) (1996), pp.1–24; S.J. Lucy, 'Housewives, warriors and slaves? Sex and gender in Anglo-Saxon burials', in Moore and Scott, eds, *Invisible People and Processes*, pp.150–68.

Although the author does not explicitly address the issue of masculinity, the following form a good starting point for a discussion of male identity and burial rite: H. Härke, 'Knives in early Saxon burials: blade length and age at death', *Medieval Archaeology* xxxiii (1989), pp.144–48; *idem*, 'Warrior Graves? The background of the Anglo-Saxon weapon burial rite', *Past and Present* 126 (1990), pp.22–43. Symbolism and grave goods are discussed in H. Härke, 'Changing symbols in a changing society: the Anglo-Saxon burial rite in the seventh century', in M. Carver, ed., *The Age of Sutton Hoo* (Woodbridge, 1992), pp.149–65; E.J. Pader, *Symbolism, Social Relations and the Interpretation of Mortuary Remains*, BAR, International Series, 130 (1982); J.D. Richards, 'Funerary symbolism in Anglo-Saxon England: further social dimensions of mortuary practices', *Scottish Archaeological Review* 3 (1984), pp.42–55.

Chapter Three: Frustrated Masculinity: The Relationship between William the Conqueror and his Eldest Son

General introductions to the life and career of William the Conqueror can be found in David Douglas, *William the Conqueror* (London, 1964); and David Bates, *William the Conqueror* (London, 1989). On Robert Curthose see C.W. David, *Robert Curthose* (Cambridge, Mass., 1920); Stephanie Mooers, ' "Backers and stabbers": problems of loyalty in Robert Curthose's entourage', *Journal of British Studies* 21 (1981), pp.1–17. Translations of the writing of Orderic Vitalis are to be found in *The Ecclesiastical History of Orderic Vitalis*, ed. and trans., Marjorie Chibnall, 6 vols (Oxford, 1968–80); his historical methodology is discussed in Marjorie Chibnall, *The World of Orderic Vitalis* (Oxford, 1984).

Anglo-Norman 'youth' and childhood are discussed in Georges Duby, 'Youth in aristocratic society. Northwestern France in the twelfth century', in his *The Chivalrous Society* (London, 1977); Ralph Turner, 'The children of Anglo-Norman royalty and their upbringing', *Medieval Prosopography* 11, no. 2 (1990), pp.17–52. Duby's *The Chivalrous Society* includes a number of translated essays originally published over the previous decade or so; of particular interest is his work on the family and the changing nature of inheritance. The ways in which William the Conqueror exploited dynastic rivalries are discussed in E. Searle, *Predatory Kinship and the Creation of Norman Power 840–1066* (Berkeley, Ca., 1988).

Pauline Stafford has highlighted the Norman impact on women in Anglo-Saxon England in her 'Women in Domesday', in *Medieval Women in Southern England, Reading Medieval Studies* 15 (1989), pp.75–94, where she emphasizes the way in which male lords controlled land through the control of women; see also her 'Women and the Norman Conquest', *TRHS* 6th ser., iv (1995), pp.221–50. She also discusses the relationships between royal mothers and sons in the early medieval period in 'Sons and mothers: family politics in the early Middle Ages', in D. Baker, ed., *Medieval Women* (Oxford, 1978), pp.79–100. The complex interplay between gender, ethnicity and social status following the Norman Conquest is revealed in a study of personal names by Cecily Clark in 'Women's names in post-Conquest England: observations and speculations', *Speculum* 53 (1978), pp.223–51.

Chapter Four: Masters and Men in Later Medieval England

A number of relevant documents for this chapter are translated in J. Goldberg, *Women in England c.1275–1525* (Manchester, 1995). A general survey of late medieval workshops is Heather Swanson, *Medieval Artisans. An Urban Class in Late Medieval England* (Oxford, 1989). A good introduction to the socio-economic history of late medieval English towns is provided by R. Holt and G. Rosser, eds, *The Medieval Town. A Reader in English Urban History* (London, 1990). Much interesting work has been undertaken recently on women in medieval towns. Of particular note are Jeremy Goldberg, *Women, Work and Life-Cycle in a Medieval Economy: Women in York and Yorkshire c.1300–1520* (Oxford, 1992); C.M. Barron, 'The education and training of girls in fifteenth-century London', in D.E.S. Dunn, ed., *Courts, Counties and the Capital in the Later Middle Ages* (Stroud, 1996), pp.139–53.

A recent study of urban life which emphasizes the childhood experiences of men and women is Barbara Hanawalt, *Growing Up in Medieval London. The Experience of Childhood in History* (Oxford, 1993). Sexuality and marriage in late medieval English towns are explored in R.M. Karras, *Common Women: Prostitution and Sexuality in Medieval England* (New York, 1996); and S. McSheffrey, *Love and Marriage in Late Medieval London* (Kalamazoo, Mich., 1995). Aspects of social structure and conflict in medieval towns are addressed in S.H. Rigby, *English Society in the Later Middle Ages. Class, Status and Gender* (London, 1995). Discussions of early modern households are to be found in R. Wall, 'Leaving home and the process of household formation in pre-industrial England', *Continuity and Change 2* (1987), pp.77–100; and L. Roper, *The Holy Household: Women and Morals in Reformation Augsburg* (Oxford, 1989).

An introduction to gender issues in the urban environment in a European context may be found in the following: M.C. Howells, *Women, Production and Patriarchy in Late Medieval Cities* (Chicago, 1986); *idem*, 'Citizenship and gender: women's political status in northern medieval cities', in M. Erler and M. Kowaleski, eds, *Women and Power in the Middle Ages* (Athens, Ga., 1988); B. Hanawalt, ed., *Women and Work in Pre-Industrial Europe* (Bloomington, Indiana, 1986). The issue of masculinity and urban political and social organization is discussed in S. Chojnacki, 'Subaltern patriarchs. Patrician bachelors in Renaissance Venice', in C. Lees, ed., *Medieval Masculinities. Regarding Men in the Middle Ages* (Minneapolis, 1994), pp.73–90. Susan Mosher Stuard discusses the importance of husbanding in the construction of masculine gender identity in mostly urban contexts in her 'Burdens of matrimony: Husbanding and gender in medieval Italy', in *ibid.*, pp.61–71.

Chapter Five: Military Masculinity in England and Northern France c.1050–c.1225

Many of the texts discussed in this paper are available in translation. See, for example: *William, Count of Orange: Four Old French Epics*, ed., G. Price (London, 1975); *The Song of Roland*, ed. and trans., G. Burgess (Harmondsworth, 1990); *Eneas: a twelfth-century French Romance*, trans., J.A. Yunck (New York and London, 1974).

A good introduction to military households is J.O. Prestwich, 'The military household of the Norman kings', *EHR* 96 (1981), pp.1–37. Knightly society, primarily in France, is examined in two books by Georges Duby: *The Chivalrous Society* (London, 1977); and *The Knight, The Lady and the Priest* (London, 1983). On the concept of knighthood in contemporary literary sources, see T. Hunt, 'The emergence of the knight in France and England, 1000–1200', in W. Jackson, ed., *Knighthood in Medieval Literature* (Woodbridge, 1981), pp.1–22; and S. North, 'The ideal knight as presented in some French narrative poems, c.1090–1240', in C. Harper-Bill and R. Harvey, eds, *The Ideals and Practice of Medieval Knighthood* (Woodbridge, 1986), pp.117–32. M. Keen, *Chivalry* (New Haven and London, 1984) explores the development of chivalry, its secular origins and the involvement of the Church. Violence and conflict in Normandy in the eleventh century are discussed in M. Bennett, 'Violence in eleventh-century Normandy: feud, warfare and politics', in G. Halsall, ed., *Violence and Society in the Early Medieval West* (Woodbridge, 1998), pp.126–40.

Charles Coulson has discussed the military aristocracy from the perspective of castle architecture in his 'Structural symbolism in medieval castle architecture', *Journal of the British Archaeological Association* 88 (1979), pp.73–90. The relationship between this and notions of aristocratic masculinity would repay further attention, as is shown by Roberta Gilchrist's discussion of gender and the use of space in castles with reference to female status and identity in her 'Medieval bodies in the material world: gender, stigma and the body', in M. Rubin and S. Kay, eds, *Framing Medieval Bodies* (Manchester, 1994), pp.43–61.

The role of women in this military world has been explored in a number of papers, which are mostly concerned with literary evidence: M. McLaughlin, 'The woman warrior: gender, warfare and society in medieval Europe', *Women's Studies* 17 (1990), pp.193–203; H. Solterer, 'Figures of female militancy in medieval France', *Signs* 16 (3) (1991), pp.522–49; M.T. Bruckner, 'Fictions of the female voice: the women troubadours', *Speculum* 67 (1992), pp.865–91. The texts discussed by these papers reveal a world which is the reverse of the norm, in which women take to the field as warriors or as the narrators of epic tales. These texts may serve to challenge the prevailing order, to respond to the existence of bellicose women in society, to make fun of the norm, or to reinforce the social order through role-reversal. On the prevalence of male stereotypes for women who wanted to pursue traditionally masculine activities, such as warfare or the running of the household, see V.R. Hotchkiss,

Clothes Make the Man: Female Cross Dressing in Medieval Europe (New York, 1996).

Chapter Six: Images of Effeminate Men: the Case of Byzantine Eunuchs

For general studies of Byzantine history see G. Ostrogorsky *History of the Byzantine State* (English edn, New Brunswick, N.J., 1954); M. Whittow, *The Making of Orthodox Byzantium, 600–1025* (Basingstoke, 1996); and M. Angold, *The Byzantine Empire 1025–1204* (2nd edn, London, 1997).

There have been numerous studies of the role of eunuchs in Byzantine society. Among the most notable are: H. Diner, *Emperors, Angels and Eunuchs. The Thousand Years of the Byzantine Empire*, ed. and trans. E. and C. Paul (London, 1938); K. Hopkins, *Conquerors and Slaves* (Cambridge, 1972); M.S. Kuefler, 'Castration and eunuchism in the middle ages', in V.L. Bullough and J.A. Brundage, eds, *Handbook of Medieval Sexuality* (New York and London, 1996), pp.279–306; P. Magdalino, 'The *Bagoas* of Nikephoros Basilakes: a normative reaction?', in L. Mayali and M.M. Mart, eds, *Of Strangers and Foreigners* (Berkeley, 1993), pp.47–63. Eunuchs have also been discussed in the context of the construction of gender identity by the following: K. Ringrose, 'Living in the shadows: eunuchs and gender in Byzantium', in G. Herdt, ed., *Third Sex, Third Gender: Beyond Sexual Dimorphism in Culture and History* (New York, 1994), pp.85–110; S.F. Tougher, 'Byzantine eunuchs: an overview, with special reference to castration and origin', in L. James, ed., *Women, Men and Eunuchs: Gender in Byzantium* (London, 1997), pp.168–84. This collection edited by Liz James is an excellent introduction to gender issues in general in Byzantium, and includes a paper on masculinity: C. Barber, '*Homo Byzantinus*', pp.185–99.

Chapter Seven: Masculinity in Flux: Nocturnal Emission and the Limits of Celibacy in the Early Middle Ages

A general introduction to the formation of the western monastic tradition is R. Markus, *The End of Ancient Christianity* (Cambridge, 1990). For discussions of early medieval monasticism see *idem, Gregory the Great and his World* (Cambridge, 1996); C. Leyser, *Community and Authority from Augustine to Gregory the Great* (Oxford, forthcoming).

Nocturnal emission has been explored in a number of recent papers: D. Brakke, 'The problematization of nocturnal emissions in early Christian Syria, Egypt and Gaul', *Journal of Early Christian Studies* 3 (4) (1995), pp.419–60; D. Elliott, 'Pollution, illusion, and masculine disarray: nocturnal emissions and the sexuality of the clergy', in J. Schultz *et al.*, eds, *Constructing Medieval Sexuality* (Minneapolis, forthcoming). The work of Mary Douglas is influential in this branch of scholarship: *Purity and Danger: An Analysis of the Concepts of Pollution and Taboo* (London, 1966); *Natural Symbols: Explorations in Cosmology* (Harmondsworth, 1970).

A number of books and articles have appeared recently which discuss gender, sexuality and the body in late Antique and medieval society: A. Rousselle, *Porneia: On Desire and the Body in Late Antiquity* (London, 1988); P. Brown, *The Body and Society: Men, Women and Sexual Renunciation in Early Christianity* (London, 1989); K. Cooper, 'Insinuations of womanly influence: an aspect of the christianization of the Roman aristocracy', *Journal of Roman Studies* 82 (1992), pp.150–64; *idem, The Virgin and the Bride: Idealized Womanhood in Late Antiquity* (Cambridge, Mass., 1996); M. Rubin and S. Kay, eds, *Framing Medieval Bodies* (Manchester, 1994); C.W. Bynum, *Fragmentation and Redemption: Essays on Gender and the Body in Medieval Religion* (New York, 1991); *idem, The Resurrection of the Body in Western Christianity, 200–1336* (New York, 1995); B. Hanawalt and D. Wallace, eds, *Bodies and Disciplines. Intersections of Literature and History in Fifteenth-Century England* (Minneapolis, 1996). Medievalists have also been greatly influenced by T. Laqueur, *Making Sex: Body and Gender from the Greeks to Freud* (Harvard, 1990).

Some of the ideas discussed in this chapter are developed for a later period in C. Leyser, 'Cities of the Plain: the rhetoric of sodomy in Peter Damian's "Book of Gomorrah"', *Romanic Review* 86 (2) (1995), pp.191–211; 'Custom, truth and gender in eleventh-century reform', in R.N. Swanson, ed., *Gender and the Christian Religion*, Studies in Church History 34 (1998), pp.75–91.

Chapter Eight: Monks, Secular Men and Masculinity, c.900

A general overview of the Church in the ninth century may be found in J.M. Wallace-Hadrill, *The Frankish Church* (Oxford, 1983). An introduction to the political, social and cultural background of the period is R. McKitterick, *The Frankish Kingdoms under the Carolingians, 751–987* (London, 1983); see also J. Dunbabin, *France in the Making, 843–1180* (Oxford, 1985). The broader political and ideological context for the discussion of the ninth-century Frankish aristocracy is provided in two collections of Janet Nelson's published work: *Politics and Ritual in Early Medieval Europe* (London, 1986); and *The Frankish World, 750–900* (London, 1996). On the life and career of King Alfred see J.L. Nelson, ' "A king across the sea": Alfred in continental perspective', *TRHS* 36 (1986), pp.45–68; and the controversial book by Alfred Smyth, *King Alfred the Great* (Oxford, 1995).

The promotion of celibacy by the Church in various periods and the experiences of men and women who attempted to adopt this ideal both within the Church and among the laity is explored in the following: J. Bugge, *Virginitas. An Essay in the History of a Medieval Ideal* (The Hague, 1976); P. Brown, *The Body and Society: Men, Women and Sexual Renunciation in Early Christianity* (London, 1989); D. Elliott, *Spiritual Marriage. Sexual Abstinence in Medieval Wedlock* (Princeton, 1993). Attitudes to warfare, ecclesiastical concern about relations with secular powers, and about involvement in violence in particular, are explored in J.L. Nelson, 'Violence in the Carolingian world and the ritualization of ninth-century Frankish warfare', in G. Halsall, ed., *Violence and Society in the Early Medieval West* (Woodbridge, 1997), pp.90–107. This collection of papers, although not specifically about gender, has important implications for the study of early medieval masculinity as it provides new perspectives on a stereotypically male activity.

The importance of performance and dress in the construction of gender is highlighted in this chapter. Recent discussions of this subject include: J. Butler, *Gender Trouble: Feminism and the Subversion of Identity* (New York, 1990); V.R. Hotchkiss, *Clothes Make the Man: Female Cross Dressing in Medieval Europe* (New York, 1996); see also Janet Nelson's paper on ninth-century knighthood, with its discussion of ritual and the signification of status through dress and appearance, 'Ninth-century knighthood: the evidence of Nithard', in C. Harper-Bill, C.J. Holdsworth and J.L. Nelson, eds, *Studies in Medieval History presented to R. Allen Brown* (Woodbridge, 1989), pp.255–66.

Chapter Nine: Men and Sex in Tenth-century Italy

The writing of Liutprand is available in translation in F.A. Wright, *The Works of Liudprand of Cremona* (London, 1930), reprinted as *The Embassy to Constantinople and Other Writings* (London, 1993); and that of Ratherius of Verona in P.L. Reid, *The Complete Works of Ratherius of Verona* (Michigan, 1991). For the general background to Italy in the tenth century see C.J. Wickham, *Early Medieval Italy, Central Power and Local Society 400–1000* (London, 1981); G. Tabacco, *The Struggle for Power in Medieval Italy* (Cambridge, 1989); also useful is H. Fichtenau, *Living in the Tenth Century* (Chicago, 1991; original German 1984). On individual bishops: Jon Sutherland *Liudprand of Cremona: Bishop, Diplomat, Historian* (Spoleto, 1988); P. Buc, 'Italian hussies and German matrons. Liutprand of Cremona on dynastic legitimacy', *Frühmittelalterliche Studien* 29 (1994); K. Leyser, 'Liudprand of Cremona: Preacher and Homilist', and 'Ends and Means in Liudprand of Cremona', in T. Reuter, ed., *Communications and Power in Medieval Europe. The Carolingian and Ottonian Centuries* (London, 1994); S.F. Wemple, *Atto of Vercelli* (Rome, 1979).

Recent discussions of gender in early medieval Italy include: P. Skinner, 'Women, wills and wealth in medieval southern Italy', *EME* 2 (2) (1993), pp.133–52; R. Balzaretti, ' "These are things that men do, not women": the social regulation of violence in Langobard Italy', in G. Halsall, ed., *Violence and Society in the Early Medieval West* (Woodbridge, 1998), pp.175–92.

Homosexuality in the Middle Ages has received much attention in recent years. However, it remains a controversial area of study; the notion of the 'homosexual' is hotly disputed, although there is no doubt that homosexual activity occurred in many spheres and was commented on explicitly and implicitly by many authors. For discussion see, R. Balzaretti, 'Michel Foucault, homosexuality and the Middle Ages', *Renaissance and Modern Studies* 37 (1994), pp.1–12; J. Boswell, *The Marriage of Likeness. Same-Sex Unions in Pre-Modern Europe* (London, 1995); *idem, Christianity, Social Tolerance and Homosexuality: Gay People in Western Europe from the Beginning of the Christian Era to the Fourteenth Century* (Chicago, 1980). On medieval attitudes to sexual activity more generally see J.A. Brundage, *Law, Sex and Christian Damnation in Medieval Europe* (Chicago, 1987); J. Richards, 'Homosexuals', in his *Sex, Dissidence and Damnation. Minority Groups in the Middle Ages* (London, 1991), pp.132–49.

Chapter Ten: Angels Incarnate: Clergy and Masculinity from Gregorian Reform to Reformation

General introductions to the Church and its role in late medieval society are P. Heath, *The English Parish Clergy on the Eve of the Reformation*

(London, 1969); R.N. Swanson, *Church and Society in Late-Medieval England* (Oxford, 1989). On the Church and the clergy in western Europe more generally see G. Tellenbach, *The Church in Western Europe from the Tenth to the Early Twelfth Century* (Cambridge, 1993); R.N. Swanson, *Religion and Devotion in Europe, c.1215–c.1515* (Cambridge, 1996). The impact of Gregorian reform and its implications for discussions of gender are discussed in C. Leyser, 'Custom, truth and gender in eleventh-century reform', in R.N. Swanson, ed., *Gender and the Christian Religion*, Studies in Church History 34 (1998), pp.75–91.

Jo Ann McNamara discusses the 'men question' and what she perceives as a crisis in the gender system with reference to changes in urban and intellectual circles in 'The *herrenfrage*: the restructuring of the gender system, 1050–1150', in C. Lees, ed., *Medieval Masculinities: Regarding Men in the Middle Ages* (Minneapolis, 1994), pp.3–29. Vern Bullough examines broader societal notions of masculinity in the same period in 'On being a male in the Middle Ages', in *ibid.*, pp.31–45.

Both the polarization of gender identities in the later Middle Ages and the acceptance of a range of possible gender identities are debated in M. Rubin, 'The person in the form: medieval challenges to "bodily order"', in S. Kay and M. Rubin, eds, *Framing Medieval Bodies* (Manchester, 1994), pp.100–22; and Joan Cadden, *Meanings of Sex Difference in the Middle Ages* (Cambridge, 1993), who also discusses medieval traditions about sexual activity and the implications of celibacy. The debates about marriage in the twelfth century, and the necessity of consummation, are discussed in J.A. Brundage, *Law, Sex and Christian Society in Medieval Europe* (Chicago and London, 1987). A collection of papers that deal with the concept of a third gender, although with little medieval content, are to be found in G. Herdt, ed., *Third Sex, Third Gender: Beyond Sexual Dimorphism in Culture and History* (New York, 1994).

The recent work of Caroline Walker Bynum has explored aspects of male and female spirituality in the later Middle Ages, with particular emphasis on confusions or inversions of gender identity. See, for example, 'Jesus as mother, abbot as mother: some themes in early Cistercian writing', in her *Jesus as Mother: Studies in the Spirituality of the High Middle Ages* (Berkeley, 1982), pp.110–68; *idem, Fragmentation and Redemption: Essays on Gender and the Human Body in Medieval Religion* (New York, 1991). The experiences of men and women in the medieval parish church are explored in M. Aston, 'Segregation in church', in W. Shiels and D. Green, eds, *Women in the Church*, Studies in Church History 27 (1990), pp.237–94. A recent paper by Pamela Graves explores the ways in which both the social use of space and participation in, and observance of, the mass contributed to the construction of social identity in the late medieval parish church; this approach could, as Aston's paper demonstrates, be expanded to include gender as an aspect of social relations: P. Graves, 'Social space in the English medieval parish church', *Economy and Society* 18 (3) (1989), pp.297–322. The performative nature of medieval religious experience and the importance of symbols and images are explored in a number of papers, which could easily be re-read with an awareness of the gender implications: R.N. Swanson, 'Medieval liturgy as theatre: the props', in D. Wood, ed., *The Church and the Arts*, Studies in Church History 29 (1992), pp.239–53.

Chapter Eleven: Clergy, Masculinity and Transgression in Late Medieval England

P. Heath, *The English Parish Clergy on the Eve of the Reformation* (London, 1969) provides a general introduction to the late medieval English clergy. See also R.N. Swanson, *Church and Society in Late-Medieval England* (Oxford, 1989); and J.A.F. Thomson, *The Early Tudor Church and Society, 1485–1529* (London, 1993). The lives and careers of minor clergy in the secular cathedrals are discussed in K. Edwards, *English Secular Cathedrals in the Middle Ages* (2nd edn, Manchester, 1967); and D. Lepine, *A Brotherhood of Canons Serving God: English Secular Cathedrals in the Later Middle Ages* (Woodbridge, 1995); see also M. Bowker, *The Secular Clergy in the Diocese of Lincoln, 1495–1520* (Cambridge, 1968); and on the problems that might develop between parishioners and their clergy see K. Wood-Legh, ed., *Kentish Visitations of Archbishop William Warham and his deputies, 1511–2*, Kent Records Society, 24 (1984). Many of the sources discussed in this chapter are readily available: R.T. Davies, ed., *Medieval English Lyrics* (London, 1966); L.D. Benson, *The Riverside Chaucer* (3rd edn, London, 1988).

The military activity of the clergy is discussed in B. McNab, 'Obligations of the Church in English society: military arrays of the clergy, 1369–1418', in W.C. Jordan, B. McNab and T.F. Ruiz, eds, *Order and Innovation in the Middle Ages: Essays in Honour of Joseph R. Strayer* (Princeton, N.J., 1976), pp.293–314; A. McHardy, 'The clergy and the Hundred Years' War', in W. Shiels, ed., *The Church and War*, Studies in Church History 20 (1983), pp.171–9.

The lay married household has been discussed as the site of social adulthood, in contrast to the disruptive sexual and other transgressions of youthful masculinity in L. Roper, *The Holy Household: Women and Morals in Reformation Augsburg* (Oxford, 1989). A discussion of conflicting and changing expectations of masculine behaviour in a modern context is to be found in L. Segal, *Slow Motion: Changing Masculinities, Changing Men* (London, 1990); see also R.W. Connell, *Masculinities* (Cambridge, 1995). Caroline Walker Bynum has highlighted aspects of gender inversion in late medieval religiosity in a variety of studies: see the references in chapter 10.

Chapter Twelve: Women and Hunting-birds are Easy to Tame: Aristocratic Masculinity and the Early German Love-Lyric

The history of twelfth-century Germany is discussed in J. Gillingham, *The Kingdom of Germany in the High Middle Ages*, Historical Association Pamphlet 77 (London, 1971); H. Fuhrman, *Germany in the High Middle Ages, c.1050–1200* (Cambridge, 1986). Also useful for the aristocratic context is J. Bumke, *Courtly Culture: Literature and Society in the High Middle Ages*, trans. T. Dunlop (Berkeley, 1991). Gayle Agler-Beck has a useful commentary and interpretation in English of the lyrics of Der von Kürenberg in *Der von Kürenberg: Edition, Notes and Commentary* (Amsterdam, 1978). The Danubian lyric is discussed in English in O. Sayce, *The medieval German Lyric 1150–1300: The Development of its Themes and Forms in their European Context* (Oxford, 1982); and M. Chinca, 'Knowledge and practice in the early German love-lyric' *Forum for Modern Language Studies* 33 (1997), pp.204–16.

The value of literature as part of the historical record is discussed in Simon Gaunt, *Gender and Genre in Medieval French Literature* (Cambridge, 1995). The role of literature in the construction and transmission of ideas about masculine status is explored in H. Spiegel, 'The male animal in the *Fables* of Marie de France', in C. Lees, ed., *Medieval Masculinities. Regarding Men in the Middle Ages* (Minneapolis, 1994), pp.111–26; C.A. Lees, 'Men and *Beowulf*', *ibid.*, pp.129–48; C. Baswell, 'Men in the *Roman d'Enéas*. The construction of Empire', *ibid.*, pp.149–68; L. Mirrer, 'Representing "other" men. Muslims, Jews and masculine ideals in medieval Castilian Epic and Ballad', *ibid.*, pp.169–86. A number of recent papers have examined notions about the body and gender expressed in medieval literature: R. Copeland, 'The Pardoner's body and the disciplining of rhetoric', in S. Kay and M. Rubin, eds, *Framing Medieval Bodies* (Manchester, 1994), pp.138–59; M. Chinca, 'The body in some Middle High German *Mären*: taming and maiming', *ibid.*, pp.187–210; S. Kay, 'Women's body of knowledge: epistemology and misogyny in the *Romance of the Rose*', *ibid*, pp.211–35. For other references to studies of the transmission of ideas about gender roles through text and its performance, see the further reading suggested for chapter 5.

Chapter Thirteen: The Medieval Male Couple and the Language of Homosociality

Many of the texts discussed in this chapter are available in translation; for the most readily available translations and editions see: *The Song of Roland*, ed. and trans., G. Burgess (Harmondsworth, 1990); *Eneas: a Twelfth-Century French Romance*, trans., J.A. Yunck (New York and London, 1974); *Daurel et Beton*, ed., A.S. Kimmel, University of North Carolina Studies in Romance Language and Literature (Chapel Hill, N.C., 1971); *Ami et Amile*, ed. P.F. Dembowski (Paris, 1969); T. Stehling, ed., *Medieval Latin Poems of Male Love and Friendship*, Garland Library of Medieval Literature, series A, 20 vols (New York and London, 1984), vii; *The Cistercian World: Monastic Writings of the Twelfth Century*, ed. and trans., P. Matarasso (Harmondsworth, 1993). Two influential recent studies of literature of this period are S. Gaunt, *Gender and Genre in Medieval French Literature* (Cambridge, 1995); S. Kay, *The Chansons de Geste in the Age of Romance* (Oxford, 1995).

For the history of France in the twelfth century, the following provide useful introductions: J. Dunbabin, *France in the Making 843–1180* (Oxford, 1985); E. Hallam, *Capetian France 987–1328* (London, 1980). Knightly society in France is discussed in G. Duby, *The Chivalrous Society* (London, 1977); *idem, The Knight, the Lady and the Priest* (New York, 1983); M. Keen, *Chivalry* (New Haven and London, 1984).

Homosexual practices in the medieval period have been much discussed in recent years; bibliographical references are given above, for chapter 9. The relationships between men expressed in late medieval literature are discussed in the following: Eve Kosofsky Sedgwick, *Between Men: English Literature and Male Homosocial Desire* (New York, 1985); R. Hyatt, *The Arts of Friendship: The Idealization of Friendship in Medieval and Renaissance Literature* (Leiden, 1994); G.A. Bond, *The*

Loving Subject, Desire, Eloquence and Power in Romanesque France (Philadelphia, 1995); J. Leclercq, *Monks and Love in Twelfth-Century France: Psycho-Historical Essays* (Oxford, 1979).

Chapter Fourteen: Love, Separation and Male Friendship: Words and Actions in Saint Anselm's Letters to his Friends

Most of the sources discussed in this chapter are available in translation: *The Letters of St Bernard of Clairvaux*, trans. B. Scott James (London, 1953); *The Letters of Saint Anselm of Canterbury*, trans. W. Fröhlich (Kalamazoo, Mich., 1990–94), 3 vols; *Aelred of Rievaulx. Spiritual Friendship*, trans. M.E. Laker (Kalamazoo, Mich., 1977). R.W. Southern's study of Saint Anselm is important background for this chapter: R.W. Southern, *Saint Anselm. A Portrait in a Landscape* (Cambridge, 1990).

The literature of love in the twelfth century and related themes are discussed in the following: R.W. Southern, *Medieval Humanism and Other Studies* (Oxford, 1970); *idem, Scholastic Humanism and the Unification of Europe* (Oxford, 1995); M.-D. Chenu, *Nature, Man and Society in the Twelfth Century*, trans. J. Taylor and L.K. Little (Chicago, 1968); C. Walker Bynum, *Jesus as Mother: Studies in the Spirituality of the High Middle Ages* (Berkeley, 1982). Friendship and its cultivation through letter-writing has received much recent attention: B.P. McGuire, *Friendship and Community. The Monastic Experience 350–1250* (Kalamazoo, Mich., 1988); J. Leclerq, *Monks and Love in Twelfth-Century France: Psycho-Historical Essays* (Oxford, 1979); J.P. Haseldine, 'Friendship, equality and universal harmony', in O. Leaman, ed., *Friendship East and West: Philosophical Perspectives* (Richmond, 1996), pp.192–214.

Three particular letter collections and friendship networks are discussed in I.S. Robinson, 'The friendship network of Gregory VII', *History* 63 (1978), pp.1–22; M. McLoughlin, '*Amicitia* in practice: John of Salisbury (c.1120–1180) and his circle', in D. Williams, ed., *England in the Twelfth Century*, Proceedings of the 1988 Harlaxton Symposium (Woodbridge, 1990), pp.165–81; and J. Haseldine, 'Understanding the language of *amicitia*. The friendship circle of Peter of Celle (c.1115–1183)', *JMH* 20 (1994), pp.237–60. K. Cherewatuk and U. Wiethaus, eds, *Dear Sister: Medieval Women and the Epistolary Genre* (Philadelphia, 1993) examines the participation of women in the cultivation of love and friendship through correspondence.

Index